TOOLS OF WAR

TOOLS
OF WAR

Instruments, Ideas, and Institutions
of Warfare, 1445–1871

Edited by
JOHN A. LYNN

UNIVERSITY OF ILLINOIS PRESS
Urbana and Chicago

Publication of this work was made possible in part by a subvention
from the College of Liberal Arts and Sciences,
University of Illinois, Urbana.

This book is printed on acid-free paper.

Library of Congress Cataloging-in-Publication Data

Tools of war : instruments, ideas, and institutions of warfare,
   1445–1871 / edited by John A. Lynn.
      p.   cm.
   Includes index.
   ISBN 0-252-01653-X (alk. paper)
      1. Military art and science—History.   2. Military history,
   Modern.   3. Technology—History.   I. Lynn, John A. (John Albert),
   1943–   .
   U39.T66   1990
   355'.009—dc20   89-4887
                                                    CIP

Contents

Preface

Tools of War challenges the concept of technological determinism in military history, 1445–1871. Its chapters juxtapose the roles played by instruments, ideas, and institutions in shaping the evolution of warfare. The authors define these key categories to cover a wide variety of factors: The category "instruments of war" goes beyond the hardware that soldiers brought to battle; it includes a diversity of technologies, from fortification to transportation. "Ideas" spans many areas, from military theory, to government policy, to formal philosophy, to popular mythology. "Institutions" includes not only the absolutist state, but also military, social, and even religious groups and practices.

Accepting these broad definitions, the authors explored a great variety of possible themes and approaches. They were not assigned specific subjects or methods; the goal here was to assemble a team of gifted historians to produce virtuoso performances, not to have them lockstep as a kind of intellectual drill team. Each chapter is unique, yet all the chapters are bound together by theme and by the shared contexts of the book's historical time frame and the limits of technology.

Generalizations concerning the balance between the instruments, ideas, and institutions of warfare tend to vary from one era of military history to another. An obvious essential in defining such an era, then, is the sophistication of its tools of war. Both primitive and advanced technologies present soldiers with alternative combat styles; rarely do they dictate single choices. However, a difference does exist. Sophisticated modern technologies with their complex weaponry and rapid pace of innovation, not only increase the deadly consequences of right and wrong decisions but emphasize narrowly technical and professional factors—and economic forces, to be sure. Less advanced and more stable arsenals allow greater play to intellectual, political, and social inputs.

The rationale for identifying the period to be discussed in this volume as 1445–1871 was largely based on reasonable dividing points in the history of weaponry. All the chapters deal with warfare after the introduction of firearms but stop short of the time when the industrial revolution transformed armed conflict.

Only in the last quarter of the nineteenth century did machines come to dominate warfare. While products of the industrial age had already arrived on the battlefield by mid-century, their arrival was but the harbinger of the later onslaught. By 1900 weaponry had changed dramatically, with the introduction of repeating rifles, machine guns, and rapid-fire artillery. Although naval warfare first felt the influence of the machine, by mid-century a most important innovation in land warfare had arrived—the railroad. Nevertheless, the railroad's impact was hampered by the need to employ traditional transportation beyond the railhead, as Dennis Showalter points out in his essay. The Crimean War, the American Civil War, and the Franco-Prussian War also constituted watersheds; they marked a dividing line, but they did not lie firmly on the side of modernity.

Before these conflicts, military technology advanced at an evolutionary, not revolutionary, pace, giving the era relative stability. To take just one example, if a gunner from the artillery train of Charles VIII in 1494 had been transported to the battlefield of Gettysburg in 1863, he could have served a muzzle-loading bronze Napoleon cannon with much the same technique as that he employed to fire his primitive culverin. A few decades later, though, and he would have been dumbfounded by the steel French "75," with its nimble breach block, recoil mechanism, and exploding shells.

Weapons development advanced so rapidly after 1871 that it often left strategic and tactical doctrine scrambling to keep up with the new weapons' potentials. The acceleration of deadly invention posed questions whose solutions were all too often left to the unfortunate process of trial and error on campaign. In the preindustrial era, when the pace of technological change had not threatened to outstrip the capacity to adjust to it, conception played a more dominant role in defining tactics and strategy. The tactical innovations associated with the Dutch Revolt and the French Revolution argue strongly in this direction.

So there is reason to argue that conclusions about the relative roles of instruments, ideas, and institutions before 1871 would be qualitatively different from those concerning the period after that date. But global comments about the instruments of warfare are best left to the afterword to this volume, contributed by Sir Michael Howard.

Every one of the essays in this volume presents ideas and institutions as more central, or perhaps simply more interesting, than the instruments of war. The authors concentrate upon development from a technological base rather than upon the base itself.

The opening chapter details army growth and proposes a pattern of expansion that lends a certain institutional unity to the period 1445–1871. In it I ascribe climbing force levels more to political and social factors than to technological innovation. Simon Adams also tackles the question of army growth, building a strong case for the primacy of political goals in determining expansion, particularly in the seventeenth century. William Maltby shifts the focus to warfare at sea. He maintains that the development of line-ahead tactics, usually explained simply in terms of the architecture of the sailing ship, was in fact a choice related to the desire to exert state control over the fleet and to put a new brand of officers in command. In this case institutional change imposed a new tactical system.

Richard Hellie summarizes his earlier works describing the role of military necessity in shaping Russian society—by bringing about the two service-class revolutions and by relegating the peasantry to serfdom. It is, in a sense, the converse of Maltby's point. But even so, advances in weaponry, including the introduction of firearms, is more a given to Hellie than a central focus. Returning to the crucial importance of manpower, Bruce Lenman argues that the key innovation that assured English dominance of the Deccan was the sepoy army. Although he factors in technological change, he sees the advantages gained by superior weapons to have been temporary at best. In another colonial example, Don Higginbotham also emphasizes the creation of local forces rather than the influence of weaponry. He suggests a change of focus in the study of American military history—the "semi-professional" tradition of colonial forces.

Returning the setting to Western Europe, my chapter on the column attack insists that tactical change during the French Revolution resulted from a complicated interaction of intellectual and institutional factors in a static technological environment. Dennis Showalter ambitiously reinterprets Prussian/German tactical history from Frederick the Great to Moltke the Elder. Although the breadth of this period encompasses the introduction of the railroad, the needle gun, and Krupp artillery, Showalter nonetheless argues for the primacy of concept over matériel.

The essay contributed by Hew Strachan is unlike the others, since it alone deals directly with the study of military history as a factor by itself, an emphasis particularly apropos to this collection. He speculates upon the degree to which writings on the peninsular campaigns and the Crimean War might have informed British military doctrine and theory in the period immediately prior to World War I. He concludes that the lessons of military history, if properly understood, could have better prepared the British to deal with the new instruments of warfare on a major scale. The fact that the most respected historical and theoretical analysis of war, *On War,* by Karl von Clausewitz, came out of preindustrial Germany lends weight to Strachan's point. Its status as a modern classic, revered by scholars and soldiers alike, demonstrates that time and technology do not negate the value of historical study in understanding warfare and military institutions.

Acknowledgments

Any credit that *Tools of War* may earn must be shared by many, for in ways both obvious and subtle, a community produced this volume. The original concept for the book grew out of conversations between Geoffrey Parker, Simon Adams, and me. That concept attracted a team of scholars from the United States and Great Britain who agreed to author essays on early modern military history. At a working conference their contributions received approval and underwent alteration, emerging as the chapters published here.

A number of organizations within the University of Illinois at Urbana-Champaign pooled resources to support this project. The College of Liberal Arts and Sciences provided the lion's share of financing for the conference and contributed to the publication of this volume. William Prokasy, former dean of LAS, backed us with enthusiasm and generosity. The Program in Arms Control, Disarmament, and International Security (ACDIS) also supplied substantial funding. ACDIS directors Edward Kolodziej and Jeremiah Sullivan aided the project on several levels. Mary Anderson and Judy Jones at the ACDIS office handled the daunting volume of organizational chores required by the conference with professional skill and personal finesse. The Office of International Programs and Studies, the School of Humanities, and the Department of History supplied additional conference moneys.

In early April 1987, the working conference "Tools of War" convened at the University of Illinois. Since it was never intended for the conference to lead to a volume of proceedings in the normal sense, the valuable contributions offered by those chairing sessions and commenting in them have not been published. Nevertheless, the authors of the essays in this book owe thanks to the following colleagues who served on the conference program: Bernard S. Bachrach, John F. Guilmartin, Robert W. Johannsen, Gerald F. Linderman, William H. McNeill, Gunther E. Rothenberg, and Samuel F. Scott.

As editor, I would like to thank Barbara MacDonald and Randy Woerner of AT&T for providing me with system-6300 word-processing equipment to assemble this volume. Also, I must credit Andrea Lynn, who assisted in editing the text of several essays in this volume. The editing efforts of Beth Bower, of the University of Illinois Press, whose hand touched every page of this book, were Herculean and professional.

I must express special gratitude to my valued friend and colleague Geoffrey Parker, the Charles E. Nowell Distinguished Professor of History at the University of Illinois, without whose assistance neither the conference nor this volume would have ever materialized.

TOOLS OF WAR

The Pattern of Army Growth, 1445–1945

JOHN A. LYNN

FROM THE DEBUT of firearms in the late Middle Ages to the detonation of atomic weapons in 1945, no military development in Western Europe rivaled in importance the growth of armies. This growth multiplied the costs of war, compelled states to centralize, spawned huge civil bureaucracies, unified peoples, altered social classes, bankrupted states, precipitated revolutions, and caused the rise and fall of great powers. In short, it shaped history.

While one brief essay cannot detail all the effects of military expansion, it can sketch the pattern of growth. In addition, this chapter reflects upon the roles played by the instruments and ideas of warfare in delineating the most fundamental institutional development of the half-millenium, 1445–1945. The curve drawn here outlines a rationale, beyond those based on industrial technology, for centering the discussion in *Tools of War* from the mid-fifteenth to the late nineteenth century. During that era, a particular quality and magnitude of growth provided a background, and at times a motif, for apparently diverse aspects of military history.

The French Case Study: Counting Heads, 1445–1945

Consider the growth of the French army as a concrete case study of military expansion. While the French pattern was unique to France, it nonetheless both illustrated and influenced Continental military trends. With the *Ordonnance* of 1445, Valois France was the first European state to establish a permanent standing army since Imperial Rome. The multiplication of France's armed forces over the next five hundred years can be usefully divided into four periods, dictated by the size and

1

character of military institutions and by their political environments. The first ran from the promulgation of the *Ordonnance* to the military expansion under Richelieu; the second, from 1624 through the onset of the French Revolution; the third, from 1789 through the end of the Franco-Prussian War; and the fourth, from 1871 to the end of World War II.

Several basic choices must be made when charting an army's growth over time. This author has elected to count all troops, not just those assembled in field armies. Full "paper" or legal strengths are usually reported without any attempt to discount or interpret them into "real" totals.[1] Also, when possible, gross numbers appear, not just those of forces "present under arms." Since figures reported here come from various authorities, they derive from different systems of calculation. Where major discrepancies exist between respectable sources, they are reported rather than resolved.

Also, in studying the expansion of French military forces it is important to distinguish the levels of troops maintained in peacetime from those marshaled for war. The comments that follow address peacetime and wartime figures separately for each of the four periods.

The First Period, 1445-1624

Remarkable stability in the size of both peacetime and wartime French force levels characterized the first, and longest, period.[2] Contamine estimated that the monarchy maintained a peacetime force of about 14,000 into the 1470s and kept an average of 20,000 to 25,000 on foot during the last quarter of the century, a figure inflated by Louis XI's short-lived attempt to maintain a peacetime army of 24,000.[3] It is hard to speak of real "peace" in the sixteenth century, but Ferdinand Lot stated that 28,000 troops remained after the conclusion of the Peace of Cateau-Cambrésis in 1559.[4] J. R. Hale has asserted that this was reduced to only 10,000 by 1562.[5] With the end of the Wars of Religion at the close of the century, Henri IV reduced the standing army to 8,500.[6]

Wartime levels during this first period probably did not top 55,000. Contamine concluded that French forces stood at 40,000 to 45,000 during years of major campaigns in the late fifteenth century.[7] Lot calculated that troops marshaled for the invasions of Italy numbered 30,000 to 40,000. He discounted the claims that Henri II assembled 60,000 to 80,000 for his campaign of 1552, setting the number at the far more modest level of 38,000.[8] Henri IV may have had as many as 50,000 troops in the field during the last phase of the Wars of Religion.[9] Sully reported that even when Henri was secure on his throne, and had amassed a sizable war chest, he planned to assemble no more than 54,600 for his great war in 1610.[10]

Number chasing for these early centuries is a risky enterprise, but it seems to reveal little if any growth in either peacetime or wartime levels; if anything, peacetime figures from the late fifteenth century probably exceeded those of the early seventeenth.

The Second Period, 1624-1789

Beginning in the 1620s, and greatly accelerating with the entry of France into the Thirty Years' War in 1635, the army experienced massive and rapid growth that stabilized at new higher levels in the 1680s. One scholar states that after the Peace of Alais in 1629, French peacetime forces stood at only 12,000.[11] Yet, in 1666, a generation later, Louvois reported peacetime levels of 72,000, already several times greater than any previous figure.[12] But this soon jumped even higher, to 131,000, after the end of the War of Devolution in 1668.[13] This impressive peacetime level is somewhat misleading since the French did not de-mobilize after the War of Devolution. Louis XIV longed for revenge against the Dutch as soon as possible, which he achieved by attacking them in 1672. In any case, from the late 1670s through the 1780s French peacetime troop levels hovered around 150,000, sometimes dipping below 140,000 and occasionally exceeding 160,000.[14]

Wartime figures also soared to unprecedented heights and remained there. During the crucial war year of 1636, one official projection for the army of Louis XIII topped 200,000 troops; another for 1640 listed 196,000.[15] Richelieu claimed that there were 180,000 troops in the king's service.[16] Commonly, for much of the war the figure of 150,000 is reported by contemporary sources and echoed today.[17] This last number seems a reasonable median for official wartime strength, even though it undeniably overstates the reality; in recent research Kroener and Parrott argue that for the era of the Thirty Years War, such paper figures must be cut in half to arrive at the number actually present for service.[18] The brief War of Devolution (1667–68) put roughly 134,000 French troops under arms.[19] Over 279,000 troops took the field at the height of the Dutch War (1672–78) according to contemporary sources.[20] The tighter character of military administration under Louis XIV gives greater credit to these later official numbers.

From the later reign of Louis XIV until the Revolution that dealt his world a deathblow, troop strength repeatedly approached 400,000 for major wars. One study put the number for the War of the League of Augsburg (1688–97) at about 396,000 and set the wartime peak of the War of the Spanish Succession (1701–14) at just over 392,000.[21] The War of the Polish Succession (1733–38) was a minor affair that brought the French army to a strength of only 205,000;[22] however, the War of the Austrian Succession (1740–48) pushed the level back up to roughly 401,000.[23] The Seven Years' War (1756–63) fell short of such military expansion, as only 330,000 troops stood by the colors during that conflict.[24]

The Third Period, 1789–1871

The third period poses new problems for the historian trying to encapsulate French military development. Not the least problem is the fact that this era witnessed six, seven, or eight distinct regimes, depending on how one chooses to count them. It is necessary to begin by considering the turbulent epoch of the Revolutionary and Napoleonic Wars in its own right. On paper, the army reached the extraordinary peak of a million troops during the summer of 1794.[25] But this unique assembly of troops did not really set a standard for wartime figures for 1789–1871. In fact, this level soon fell precipitously; Minister Petiet stated that the army had fallen to 484,000 by August 1795, to 396,000 by August 1796, and to 382,000 in 1797.[26] Napoleon never matched the number of French troops mobilized by the Republic of Virtue; the French contingents of his Imperial army seem to have stood at no more than 600,000 to 650,000 at any one time.[27]

Only after Waterloo is it possible to speak of a true peacetime army again. In the aftermath of the final Napoleonic defeat, the army collapsed to a level of 75,000 by January 1816, but the military law of 1818 jacked up its legal peacetime level to 240,000.[28] In urging the adoption of the 1832 military law that bears his name, Marshal Soult stated that the army stood at only 224,000.[29] The Soult Law stipulated an army of about 300,000, and a military ordinance of 1841 raised that level to 334,000.[30] Official figures, however, reported the number as higher, averaging 352,000 from 1831 to 1847.[31] The average for the periods of relative quiet during the Second Empire rose to 412,000.[32]

It is more difficult to arrive at a clear comparison of wartime highs, since no conflict between Waterloo and the Franco-Prussian War posed a lethal threat or lasted long enough to warrant full mobilization for war. Under the July Monarchy mobilization projections were based on putting 500,000 men into the field.[33] According to the Delbousquet report, the army reached about 590,000 at the peak of the Crimean War and 540,000 for the 1859 Italian War.[34] Mobilization tables for the early 1860s claimed that with its reserve the French army could have put 625,000 to 650,000 men into the field.[35]

On the eve of the Franco-Prussian War, Napoleon III pushed for a major military reform intended to double the number of troops that could be mobilized. However, the resultant 1868 Neil Law accomplished little.[36] It intended to raise the force of the peacetime army and expand the reserve, so that by 1875 the mobilized army would have amounted to 800,000, backed by a Garde Mobile of 500,000.[37] However, these gardes could claim only minimal training.[38] In 1870, when war came, the number the French put in the field fell far short of Prussian levies. The potential 1,100,000 was largely fiction, counting as it did the useless Garde Mobile. The most reliable figure is 567,000, a total reported in an official troop report of 5 July 1870.[39] It may not be fair to judge what forces the French state could have produced by reference to the Franco-Prussian War, since it ended too soon to test the government's capacity to mobilize on a Revolutionary or Napoleonic scale.

The Fourth Period, 1871–1945

Immediately after the Franco-Prussian War, the peacetime level set by the fairly conservative 1872 military law stood at about 400,000, with a five-year service term. However, military laws of 1889 and 1905 reduced service to three years and then to two, raised the number of troops in uniform to some 500,000 by 1911, and expanded the reserve.[40] In 1913 the term of service was lengthened to three years so that the French might increase their standing army to match that of the Germans. This created a force of about 731,000 in early 1914. After World War I, the French decreased the time in service required of conscripts to eighteen months in 1923 and then to twelve months in 1928. The size of the French army in uniform authorized by the law of 1928 fell to just under 524,000. About 450,000 actually served in 1933.[41]

With the reserve system in place, the difference between peacetime and wartime levels exceeded all previous levels. France mobilized some 3,580,000 men in the late summer of 1914, about four and a half to five times the number of troops in the standing army earlier that year.[42] In 1939–40 the French mobilized more men—at least 4,000,000.[43] Combat units stood in 110 divisions. The uniformed Free French forces that fought alongside the Allies never amounted to more than a small fraction of the numbers mobilized in 1940. In 1945, the largest French force, De Lattre de Tassigny's First Army, amounted to only two corps, totaling eight divisions.[44] While some credit the nonuniformed resistance fighters as the equivalent of fifteen more divisions, this figure is largely subjective.[45]

Characteristics of French Military Expansion

Between 1445 and 1945 the scale of armies changed dramatically. This expansion seems more inevitable than surprising, considering the great technological, intellectual, institutional, and demographic developments that transformed Europe during these five centuries. The figure at right summarizes the growth of the French army over half a millennium.

The first period set peacetime numbers in the range of 10,000 to 25,000, with wartime figures of 30,000 to 55,000. While historians continue to offer differing estimates of troop strengths, one thing is clear: there was no significant expansion over this era of more than 170 years. By contrast, the second period brought an unprecedented rise of force levels. In percentage terms, this expansion would never be equaled again. After 1678, the peacetime standing army marshaled about 150,000, to be multiplied to 400,000 in wartime. This constituted a 700 to 1000 percent increase over base levels set between 1445 and 1624. So extraordinary was this expansion that it qualifies as the French phase of the military revolution.[46]

The confusing third period saw average peacetime levels climb to 352,000 to 412,000, while wartime highs under Napoleon I and Napoleon III did not exceed 650,000. The spike of a million men in the summer of 1794 proved to be an anomaly. Therefore, while the third period brought increases, they fell into the range of only 150 to 250 percent. These increases appear more modest when one realizes that from 1830 on the army carried major colonial responsibilities—especially in North Africa—not borne under earlier regimes. So, for example, the troops marshaled to fight the Franco-Prussian War included 50,000 troops who garrisoned Algeria.[47] With its capacity to

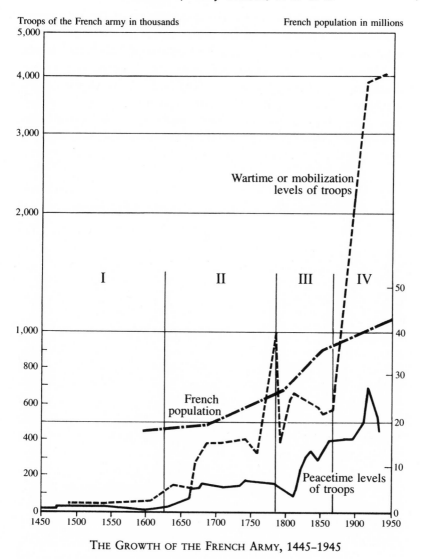

Troops of the French army in thousands

French population in millions

THE GROWTH OF THE FRENCH ARMY, 1445–1945

call upon a mass army, the Third Republic mobilized as many as 4,000,000 soldiers for the world wars of the twentieth century. This amounted to a rise of 600 to 700 percent in initial wartime strength. However, peacetime figures rose much more modestly to average about 400,000 to 600,000, a comparatively low 150 percent, at the most, of those maintained in the previous period.

Just how typical is this story of expansion? While its exact pattern of growth is unique to France, the timing and proportion of expansion were still part of a larger European phenomenon. The Russian army only reached the Western European scale under Peter the Great. During the eighteenth century, its wartime troop figures grew from about 200,000 in the early 1700s to 400,000 by 1800.[48] To resist Napoleon's invasion, the Russians marshaled only about 410,000 troops.[49] These forces continued to grow as Russia became the most populous state in Europe. By 1826 its active forces and reserves numbered over 850,000 on paper, and they remained at that level until the Crimean War.[50] These troops were long-service conscripts, serving twenty-five-year hitches, which were later reduced to fifteen years; Russian reserves were comparatively small.[51] In reaction to the Crimean defeat and later Prussian victories, the Russians labored to create a mass reserve army on Prussian lines. In 1874 the service term was reduced to six years. When war broke out in 1914, the tsar mobilized more divisions than either France or Germany.

The Austrian army had much the same proportions in the nineteenth century as the French army. The Austrians possessed only a small reserve. Regular forces were similarly composed of long-service professionals recruited through conscription; however, before 1845 the number of years of required service varied. German areas within the Austrian Empire sent their sons for fourteen years' service; Hungarians, for life. After 1845 service was standardized at eight years.[52] In 1813 the Austrians put 550,000 men in the field against Napoleon; they did not better this against the Prussians in 1866, when the most charitable figures add up to only 528,000, mobilized in seven weeks.[53] They adopted the mass army concept with reforms that began in 1868.

A comparison of the French case with that of France's ultimate rival, Prussia/Germany, reveals some parallels and significant differences. Of course, the Prussian/German example is more complicated than the French case because state boundaries and resources changed so greatly over time. From quite different beginnings, Prussian forces also swelled in the seventeenth century under the Great Elector, to a standing force of 31,000.[54] While the French army stabilized in the eighteenth century, Prussian battalions continued to multiply. Frederick William I began with an army of 38,000, which he doubled to 80,000 by 1740.[55] Under Frederick II, Prussia added Silesia and also Polish territories and doubled the size of the standing army again to 162,000.[56] At a time when the

French maintained a standing army of 350,000, the restored Prussia of the 1830s and 1840s maintained one of 200,000.[57] While the reformers of the early nineteenth century established the principles of conscription and large reserves, the Prussian army had not yet realized the potential of this system because the state called up only part of the annual contingent of potential recruits and was still relatively limited in resources. Prussia raised 355,000 men to fight Austria in 1866—a sizable force, but still one of only Napoleonic scale.[58] German forces mobilized to fight France in the years 1870–71 were much larger, totaling nearly 1,200,000.[59] With the creation of the German Empire came still greater numbers. The standing army totaled about 400,000 in 1875 and grew to more than 750,000 in 1913.[60] In 1914 Germany mobilized a massive force of about 3,800,000 troops.[61]

Thus the growth of the French army from 1445 to 1945 reveals the directions and dimensions of a Continental trend; it also says something about the dynamics of phenomenon. After the creation of the standing army in 1445, each of the major upturns in army size was associated with a major political change. It could be argued that even the acts that created Europe's first permanent army in the mid-fifteenth century constituted a political watershed. Certainly the grant of a regular tax base and the founding of a standing army both recognized and extended the growing power of the Valois monarchy. Nevertheless, Contamine argues, the forging of the *compagnies d'ordonnance* is better seen as an attempt to regularize the organization of forces already existing at the end of the Hundred Years' War than as an attempt to bring an army into being.

The military expansion at the start of the second period, beginning in the 1620s and accomplished by the 1680s, created the absolutist state. Through a long administrative, fiscal, and political process, the French state struggled to support armed forces seven to ten times greater than any it had maintained in the past. To do so the Bourbon monarchy sponsored a dramatic political metamorphosis under Louis XIII and Louis XIV. In fact, even after the forging of the absolutist state, the monarchy's financial resources never equaled the needs of its armed forces, and war continually threatened the state with bankruptcy.

In 1789, the Revolution—largely brought on by the fiscal crisis of the monarchy—changed the given assumptions and methods of French government and society, thus making possible the military expansion of the third period. Though much is said of the revolutionary élan of the mass army that rose to defend the new France, the emotional peak of revolutionary enthusiasm could not endure for long. From a military point of view, the most lasting accomplishments of the Revolution were the elimination of traditional restraints upon the central government's ability to tap the resources of France, the exploitation of nationalist sentiment, the introduction of regular conscription, and the democratization of the officer corps. Interestingly, while regimes changed in political assumptions from Napoleon I through Napoleon III, they maintained very similar concepts about the nature of military institutions, favoring long-service professional forces composed of volunteers and conscripts, augmented by modest reserves in wartime. Changes in regime and political principle did not always bring change within military institutions.

With some reluctance, the French fashioned the Third Republic in the 1870s, ushering in a new political and military period based on new principles. The unrevolutionary Third Republic gave France what the revolutionary First and Second Republics failed to provide—the Jacobin ideal of an army based on a massive citizen-reserve force. Faced with the example and threat of Imperial Germany before them, the French redefined the regular army as a training organ, designed to produce a great reserve force at the outbreak of war. They created a nation at arms—not simply as a short-lived reaction to crisis, as in 1792–94 or 1870–71, but as an ongoing reality.

So in each case, the creation of a larger army did not come about as the result of just doing the same but more so. New levels of military force implied new assumptions about the army and new principles of government.

Influences Compelling the Expansion

"How" is a much less ambitious interrogative than "why." While a thorough examination of why the army grew exceeds the scope of this essay, some probable causes demand at least a brief discussion.

An obvious explanation for growing armies might simply be that they result from a growing population. The French increased their numbers nearly threefold between 1600 and 1950, from roughly 18 million to 42 million.[62] Surely that is an important part of the story, but not all of it. For while higher numbers of people make it much easier to field greater armies, they do not necessarily create greater armies. The largest percentage increase in French military force came at a time when the population remained relatively stable, or may even have declined somewhat, in the mid-seventeenth century, while the impressive population growth of the mid-nineteenth century saw only a modest rise in the troop levels of the French army. And even if one argues plausibly that a time lag existed between population growth and later military expansion, or that multiplying battalions fed on marginal population increases rather than on total sums, this still does not account for the exact pattern of military expansion in France. Increases would seem to have more to do with politics than with population.

Could it be that technology—the tools of war—imposed military expansion? Much of the debate over the military revolution, 1560–1660 (a term coined by Michael Roberts) revolves around the growth of armies and the rationale behind it. Geoffrey Parker has argued forcefully that the spread of modern fortifications in the sixteenth and seventeenth centuries imposed larger armies on the great states of Europe. Briefly put, he contends that the polygonal fortresses designed according to the *trace italienne* came to dictate the course of wars in this period and that the attack or defense of such works required huge numbers of troops. In this volume, Simon Adams rebuts Parker's assertions. First, Adams questions the timing of military expansion, suggesting that while Spain's armies grew to maintain the Spanish school of strategy in the sixteenth century, for most of Europe, expansion only became clear in the latter half of the seventeenth century. Second, he insists that the political goals of rulers during the Thirty Years' War—not fortresses—required the unprecedented scale of forces. Bourbon policy, for example, not the existence of new fortifications, drove up French army size after 1635. So far as army expansion is concerned, Adams concludes that the instruments of war exerted less influence than ideas did.

To be sure, the instruments of war clearly set limits on army expansion, and new technologies often opened up new possibilities. While the attempt to explain military growth during the seventeenth century by appeal to supposed improvements in the European road system hits wide of the mark, roads—and later, railroads—played a major part in warfare. Railroads made it possible to marshal, deploy, and sustain armies in the millions by the twentieth century. But it is worth noting that the concept which inspired the mass army—the notion of an army based on great reserves, to be trained in peacetime and mobilized for

war—came out of the Napoleonic era. Railroads alone did not transform warfare. Though a railroad network covered France by 1848,
force levels remained constant from the 1830s into the 1870s. Showalter
argues that even the first masters of the military possibilities of the
railroad, the Prussians, still had to proportion their armies in relation
to other means of transportation through the Franco-Prussian War.

Administrative efficiency also is put forward to account for the
growth of armed forces. Certainly, mushrooming troop levels required
larger and more active bureaucracies to support them. In no case was
this truer than with seventeenth-century French military expansion.
Louis XIV's great ministers of war, Le Tellier and Louvois, justly deserve
mention alongside Condé, Turenne, and Luxembourg. However, it is
by no means clear that administrative capacity caused numbers to
multiply as they did. There is good reason to believe that the converse
is true—that needs imposed by a growing army generated the mixture
of power and bureaucracy known as absolutism. The robbery and
rapine the army inflicted on the French people, particularly during the
Thirty Years' War, testified to the fact the army grew more rapidly
than the financial and administrative apparatus designed to equip, feed,
and house it.[63] To satisfy their unmet needs, soldiers extorted money,
food, and lodgings from the unfortunate subjects of the very king they
served. At least into the 1680s, the bureaucracy of the fledgling absolutist state seemed forever to be trying to catch up with the demands
imposed on it by an army of unprecedented scale.[64]

This brings the argument back to the point raised by Simon Adams—
the necessity of viewing the military revolution in its political context.
Styles of warfare and the proportions of armies changed to meet political goals. In other words, the role of ideas must be given heavy
emphasis. An understanding of the growth of the French army during
the second period requires a consideration of the foreign policy assumptions and goals of the Bourbon monarchy. Louis XIV's bid for
territorial aggrandizement and European hegemony demanded an army
of 400,000. A century later, Napoleon's imperial designs required a
force of 650,000. For the period of greatest numerical increase, population, technology, and government provided a context in which concepts of political goals and military institutions played crucial roles.
Competition between states was also a factor: for example, France set
the standard for the seventeenth century, but in the period 1871–1914
she fashioned her army and set its proportions to match those of

Germany. Through international competition, the *goals* of a leading state impose that state's *means* on its rivals. And decline, once raised to a new level, becomes difficult and dangerous in a kind of Clausewitzian ratchet effect.

Composition of Forces

Major changes in force levels usually bring changes in the social composition of armies. Choices concerning the number of men who will be called to arms require decisions about the kind of men they will be. No issue of military expansion can be more complex or have more enduring consequences in military, political, and social spheres.

French military expansion during the early years of the Revolution provides a particularly concrete example of the link between army growth and the transformation of troop composition. The regiments of Louis XVI were composed of common soldiers from the lower ranks of society, who, while not the total outcasts they are frequently portrayed as, were castoffs of the economy. Their aristocratic officers saw themselves as socially superior and increasingly professional. In 1781, the aristocrats won an important victory with the Ségur law, which barred both non-nobles and those who had recently purchased a patent of nobility from wearing an officer's epaulet.[65]

Revolution brought with it a redefinition of the soldier, the officer, and military duty itself. Once condemned as insensitive tools of an autocratic regime, soldiers now won praise as inspired defenders of a new society. In short, they became model citizens. The idea of the citizen soldier—and its corollary, that every citizen bore the duty to serve as a soldier in times of crisis—made the *levée en masse* possible. Technology did not impose or encourage this decision. The stakes were high enough to generalize the selection of soldiers to the entire male population of suitable age, health, and family status. Even before war broke out, the barriers that excluded non-nobles from officers' commissions fell. Egalitarian principles of the Revolution dictated this measure. As the army greatly exceeded ancien régime proportions, the new social definition of an officer allowed the Republic of Virtue to provide a sufficient number of leaders for an army of a million men.

In his essay, Dennis Showalter draws the contrast between the army of Frederick the Great and that of the early nineteenth-century reformers in a similar fashion, describing the eighteenth-century Prussian soldier and officer in much the same terms as those that apply to the

French. The new army of the reformers was also linked to a liberal redefinition of the soldier. And while the barriers against non-noble officers did not disappear as they did in France, they were significantly breached at the height of military reform in Prussia. Of course, Prussian military reform came directly as a result of the French threat.

While the transformation of the French military during the Revolution came as a product of social upheaval, history can reverse that causal link. Creation of the middle-service cavalry in Russia, as described by Richard Hellie in his essay, exemplifies the social impact that the creation of new military forces can exert. He describes how the need to produce the maximum number of cavalry in the late fifteenth and sixteenth centuries led to the purchase of military service through grants of land and labor. Peasants became serfs as a consequence of this military bargain. This choice of weapons and warriors put its stamp on peasant social structure until 1906.

Turning to Asia, Bruce Lenman demonstrates that the key to creating an armed force large enough to extend British control over all of India lay in a dramatic redefinition of who would be a soldier. While the British gained a foothold in India through naval power, transported European troops, and clever diplomacy, the domination of the subcontinent demanded larger forces than could be imported across the oceans. Although the British held a great technological advantage at sea, on land the East India Company did not conquer simply through overwhelming superiority in terms of the instruments of war. Native armies eventually possessed muskets and artillery to match their European foes. Lenman describes how a great army was forged in the late eighteenth century by raising regiments of sepoys. Only by marshaling the financial and manpower resources of Bengal could the British conquer and control the Deccan.

The effect of personnel choices can extend beyond the creation of larger armies; they can change the way an army — or navy — fights. William Maltby discusses how a change in the origin and character of English naval officers encouraged the choice of sailing-ship tactics in the seventeenth and eighteenth centuries. In its drive to create a larger and more controllable fleet, the English government turned away from the earlier merchant sailors, or "tarpaulins," to captain its ships, promoting instead gentlemen officers, who may have mastered less of the mariners' trade but who were more obedient and better versed in the literature of the military art. This, Maltby argues, was a major factor in tipping the balance in favor of line-ahead tactics, which though less decisive than melee fights, required a lower level of seamanship. Consequently, he denies that the line ahead inevitably resulted from naval technology in the era of sail.

This author will contend that the French "revolutionary attack" developed in a similar manner, as a consequence of a change in the personnel and character of the officer corps. This combination of skirmishers and assault columns did not evolve simply in response to the massive influx of untrained soldiers, as has long been believed; the "revolutionary attack" accorded well with the spirit of the citizen-soldiers who employed it in battle.

Growing Armies and Military Professionalism

The growth of armies influenced the development of military professionalism, but their relationship is not a simple one. Even the very term "professional" belies easy definition. If by "professional" all that is meant is long service, then it is difficult to argue that the *compagnies d'ordonnance* were any less professional than the regiments of Louis XV. However, if the definition stipulates a special educational preparation, value system, and corporate sense, then the soldiers of the eighteenth century were clearly more professional than their predecessors.

To gain some understanding of the problems involved in hasty generalizations, briefly consider certain aspects of professionalism within the French officer corps. Captains in the smaller sixteenth-century army functioned much as independent entrepreneurs. The absolutist state exerted greater control over, and demanded increased proficiency from, its commanders, since the growing number of troops and the higher level of skills typical of seventeenth-century warfare made this necessary. The process was aided by the fact that larger standing armies fostered professionalism simply by providing steady careers for higher numbers of officers. In addition, the technical needs of artillery and of engineers encouraged the creation of a series of military schools in the eighteenth century.

Yet at the same time, the need to increase to unprecedented wartime strengths periodically meant that many individuals without training or commitment received commissions during the late seventeenth and eighteenth centuries. They returned to civilian life upon demobilization. The purchase of commissions gave the advantage to the wealthy, not the skilled, particularly during periods of rapid mobilization. This led to conflict between aristocratic professionals and individuals they viewed as rich parvenus. Eventually the Ségur Law of 1781 gave victory to the dedicated noble officers of old families.

The Revolution swept aside the class prejudices of the ancien régime officer and attempted to substitute the goal of a citizen army. But the stress of war encouraged a new professionalism. The combination of noble emigration and military expansion opened slots for an enormous number of new officers. Most often these men came from the cadre of noncommissioned officers who had served in the ancien régime. Some rose through the ranks at a meteoric rate, but most spent considerable time in grade. Seniority and selection by brother officers replaced election by the rank and file of the early Revolutionary days.

The smaller long-service armies of the period 1815–70 provided a good base for professionalism. The nobility did not reestablish its former dominance. Military schools (Saint Cyr and the Polytechnique) prospered, and a substantial percentage of officers came up from the ranks. There was a certain self-perpetuating character to the officer corps, at least under the Second Empire.[66]

After 1871 the reliance upon great reserve forces both promoted and corroded aspects of professionalism. On the one hand, the development of a general staff and of advanced military education raised the technical character of the higher echelons. On the other hand, the dependence upon reserves meant that long-service officers were now to be seconded by part-time amateurs on an unprecedented scale. While formal training and compliance with certain professional values could be required of part-timers, they could not be expected to hold the same values as soldiers who made the military an exclusive career.

The Mobilization of Forces to Wartime Levels

Charting the growth of the French army from 1445 to 1945 drives home the point that a study of military expansion must confront the difference between peacetime and wartime figures. Obviously, troop strengths during war far exceed the numbers maintained by the standing army in quieter times. An attempt to maintain forces at wartime peaks between conflicts could only have bankrupted the state. Less obviously, peacetime and wartime curves describe separate patterns; that is, they can rise or fall at different rates. This contrast becomes particularly apparent when comparing the third period, with its emphasis on long-service professional soldiers, and the fourth period, with its emphasis on short-term soldiers and large reserves. The varying distances between peacetime and wartime figures pose an important question: how does an army jump that gap, expanding from its peacetime to its wartime footing? The answer hinges on pivotal conceptions of an army's nature and function.

The peacetime army of ancien régime France performed several functions. Troops garrisoned towns and fortresses—a role with both military and civil dimensions. In the eighteenth century each regiment changed its garrison at least once a year.[67] Political rationale would seem to explain this constant rotation: changing posts broke the bonds between units and localities, while the resultant moves regularly filled the French roads with an impressive show of military force. This was valuable for an army intended to buttress the power of civil government administration. Beyond its double-edged garrison role, peacetime forces provided the only troops who would be ready to meet the challenge of warfare at the outbreak of hostilities. Lastly, the peacetime army served as a repository for the skills that had to be imparted to the newcomers who filled the wartime ranks.

Relying on long-service volunteers, the Bourbon army lacked a competent trained reserve which could be immediately added to standing forces at the onset of war. From 1688 to the Revolution, the French experimented with both conscription and reserves through the institution of the *milice*. Earlier regimes had attempted to raise effective national militia forces—witness the fifteenth-century *francs-archers* and the sixteenth-century legions—but the *milice* proved to be much longer-lived than these predecessors. Chosen by lot and compelled to drill in local units during peacetime, *miliciens* resented service. The role and organization of the ill-prepared and unpopular *milice*—which stood at 40,000 to 60,000 during periods of peace in the mid-eighteenth century—changed repeatedly during its hundred-year history.[68] By the end of its existence, the *milice* had become an organized semitrained pool of recruits to be integrated into regular regiments during wartime.[69]

Under these circumstances, it took considerable time for the army to expand from peacetime to wartime proportions. Accepting the average of 140,000 to 150,000 for a peacetime baseline and 400,000 for a wartime high, force levels had nearly to triple after war began. The army expanded by increasing the number of men in existing companies and battalions, by adding new battalions or squadrons to existing regiments, and by raising entirely new, and generally temporary, regiments. All this consumed months and even years. For example, just before the War of the Spanish Succession, French forces stood at 140,000, and Louis ordered the first new levies in October 1700. By January 1702, the king's army stood at 220,500; during the remainder of that year one hundred new regiments appeared on the army list. However, the French army probably only hit the wartime high of 392,000 in 1709 and 1710.[70]

While the French pattern exemplifies the primary Continental means of expansion, it does not cover the entire repertoire of mobilization in Europe and its colonies. During the eighteenth century, the British created forces by enlisting sepoys in India and by hiring entire German regiments for warfare in America. The thirteen American colonies evolved their own unique system for moving from peacetime to wartime footing. Don Higginbotham characterizes it as a semiprofessional tradition. Although Americans boasted of them, their militias were stay-at-home units intended for defense or for civil control, as in the case of slave patrols in the South. Before their revolution, Americans moved to a war footing, not by calling out the militia, but by creating full-time units for particular campaigns. They were led by officers who learned their craft through what Higginbotham terms the "tutorial system"—officers who returned to civilian life at the end of the war. The only professional standing forces in peacetime were British regulars. Still, the militia so captured the popular imagination that it became a potent mythology blinding Americans to the reality of their peculiar mobilization.

The Revolutionary and Napoleonic eras ushered in the age of large-scale conscription and mass reserves to Western Europe. While the French Revolution brought full-scale conscription to Western Europe, the high level attained in the summer of 1794 was the product of the extraordinary revolutionary measures of the *levée en masse*—measures that would not be repeated. Without an ongoing system for levying new recruits to sustain it, such a high tide of manpower was bound to ebb. It was this decline that called forth a more regular system of conscription in the Jourdan Law of 1798. Napoleon relied on conscription to complete his ranks and raised impressive numbers, particularly during the later years of his dominion. Between 1800 and 1814, he raised some 2,000,000 Frenchmen.[71] Between 1815 and 1870, military legislation continually adjusted conscription to produce desired yearly levies. The system was employed to compel unlucky young men to sign on for long terms of enlistment. Thus, it became a recruiting device for a professional army, not a citizen army in the revolutionary sense. There was a significant reserve, but it amounted to only about half the strength of the standing army at best. Thus a standing army of 410,000 in 1867 was to be backed by a reserve of about 212,000.[72]

It is ironic that the French invention of conscription was better maintained and perfected by Prussia, France's archenemy. The reform era endowed the Prussian military with a short-service conscript army composed of men raised by conscription who then passed on to the reserves and eventually the Landwehr after active service. As Showalter demonstrates, this accorded with a political agenda as well as with military theory. This involved a redefinition of the function of the standing army. Not only was it seen as fulfilling the duties associated with a "force in being," it was also viewed as a training ground for the men bound to two or three years' service in its ranks. The wartime army could multiply in size severalfold by mobilizing the army reserve and calling out the Landwehr. The Landwehr may have proved a faulty institution in the long run, but it set the principle for a new style of army — a style copied by others after the Prussian victories of 1864–71.

It took a number of years for the French to restructure their manpower policy after the Franco-Prussian War. The long-service army died hard in France. By 1889 the French Third Republic came to rely on a pool of reserves to greatly bolster active troops in wartime. This explains the great contrast between peacetime and wartime figures in the fourth period. Thus in contrast to the period 1624–1789, when the wartime army was only 250 or 300 percent larger than the peacetime force, or that of 1789–1871, when mobilized forces were to stand at only about 150 to 200 percent of the standing army, wartime mobilized troops levels were to be 600 to 800 percent of peacetime strength.

Conclusion

During the centuries between 1445 and 1871, officers and soldiers constituted the ultimate instruments of war, more so than the weapons they wielded. Authors of the essays in *Tools of War* repeatedly return to this theme. A discussion of the instruments, ideas, and institutions of warfare, therefore, must take into account the quality and quantity of men who marched into battle.

A pattern of army growth aids in delineating the period examined in this volume. After the decline of the Roman Empire, permanent military establishments did not exist in Western Europe until the *Ordonnance* of 1445. The companies it authorized constituted the first standing army. Succeeding centuries brought army increases, and the institutional changes that were fashioned by expansion promoted even further growth. Just as in the case of the industrial technology of warfare, the keys which were to unlock the gates to a very different future had been forged by 1871; however, the gates had yet to be opened fully. After 1871 Continental European states welcomed the concept of the mass reserve army, already pioneered by Prussia; thus World War I would be fought by armies numbering in the millions. Between those two milestones along the course of Western military history, the pattern of army growth marked a path along which military institutions were compelled to travel if they were not to perish.

NOTES

1. See John A. Lynn, "The Growth of the French Army during the Seventeenth Century," *Armed Forces and Society* 6 (Summer 1980), for a discussion of the merit of emphasizing "paper" figures as opposed to discounted estimates of men actually in the field. We will never know exactly how many men were at the front in past armies, but official paper figures at least give us an index by which we can compare the relative size of forces.

2. For a discussion of the sources to be used and the problems encountered in establishing troops strengths for the first three periods, see Lynn, "The Growth of the French Army."

3. Philippe Contamine, *Guerre, état et société à la fin du moyen âge* (Paris, 1972), 278–83, 286, 290–93, 298–301, and 317; Philippe Contamine, *War in the Middle Ages*, trans. Michael Jones (Oxford, 1986), 169–71. One has to wonder if this high figure includes forces for Louis XI's military venture in the Netherlands and Charles VIII's "Mad War," since the attempt by Louis XI to actually maintain peacetime forces of about 24,000 occurred only during the last two years of his life and was quickly abandoned at his death.

4. Ferdinand Lot, *Recherches sur les effectifs des armées françaises des Guerres d'Italie aux Guerres de Religion, 1494–1562*, 189–92.

5. J. R. Hale, *War and Society in Renaissance Europe, 1450–1620* (Baltimore, 1985), 66.

6. Maximilien de Béthune, duc de Sully, *Mémoires* (London, 1747), 2:26. Even this figure may be too high, since La Noue was pleading for a mere 6,500, as if there were not even this many men on foot. Hale, 67. Joseph Servan, *Recherches sur la force de l'armée française, depuis Henri IV jusqu'à la fin de 1806 en Tableau historique de la guerre de la révolution de France* (Paris, 1808), 1:2–4,

gives the figure as 9,737. The bulk of this volume was the work of Philippe Henri de Grimoard, work undertaken on orders of the secretary of state for war in 1774 as an in-house piece of historical research. Joseph Servan later appended material for the periods 1600–59 and 1774–1806 and published it under his name. For the period from the late seventeenth century through the onset of the French Revolution, *Recherches* seems to be both consistent and reasonably reliable. See Lynn, 571–73, for a discussion of Servan.

7. Contamine, *Guerre, état et société*, 316–17.

8. Lot, 15–21, 41, 69–70, 125–34.

9. Edouard La Barre Duparq, *L'art militaire pendant les guerres de religion, 1562–1598* (Paris, 1863), 24.

10. Sully, 3:390. Hale, 63, states that "Sully was planning an army which, with contingents from allies, would comprise 190,000 men." These certainly were not all French.

11. Michel L. Martin, "Note de démographie militaire: Les variations d'effectifs en France depuis le quinzième siècle," *Revue des sciences politiques* no. 8 (1983): 24. To my knowledge, the Martin article is the only one that undertakes the important task of discussing French army growth over the long run. While Martin made use of my 1980 article for the period 1445–1789, he often records figures that differ from mine, and we also clash from time to time for the years after 1789. Unfortunately, Martin does not always cite his sources.

12. This estimate was given by Louvois in Camille Rousset, *Histoire de Louvois* (Paris, 1861), 1:97. In support of this level, see also Bibliothèque Nationale, manuscrits, fonds français (BN ff.), 4255, and Bibliothèque de la Ministère de Guerre (BMG), "Tiroirs de Louis XIV," pieces 36, 37, 39, and 40. Servan, 52–53, states that 125,000 were on foot immediately after the Peace of the Pyrenees.

13. Servan, 54.

14. Representative figures for the peacetime standing army during this era include the following: 138,000 during the early 1680s; 140,216 in 1700; 132,959 in 1715; 142,653 in 1739; 167,528 about 1750; 159,016 in the late 1760s; and 154,910 in early 1789. Servan, 55, 58, 60, 61, 64, 68–69, 96. For consistent comparison, all these peacetime levels, 1679–1789, have been taken from Servan. Servan's *Recherches* usually presents these figures as levels maintained after major conflicts, making it necessary to hedge at times concerning exact years. For archival confirmation see Archives de la guerre (AG), MR 1777; AG, $A^1$3686, 11; AG, $A^1$3712, 128; BN ff. 14199; AG, $A^4$80; AG, $A^1$3671, 39; AG, $A^4$84; BN ff. 6198.

15. A *contrôle* for 1636 (an official estimate of troop size and finance) projected 172,000 infantry, 21,000 cavalry, and another 12,000 cavalry separately financed; this yields a paper total of 203,000. David Parrott, "The Administration of the French Army During the Ministry of Cardinal Richelieu," D.Phil. diss., Oxford University, 1985, 99–100, 140.

Bernard Kroener, in his "Die Entwicklung der Truppenstärken in den französischen Armeen zwischen 1635 und 1661," in Konrad Repgen, ed., *Forschungen und Quellen zur Geschichte des Dreissigjährigen Krieges* (Munster, 1981), 201, presents detailed records, *états*, of troop strengths for 1638 and 1639 that he located in the Archives des Affaires Étrangers and the manuscript collection of the Bibliothèque Nationale. They list 160,010 (123,450 infantry and 36,560 cavalry) for 1638; 148,180 (125,800 infantry and 22,380 cavalry) for 1639; and 195,950 (169,800 infantry and 42,150 cavalry) for 1640.

16. In his "Succinte narration" in Petitot, ed., *Collection des mémoires relatifs à l'histoire de France*, 2d ser. (Paris, 1821), 11:317, Richelieu lists 150,000 foot, both garrison and field armies, and 30,000 horse, at a cost of 60,000,000 livres per year.

17. See BN ff. 6385; BMG, Collection des ordonnances militaires, vol. 14, piece 87; Servan, 25; Jacques Boulenger, *The Seventeenth Century in France* (New York, 1963), 71; Michel Carmona, *La France de Richelieu* (Paris, 1984), 150.

18. Kroener's is the most exhaustive study of the difference between paper figures and the number of men actually in the field. For example, his comparison of the actual effectives (as reported in a June 1641 review of Châtillon's troops) with official strengths (Kroener, 204–5) startles the reader. One infantry regiment reported only 8 percent of its supposed total of 1,200. On average the other seven regiments produced only 44 percent of their official strengths for review. Parrott ("The Administration of the French Army," 142) also argues that reality fell far short of paper possibilities. He suggests that the numbers of men actually maintained, as demonstrated through review reports, stood at only 50 percent of the numbers in the *contrôles* for the years 1630–38.

Here we have the problem of paper versus reality. I prefer paper figures as an index. But even if we accept the worst case of Parrott, there were still about 100,000 men actually reported as being under arms in 1636. In any case, even Parrott's discounted totals represent a major increase over the forces projected by Henri IV. More to the point, the less one credits expansion during the ministry of Richelieu, the more impressive become the totals assembled by Le Tellier and Louvois, at least after 1659.

19. BMG, "Tiroirs de Louis XIV," pieces 46–48, 50–54.

20. BMG, "Tiroirs de Louis XIV," piece 110. Of this figure, 163,240 were listed as being on campaign, while 116,370 were in garrison.

21. Servan, 58, puts them at 395,865 and 392,223. A 1710 *état*, or muster report, stated that 319,531 infantry and 57,564 cavalry were in the army at that point. AG, MR 1701. This falls 4 percent short of the Servan estimate, but it essentially corroborates it. In my experience the figures shown in the *Recherches* usually run a bit higher than this type of *état*, wartime or peacetime.

22. Ibid., 60.

23. To be precise, 401, 215. Ibid., 63–64. There are ample sources to justify such a high level. AG, Ya359 sets the number of the still-expanding army troops in 1743 at 320,994. AG, A⁴80 approaches the Servan estimate for 1748, cataloging 390,714 troops. BN ff. 14210, exceeds Servan for 1748, listing 426,815 troops. All these totals include the *milice* since these are wartime levels. The *milice* presents a problem for anyone attempting to count heads in the eighteenth century. It seems most reasonable to count them in force totals only during wartime because the peacetime *milice* was only put in the field during wartime.

24. Servan, 67. As is often the case, my research differs from Martin's; he credits the French with only 320,000 for the War of Austrian Succession and 350,000 for the Seven Years' War. Martin, 25.

25. Jacques Godechot, *Les institutions de la France sous la Révolution et l'Empire* (Paris, 1968), 362. Godechot lists a total paper strength of 1,169,000.

26. Petiet, "Rapport sur l'administration de son département," a report dating from year V of the revolutionary calendar (1796-97), in Jean-Paul Bertaud, *La Révolution armée* (Paris, 1979), 271. These figures were rounded off to the nearest thousand. Petiet discounted the 1794 high to 732,474. Godechot, 362, also discounts the million figure, arguing only that 750,000 men "at least" were actually under arms.

27. The military historian Owen Connelly accepts 600,000 as the figure for the "standing army" from 1805 on. Owen Connelly, *French Revolution: Napoleonic Era* (New York, 1979). Martin credits Napoleon with 700,000 to 1,000,000 troops, but he never distinguishes French from allied levies. Thus he states that Napoleon crossed the Nieman in 1812 with 700,000, but fails to note that only half of these were French. Martin, 25. Napoleonic correspondence puts the level of Imperial French soldiers in 1810 at 622,000. Correspondance 14311, 14601, 14754, cited and totaled by Jean Morvan, *Le soldat impérial* (Paris, 1904), 1:66. After the debacle of 1812, Napoleon undertook the herculean task of forging a new army to meet the inevitable counterattack; he set as his goal an army of 656,000. David Chandler, *The Campaigns of Napoleon* (New York, 1966), 866-67.

28. Gabriel Hanotaux, ed., *Histoire de la nation française* (Paris, 1927), tome 8, *Histoire militaire et navale*, 2:245-46.

29. Ibid., 251, 258. An 1824 law set the ambitious goal of a standing army of 480,000, but this was not reached.

30. Ibid., 259-60, 268-70. Hanotaux estimated the number of troops actually on foot in 1848 at 292,000 in early 1848. Ibid., 334.

31. The low point sank to 280,405 in 1836, and a high point of 428,315 was reached in 1841. La Chapelle, *Les forces militaires de France en 1870* (Paris, 1872), 106, presents a report on troop strength dated 24 September 1868 and signed by J. Delbousquet, *chef de bureau du recrutement*. It states active army and reserve figures for each year from 1830 through 1869.

32. The extremes ranged from 361,468 in 1853 to 467,579 in 1861. For 1853, see Delbousquet figures in La Chapelle, 106; for 1860-69, see Pierre Lehautcourt, *Histoire de la Guerre de 1870-1871* (Paris, 1902), 2:399, which is itself a good discussion of the strength of the French army. See also the 1848-66 figures for *effectifs moyens* supplied by Minister of War Randon in his *Mémoires du maréchal Randon* (Paris, 1877), 2:183. The years 1848-49, 1854-56, and 1859-60 have not been counted as years of peace because they witnessed revolution, war, or slow demobilization from conflict levels.

Both Randon's and Delbousquet's figures for French strength in the mid-1860s stand in very sharp contrast to the figure of 288,000 stated by the Castelnau report of 11 September 1866 in Germain Bapst's *Le maréchal Canrobert* (Paris, 1898), 4:53, and the figure given by Michael Howard, *The Franco-Prussian War* (London, 1981), 29-30. Randon, 2:182, discusses this estimate as a statement of troops available to take the field in France out of a total army strengh of 400,000.

33. Both the Soult Law of 1832 and the ordinance of 8 September 1841 stipulated mobilizable forces of 500,000, and Lamartine argued for a mobilized

army of 530,000 in the early days of the Second Republic. Hanotaux 259, 269, 334.

34. Delbousquet in La Chapelle, 106. Randon, 2:183, agrees with the Crimean War estimate but puts the Italian War figure higher, at 600,000. The Crimean War was a considerable venture for the French, but still the most that French troops numbered in the Crimea at any one time was 140,000 in November 1855. C. E. Vulliany, *Crimea* (London, 1939), 341. The 1859 Italian War, to which the French committed an army of 120,000 to aid the Piedmontese, lasted only three months from the Austrian ultimatum to the Armistice of Villafranca. Letter of Emperor Napoleon III, 15 May 1859, in Hanotaux, 372. Wanty argues that the army totaled 150,000 in six corps. Emile Wanty, *L'art de la guerre*, 3 vols. (Paris, 1967), 2:18.

35. Delbousquet figures in La Chapelle, 106. At this time the French believed that the Prussians could field 1,200,000. Howard, *Franco-Prussian War*, 29. Howard, 22, gives the actual figures of men mobilized against France as 1,183,389, of which 983,064 were from the North German Confederation.

36. For brief discussions of the Neil Law, see Hanotaux, 402–6 and Pierre de la Gorce, *Histoire du Second Empire* (Paris, 1913), 5:317–45. An accessible and good account of this vaunted law can be found in the article "Army Reform" in William E. Echard, ed., *Historical Dictionary of the French Second Empire* (Westport, Conn., 1985), 20–24. It dismisses the Neil Law as "largely fruitless."

37. Of the 800,000, 500,000 would be active army and the rest reserves. The Neil Law created an active army based on men serving for five years, plus a reserve composed of men who had served their five-year commitment and men who served only five months of active duty and passed directly into the reserve. In contrast, Delbousquet stated a mobilization figure of 627,250 for 1866, of which 391,400 were active army. La Chapelle, 106.

38. Echard, 20–24.

39. The exact figure was 567,131, according to the *état* of 1 June 1870 signed by Colonel Hartung, *directeur adjoint du personnel,* and by Delbousquet in *Enquête parlementaire sur les acts du gouvernement de la défense nationale* (Versailles, 1872), 1:67–68. This total is a paper one, good for comparison with other paper figures but overstating how many troops were actually under arms to face the Prussian invasion. The *état* reduces this to 492,585 by subtracting 74,546 "*non valeurs*." Of the 492,585, 50,000 are tolled off for Algeria and 6,500 for Rome. Marshal Leboeuf informed the government that the final figures for the mobilized army stood at 662,000, of whom 370,000 could be utilized in field armies against the Prussians. This is a much-cited figure. See, for example, William McElwee, *The Art of War from Waterloo to Mons* (Bloomington, Ind., 1974), 43.

40. For a good brief discussion of French manpower policy see Adolph G. Rosengarten, Jr., "The Evolution of French Manpower Policy from 1872 to 1914," *Military Affairs* 45 (December 1981).

41. Except for the early 1914 level, all the figures stated in this paragraph were taken from the D. S. Newhall article, "Army: Organization," in Patrick Hutton, et al., eds., *Historical Dictionary of the Third French Republic,* vol. 1 (New York, 1986). It is a very useful summary of recent scholarship on the size of French forces under the Third Republic. Rosengarten, 184, states the early 1914 figures as 712,000 enlisted and 19,000 officers. Newhall pushes the total up to 800,000,

for reasons unclear to this author. Robert Doughty, *The Seeds of Disaster* (Hamden, Conn., 1985), 22, states that by 1933 there were only 320,000 troops in France and the Rhineland. Wanty, 2:265–66, gives a high 1930 total, 651,000, with 405,000 in the Metropole.

42. Hutton, 43. Wanty, 2:95, gives the 1914 figure as 3,800,000. Both of these are total figures for frontline troops, reservists, and rear echelon units. Only about 1,500,000 French troops were in combat units ready to fight in August 1914.

43. Hutton, 43. Determining the size of French forces mobilized in 1939–40 depends on what is counted and when it is counted. B. H. Liddell Hart, *History of the Second World War* (New York, 1970), 18, gives the total as 5,000,000 in 110 divisions. Henri Michel, *The Second World War*, trans. Douglas Parmée (New York, 1975) states the total as 5,700,000, of whom 5,100,000 were French. However, French mobilization was not entirely military in the narrow sense; according to Michel, 1,400,000 of the 5,700,000 were assigned to "reserved occupations" and thus did not serve in uniform. This gets us back to the roughly 4,000,000 stated by Newhall. Also, as time went on, the French were able to mobilize more men. It should be remembered that 9 months passed between the outbreak of war on 1 September 1939 and the French request for an armistice on 16 June 1940.

44. The United States equipped eight full divisions of French forces in North Africa, while three more were formed in France after D-Day.

45. Peter Calvocoressi and Guy Wint, *Total War* (New York, 1979), 322, credit the French Forces of the Interior with mobilizing 200,000.

46. The debate over the military revolution is one of the most important in early modern military history. It was initiated by Michael Roberts with his essay The Military Revolution, 1560–1660 (Belfast, 1956), reprinted in his *Essays in Swedish History* (London, 1967). Geoffrey Parker picked up this issue later, "The 'Military Revolution' 1560–1660—A Myth?," *Journal of Modern History* 48 (June 1976), and he has recently expanded his discussion in *The Military Revolution: Military Innovation and the Rise of the West, 1500–1800* (Cambridge, 1988). See also Lynn, "The Growth of the French Army," cited above, and John A. Lynn, "Tactical Evolution in the French Army, 1550–1660," *French Historical Studies* 14 (Fall 1985).

47. *Enquête parlementaire*, 67.

48. Christopher Duffy, *Russia's Military Way to the West* (London, 1981), 125. At the end of Catherine's reign, Langeron estimated the size of Russian forces at 178,000. Ibid.

49. Chandler, 750, gives the figure of 409,000 troops for all field, garrison, and auxiliary troops on all fronts.

50. John Shelton Curtiss, *The Russian Army Under Nicolas I, 1825–1855* (Durham, N.C., 1965), 107, 108, gives the 1826 figure as 885,000 with reserves, and 820,000 to 859,000 for 1850, when the Russian population was nearly double that of France.

51. Ibid., 110, 111.

52. Alan Sked, *The Survival of the Hapsburg Empire* (London, 1979), 34, 35, and John Gooch, *Armies in Europe* (London, 1980), 77.

53. Gunther Rosenberg, *The Art of Warfare in the Age of Napoleon* (Bloom-

ington, Ind., 1978), 173, and Gordon Craig, *The Battle of Königrätz* (Philadelphia, 1964), 7.

54. Herbert Rosinski, *The German Army* (New York, 1966), 21.

55. Ibid., 21, 27. Rosinski gives a figure of "more than 76,000" on p. 21 and 80,000 on p. 27.

56. Theodore Ropp, *War in the Modern World* (New York, 1962), 46. Rosinski, 33, gives the size of the Prussian standing army as 132,000 in 1751.

57. Howard, *Franco-Prussian War,* 12.

58. Craig, 17.

59. Howard, *Franco-Prussian War,* 22. The total was 1,183,389, of whom 983,064 were from the North German Confederacy.

60. Wanty, 2:94.

61. Ibid., 2:95. Telford Taylor, *The March of Conquest* (New York, 1958), 18, gives the size of the German army in April 1940 as 3,750,000 active men on duty. Howard, *War in European History* (Oxford, 1977), 99, gives the German forces as 3,400,000 in World War I.

62. For the era before the seventeenth century, population figures are little more than guesswork. Michel Morineau estimates French population in 1580 as between 16 and 20 million, Charles Wilson and Geoffrey Parker, eds., *An Introduction to the Sources of European Economic History 1500–1800* (London, 1977), 155. Charles Tilly, *The Contentious French* (Cambridge, Mass., 1986), 64, 65, estimates the figures at 18 million in 1600 and 19 to 20 million in 1700. B. R. Mitchell, *European Historical Statistics, 1750–1975,* 2d rev. ed. (New York, 1980), 30, reports the following census figures: 27,349,000 in 1801, 35,783,000 in 1851, 38,451,000 in 1901, and 42,781,000 in 1954.

63. Two recent dissertations challenge the picture painted by Louis André, in his *Michel Le Tellier,* that this great war minister did bring about an administrative revolution before 1659. The first and more important is David Parrott, "The Administration of the French Army During the Ministry of Cardinal Richelieu." D.Phil. diss., Oxford University, 1986, which demonstrates convincingly that the Richelieu years brought no great change in military administration. He argues that, in fact, the lack of adequate institutional adjustment limited French strategic success. His study ends in 1637, but its implications cover the period until the Peace of the Pyrenees in 1659. A less impressive, but still good, French dissertation—Patrick Landier, "Guerre, Violences, et Société en France, 1635–1659," doctorat de troisième cycle, Université de Paris IV, 1978—provides many examples of problems from the period 1635–59.

64. In the words of Charles Tilly, "As they fashioned an organization for making war, the king's servants inadvertently created a centralized state. First the framework of an army, then a government built around that framework—and in its shape." Tilly, 128.

65. On the Ségur law see David D. Bien, "La réaction aristocratique avant 1789: l'exemple de l'armée," *Annales: économies, sociétés, civilisations* 29 (1974): 23–48, 505–34.

66. William Serman, *Les origines des officiers français, 1848–1870* (Paris, 1979).

67. Claude Sturgill, "Changing Garrisons: The French System of Etapes," *Canadian Journal of History* 20 (August 1985).

68. For example, archival figures place the *milice* at the following strengths: 52,200 in 1751, BN ff. 14200, BN ff. 14213; and 43,888 in 1771, AG, A⁴83 bis. In computing troop levels here, I have not counted the *milice* in calculating peacetime levels, but I have included it in wartime figures.

69. At times, the *milice* was little more than a device to draft men for wartime service in regular army units. At other times it was intended primarily to provide integral battalions to perform rear-echelon duties. During the War of the Austrian Succession, 80,000 *miliciens* were incorporated into the regular army. André Corvisier, *Armies and Societies in Europe, 1494–1789,* trans. Abigail Siddall (Bloomington, Ind., 1979), 54. By the end of its existence, the *milice* had became an organized semitrained pool of recruits to be integrated into regular regiments. Only the elite grenadier companies of *milice* battalions regularly fought on the battlefield—as *grenadiers royaux.* While service in the *milice* was not very demanding during peacetime, being drawn for service at one of the village lotteries that chose *miliciens* was considered a sorry fate. Exemptions and substitutions guaranteed that the duty fell almost exclusively upon the poorer peasantry. *Cahiers* written on the eve of the Revolution leave no doubt that the *milice* was one of the most hated institutions of the ancien régime; the French population did not readily accept the concept that the people owed military service to the state.

70. The 1702 level is from a contemporary "Mémoire des trouppes que le roy a sur pied," dated January 1702, in Georges Girard, *Le service militaire à la fin du règne de Louis XIV: Racolage et milice (1701–1715)* (Paris, 1922), 5–7.

71. Godechot, 603.

72. Delbousquet figures in La Chapelle, 106.

Tactics or Politics?
"The Military Revolution"
and the Hapsburg Hegemony,
1525–1648

SIMON ADAMS

THE CAMPAIGNS INITIATED by the landing of Gustavus Adolphus at Peenemünde in June 1630 are among the best-known events of the Thirty Years' War. The Swedish victory at Breitenfeld was, S. R. Gardiner concluded a century ago, "no common victory." Like Naseby, it was "the victory of disciplined intelligence," the success of which "could not be confined to mere fighting. It would make its way in morals and politics, in literature and science."[1] If Gardiner's Protestant liberalism now has a distinctly dated ring, the Swedish intervention has not lost its wider significance. In his magisterial biography of Gustavus Adolphus, Michael Roberts discovered in the campaigns of 1630–32 the focal point of what he identified as the "military revolution" of the century 1560–1660. By the end of the sixteenth century, he argued, "tactics had withered, strategy had atrophied." Following the military reforms that underlay the Swedish victories, war became once more an effective instrument of policy.[2]

A decade ago Geoffrey Parker subjected the Roberts thesis to a searching critical reappraisal. Parker identified four main elements in Roberts's military revolution: a revolution in tactics, a revolution in strategy, a dramatic increase in the scale of armies, and a transformation of the state. He queried both the novelty and the success of Swedish tactics and strategy but accepted the growth of armies and their impact on the state, though for somewhat different reasons.[3] For Parker the military revolution was above all logistical; as he has most recently

28

concluded, "The states of early modern Europe had discovered how to supply large armies but not how to lead them to victory."[4]

Other assessments of tactical evolution in the period have reinforced Parker's argument that they were both more diffuse and adopted earlier than Roberts allowed for. Deployment by battalions, for example, appears to have been widely accepted by the end of the 1590s.[5] On the other hand, one aspect of the orginal thesis has survived more or less intact: the argument that, to quote Martin van Creveld, the military revolution "was characterised above all by the immense growth in the size of Europe's armies."[6] Roberts argued that Philip II "had dominated Europe in his day with the aid of an army which probably did not exceed 40,000: a century later, 400,000 was esteemed necessary to maintain the ascendency of Louis XIV," though he also conceded that it "may perhaps be legitimately objected that the instances I have chosen to illustrate the growth of armies are hand-picked."[7] Parker came to the same conclusion: "Between 1530 and 1710 there was a ten-fold increase both in the total numbers of armed forces paid by the European states and in the total numbers involved in the major European battles. . . ."[8] Creveld compares the 10,000 men the duke of Alba took to the Netherlands in 1567 with the armies "far in excess of 100,000 men" that Gustavus Adolphus and Wallenstein commanded in 1631–32 and with the French establishment of 400,000 in the 1690s. He also concludes: "More and better statistics could be adduced, but they would only serve to prove what is generally recognized: namely, that apart from a period of twenty-five years between 1635 and 1660, Europe's armies multiplied their size many times over between 1560 and 1715."[9]

That there was a particularly dramatic increase in numbers in the latter half of the seventeenth century is undeniable. But if attention is focused on the period 1525–1648, certain other trends in the size of armies can be detected that provide significant grounds for reexamining the context of the military revolution. The evidence must, however, be approached with caution, for the subject is fraught with technical difficulties. The first is the apparently simple question of the definition of an army. Here a distinction must be drawn between the total number of military forces an individual government, paymaster, or commander could raise in a given year, which might be spread over a wide geographical area, and a force that campaigned, maneuvered or gave battle as a unit—a camp, an *armée de campagne,* a *feldleger,* or (as Wallenstein described it) a *Hauptarmada.*[10] The difference is that between, for example, the total number of men Gustavus Adolphus and his allies had under arms in 1632 and the army that invaded Bavaria and later fought the battle of Lützen.

Accurate measurement of either type of army is not easy. The literary sources and contemporary narratives from which the numbers of combatants in major battles have generally been drawn are notoriously inaccurate, owing in part to the understandable desire of the participants to magnify the opposing army in order to glorify victory or justify defeat.[11] For many engagements (Pavia, for example) the size of the forces employed has been a matter of some debate.[12] Frequently, the best figures available are estimates that may be several thousands out.

There are, however, two further reasons for caution in the use of the numbers involved in any particular battle. First, there is the distortion caused by eve-of-battle diversions. An obvious example is the controversial detachment of 6,000 men from the army of Francis I during the siege of Pavia. Similarly, Wallenstein faced Gustavus Adolphus at Lützen with only part of a widely dispersed army. Bernard of Saxe-Weimar refused to wait for reinforcements at Nördlingen.[13] But the converse is also true—and has a particular relevance for this period. "Armies" assembled at one place to lay siege or give battle were frequently the result of a recent junction of allied forces, and thus no guide to "national armies." Charles V's army at Metz in 1552 included the 15,000 of Albert-Alcibiades of Brandenburg-Kulmbach. Both armies at Breitenfeld were composites: Gustavus Adolphus's consisted of both his own and that of the elector of Saxony, and Tilly's the army of the Catholic League and the Imperialists under Fürstenburg. At Nördlingen, three years later, a more complex concentration occurred that makes even the description of the opposing sides difficult. The "Catholic" army was composed of three separate armies (Spanish, Imperial, and League) while the "Protestant" was composed of four (the Swedish army and three provided by various German Protestant allies).[14] The largest battle of the English Civil War—Marston Moor—was fought by a combination of two Royalist armies (Prince Rupert's and the earl of Newcastle's) and three Parliamentarian ones (the Scottish, the Eastern Association, and Sir Thomas Fairfax's).

We are on no firmer ground with the statistics of total forces raised, for the projections of treasuries, accounts of paymasters, and rolls of mustermasters are not necessarily more accurate. Many projections were never realized, and the figures given in state papers are frequently mere paper strengths. The reliability of accounts varied widely from army to army. The Army of Flanders, Geoffrey Parker has argued, undertook musters rigorously, and therefore its records can be used with some confidence.[15] The same may also be true for the Dutch army of the early seventeenth century, though clearly not for the French in the 1630s, let alone the more entrepreneurial German armies.[16] Wastage—however the rate is estimated or computed—makes it extremely difficult to translate recruiting targets into effectives.[17]

Nevertheless, if these caveats are borne in mind, several important points emerge from an examination of field armies and battle strengths. First, there is no dramatic contrast between strengths in the sixteenth and seventeenth centuries. Second, the upper limit appears to have been in the region of 35,000 to 40,000. At Pavia, which will act as a base point, the Imperialists had between 20,000 and 25,000; the French, between 25,000 and 30,000, and possibly slightly more.[18] The French and Imperial armies in the Picardy campaigns of 1543–44 were both in the region of 30,000, though the English sent to aid Charles V may have raised the Imperial total. Henry VIII fielded an enormous army of over 40,000 for the siege of Boulogne in 1544–45. Similar numbers were reached in the 1550s. Henry II took nearly 38,000 (including the Household) on the *voyage de Metz* in 1552, and Charles V raised over 50,000 (15,000 of which formed the army of Brandenburg-Kulmbach) to recover the city later in the year. In the St. Quentin campaign of 1557, Philip had some 40,000 (including 7,000 provided by his English ally). What is also clear, however, is that the raising of armies was scraping the limits of the practical. Both Henry II in 1552 and Philip II in 1557 could afford to keep forces of this scale in the field for only a few months.[19] Even a rapid demobilization did not enable them to escape bankruptcy.

The forces involved in the battles of the French Wars of Religion and the early engagements of the Dutch Revolt were considerably lower, for these were civil wars in which the rebel side frequently had considerable difficulty in putting large forces into the field. Alba's 10,000 of 1567 was only a cadre; an army of 66,000 had been proposed originally as necessary for the pacification of the Netherlands.[20] For his two campaigns in France in 1590 and 1592, the duke of Parma took first 11,000, then 30,000.[21] The figures for the major battles of the Thirty Years' War see a return to those of the first half of the sixteenth century, but no dramatic increase. The White Mountain (1620) was fought between armies numbering 28,000 and 21,000. Breitenfeld, probably the largest, involved 42,000 in Gustavus Adolphus's combined army, and 35,000 in Tilly's. The next year Gustavus invaded Bavaria with 37,000, but Lützen was fought by much smaller numbers. Gustavus had 19,000 men, while Wallenstein could muster only 16,000, plus the 3,000 cavalry that Pappenheim brought to his aid after the battle had begun.[22] Nördlingen was slightly larger in scale than the White Mountain: the Catholic army numbered 33,000; the Protestant, only 25,000.[23] R. A. Stradling considers that the army of 40,000 Olivares was preparing in Germany for the invasion of France in the winter of 1634–35 was "more than twice the size of the average field army of the time."[24] Of the later battles, only Wittstock (October 1636) and Zusmarshausen (May 1648) approached the scale of Breitenfeld and Nördlingen. To conclude with two further examples, Rocroi (1643) was fought by 24,000 French and 17,000 Spaniards, and Marston Moor (1644) by 28,000 Parliamentarians and 18,000 Royalists.

The significance of these figures lies in their nearly static quality. Rarely did the numbers rise above 40,000, and even 30,000 to 40,000 was by no means usual. Occasionally there may have been temporarily greater combinations. The three separate armies campaigning for the king of Bohemia in the spring of 1622 (the count of Mansfeld's, Christian of Brunswick's, and the margrave of Baden-Durlach's) may have reached a total of 70,000.[25] So, too, may the combined forces of Tilly and Wallenstein in the invasion of Denmark in 1627–28. The French and Dutch planned to invade the Spanish Netherlands with a combined army of 60,000 in 1635. Jonathan Israel has described this as "one of the largest field armies ever seen in Europe," but David Parrott's research reveals that the French were unable to field more than half their contribution of 30,000 men.[26] It is difficult to avoid the conclusion that 30,000 may have been a natural effective limit for a field army throughout the period. There is some evidence to suggest that contemporaries considered 20,000 to 30,000 the right size for a manageable balanced force. In January 1621 an English council of war presented a detailed report on the size of a field army to be sent to defend the Palatinate: its conclusion was 25,000 foot and 5,000 horse.[27] Sir James Turner, the Scottish veteran of the Swedish service, wrote that an "army royal" should consist of 18,000 foot and 6,000 horse.[28]

The New Model Army was first established at 25,000 (16,000 foot and 9,000 horse) but later reduced to 21,000. Its initial-establishment strength is strikingly close to Wallenstein's original commission of 1625.[29]

Total strengths present a more complex picture. The best-researched army of the period—the Army of Flanders—occupies an equivocal position, for it was somewhere between a field army and a full establishment. Geoffrey Parker's and Jonathan Israel's figures show it exceeding 80,000 men on three occasions: 1574, 1624, and 1639–40. It reached 60,000 frequently during the Dutch Revolt. During the Thirty Years' War it initially rose to the old establishment of over 60,000, but was then reduced in the later 1620s by as much as a third, though it expanded again in the 1630s.[30] The overall strength reached by Spanish forces is a more difficult question. Charles V claimed on several occasions to have more than 100,000 under arms.[31] In 1627 Philip IV boasted he had 300,000, but J. H. Elliot observes that the figure "seems wildly implausible."[32] In the winter of 1634–35 Olivares planned a concentric invasion of France with 100,000 men. Upon the outbreak of war in 1635 the establishments in Germany, Italy, and Catalonia were to be 79,000, which together with the Army of Flanders would have produced a total of nearly 150,000; but there is no evidence this figure was reached.[33]

The experience of the lesser states was more varied. The Venetians raised totals of nearly 30,000 in 1509 and 1529, 35,000 in 1570, but only 26,000 in 1617.[34] The United Provinces possessed no standing forces at the beginning of the Revolt of the Netherlands. Up to 1609, their army reached 60,000 only once (1607); for most of the 1590s their total ranged between 30,000 and 35,000. In 1621 it rose to 48,000, and then to 58,000 in 1627, and to over 70,000 from 1629 to 1643.[35] A similar dramatic increase can be found among the Swedes; it reached its peak in the ambitious projections of Gustavus Adolphus. At the beginning of 1632 he planned to raise a combined allied army of 210,000 (including a Saxon contingent of 40,000). He appears to have obtained no more than 120,000 allied troops and 20,000 Saxons.[36]

Both the Swedes and the Spaniards projected overall establishments considerably in excess of 150,000 in the 1630s. They were not alone; similar claims have been made for both Wallenstein and Louis XIII. It has recently been argued that between 1625 and 1630 Wallenstein's army grew from 61,000 to 150,000.[37] The source for these figures, the annual Imperial army lists (*Lista Kayserlichen Kriegs-Armada*), should, however, be handled cautiously. They outline the deployment of the army, regiment by regiment and company by company, but the strengths (which are purely paper) appear to have been obtained by interpolation from the assumption that the infantry companies were the standard 300 men of the German establishment.[38] Although Wallenstein was appointed commander of the Imperial army in July 1625, these troops were not so much his own army as forces in garrisons throughout the empire, from the Hungarian frontier to Jutland. How many were actually employed directly under his command in the Danish war is another question. Wallenstein's initial commission was to raise 24,000 men, which included 12,500 already on hand. By the end of 1625 he was talking about employing 50,000 in the campaign of 1626.[39] He may have reached 60,000 by the spring, but he only had 20,000 at Dessau Bridge, and he conducted his pursuit of Mansfeld later in the year with the same number.[40] That November he is said to have proposed the raising of an Imperial standing army of 70,000. His contribution to the invasion of Denmark in 1627, on the other hand, may only have amounted to 40,000; a force which, interestingly enough, he regarded as too large to campaign as a unit.[41] Last, although the Imperial army of 1628–30 may have had a paper strength of 130,000 to 150,000, much of it had already been dispersed to Italy, the Netherlands, and Poland by the summer of 1629, a year before Wallenstein's dismissal.[42]

The French war effort of the 1630s was no more successful. The standing army at the beginning of the century numbered under 10,000, less than it had been in 1559.[43] For his intervention in the Cleves-Jülich crisis in 1610 Henry IV planned to mobilize 54,000, of which 30,000 was to form his main field army.[44] Until the early 1630s this figure appears to have been accepted by French ministers (including Richelieu) as the upper limit of the possible, a total not greatly in excess of the forces raised by Francis I and Henry II.[45] In 1635–38 really massive increases in strength were projected, averaging over 150,000 and reaching just under 200,000 in 1636. The research of David Parrott has shown, however, that this was also a massive overestimation of what was practical, and that the effective strengths of French armies in the later 1630s were little more than half the projections.[46] Throughout the "French intervention" French armies campaigned at levels no greater than those of their opponents.

II

The conclusion that suggests itself is an important one. Certain aspects of the increase of armies can be accepted. The greater number of combatant powers in the 1630s may have led to a larger overall number of men serving in one army or another than had previously been the case. For some states (the United Provinces or Sweden) there was undoubtedly a novel increase in their military forces in the period that may have had a revolutionary impact.[47] But it appears equally clear that while the size of field armies remained relatively static throughout the period, the Thirty Years' War saw a dramatic increase in projected overall establishments. Moreover, this new policy appears to have met with only limited success; the number of effectives rose but little, and the scale of battles and campaigns was unchanged. The disparity between the strategic ambitions of governments and their abilities to realize them reached a dramatic peak.

The question of whether there were indeed logistical and organizational imperatives that made 35,000 to 40,000 a natural rather than accidental upper limit for field armies in this period has been addressed elsewhere.[48] What will be examined here are the reasons for the increase in projections in overall strength. Despite the widespread acceptance of the expansion of armies, more attention has been devoted to its impact than to its causes. Only Geoffrey Parker has attempted an overall explanation; his thesis is both clever and sophisticated. The initial expansion in the first decades of the sixteenth century he attributes to a decrease "both absolutely and relatively" in the numbers of cavalry, and their replacement by cheaper pikemen. Thereafter the growth of infantry was the product of the development of the new artillery fortifications: "an increase necessitated by the vast number of men required to starve out a town defended by the *trace italienne.*" The increases were not progressive. There was a dramatic expansion in the 1530s, but then a stagnation until the 1580s, when new administrative procedures and improvements in logistics enabled further growth in the following century.[49] David Parrott, on the other hand, finds the reasons for expansion "obscure" and suggests that "it probably owed most to the drastic expansion of war aims, and the imposition of new, unpopular regimes over entire states."[50]

The two key elements in the Parker thesis—the decline of cavalry and the growth of the *trace italienne*—are most clearly observable in the Netherlands campaigns. Except for the 1570s and 1640s, the cavalry complement of the Army of Flanders was well under a tenth of the strength of the foot. The proportion in the Dutch army was roughly similar.[51] Yet in the Thirty Years' War, as Roberts has observed, the proportion of horse was, on the other hand, on the increase.[52] At Lützen, half of Wallenstein's 16,000 and one-third of Gustavus's 19,000 were cavalry, while Pappenheim's reinforcement was entirely horse. Similar proportions are found at Nördlingen: 13,000 of the Catholic army's 33,000 and 9,000 of the Protestant army's 28,000. The establishments of both Wallenstein's 1625 army and the New Model Army consisted of one-third horse to two-thirds foot.

The reasons for the revival of cavalry in the armies of the 1630s and 1640s are not obscure. First, the more open circumstances of the Thirty Years' War and the English Civil War gave greater room for the use of cavalry; the fact that the proportion of horse was not higher was due to the difficulties in raising cavalry rather than a decision to dispense with it.[53] Second, the proportion of cavalry to infantry would be higher in field armies than in overall establishments. The question that needs to be addressed, therefore, is really that of the "excess" infantry. Here there are two related, if contradictory, theses. Roberts points to a general phenomenon of the "bleeding" of field armies by garrisons; Parker argues for the demands of sieges.[54]

What is at issue is the role of the *trace italienne* fortress, a role which was fundamentally ambiguous. Its spread throughout Europe in the century after 1500 was patchy, for the expense involved could bankrupt a small principality or a city-state (as it did Siena in the 1550s and Geneva in the 1580s), and no major city could afford a complete enceinte.[55] Such fortifications were undertaken only when necessary, and their strategic role was largely dependent on geography, both political and physical; the classic examples being Italy, Piedmont, and the Netherlands. Yet even in the Netherlands their expansion was limited. As late as the 1586 campaign towns like Doesburg or Deventer were devoid of modern fortifications.[56] Their relative absence in Germany on the eve of the Thirty Years' War, and in England on the eve of the Civil War, meant that sieges lacked the central strategic significance that they possessed in the Netherlands campaigns.

The stopping power of sieges can also be overestimated. Of the centrality of such sieges as Ostend (1601–4) and Breda (1625) to the Low Countries wars there can be little doubt, but, if our scope is extended, the impact of sieges is more diffuse. In some cases their significance was primarily political: the French occupation and the Imperialist siege of Metz in 1552, for example. The disastrous defeat of Charles V has been legitimately attributed to his own rashness in trying to mount a major siege in winter.[57] The same is true for fortresses in the later stages of the French Wars of Religion, particularly the 1620s phase, when the fortified Huguenot towns derived much of their importance from their status as *places de sûreté* under the Treaty of Nantes.[58] As with the examples of Haarlem, Alkmaar, and Leiden in 1573–74, the long defense of La Rochelle in 1627–28 owed as much to the intransigence of the civilian population as to the inherent strength of its fortifications. In several celebrated instances, political unwillingness to conclude the siege on the part of the besiegers accounted for the apparent success of the defense: Magdeburg in 1549–50, La Rochelle in 1573, or Stralsund in 1628–29.[59]

The popularity of the new fortifications in the middle decades of the sixteenth century owed much to the mistaken belief that they provided a cheaper means of defense than a field army. The belief was held particularly strongly by smaller states, Siena in the 1550s, or Venice, for example. The duke of Somerset's occupation of Scotland between 1547 and 1550 was a bold attempt to use garrisons offensively. However, both the Sienese Revolt and Somerset's defeat revealed the limitations of this strategy; and later campaigns, in the Netherlands in particular, confirmed the lesson. Without a field army to relieve them or provide diversions, immobilized and isolated garrisons were extremely vulnerable to being picked off one by one.[60] The "bleeding of field armies" was a consequence of the need to maintain both garrisons and the necessary mobile force.

The problem was more one of frontiers than communications. The long supply lines the Swedish army possessed in Germany in the 1630s and 1640s were the exception rather than the rule. The greatest line of communications of the period—the famous Spanish Road—was too large to garrison; its security depended on diplomacy. What further complicated the defense of frontiers was the other aspect of the new fortifications—the use of citadels for the intimidation of the local population. In some of the Italian cities this was a long-established practice, but its spread during the sixteenth century throughout Europe (as, for example, in the Hapsburg citadels in Siena in 1549 and Antwerp in 1568–69), and the similar use of garrisons in counterinsurgency warfare (as the English employed in Ireland), marked a major increase in the demands on existing military resources.[61]

The significance of garrisons in their twin roles of defense of territory and control of populations can be seen most clearly in the growth of standing armies in the sixteenth century. Although regiments or tercios could be either administrative or tactical units, the assigning of territorial designations to permanent formations reveals that their function was essentially that of static garrisons. The old Spanish tercios of Lombardy, Naples, or Sicily; the French legions, *bandes,* or regiments of Piedmont, Picardy or Champagne; and the Dutch provincial regiments of North Holland, Friesland, Utrecht, or Zeeland derived their names from the provinces they garrisoned, not from the ones where they were recruited.[62] In the French case they were frontier garrisons; in the Spanish, they were those of occupied provinces.[63] As I. A. A. Thompson has shown, apart from a skeletal royal guard, there were no standing forces in peninsular Spain in the sixteenth century.[64] Standing armies were essentially garrison armies. Even the French gendarmerie was employed as a police force in the sixteenth century, beginning a long and notorious tradition that culminated in the *dragonnades* of the 1680s.[65] The much more limited growth of an English standing army under the Tudors was also part of the same process. It involved the spread of the Pale system of a permanent garrison from Calais to Ireland in the 1530s, then to Boulogne between 1545 and 1550 and Berwick after 1551.[66]

III

If the growth of garrisons provides an explanation for the "excess infantry," the strategic context of this expansion demands further attention. The battles of the Italian wars (La Bicocca, Pavia, and Ceresole) demonstrated conclusively that firearms and field fortifications made offensive campaigns a dubious enterprise. Thereafter it is difficult to detect a major advance in tactics or technology that altered the balance.[67] It is to the peculiar political concerns of the period 1525 to 1648—and two major international questions in particular—that changes in strategy are to be attributed.[68] They were not questions to which there were immediate objective answers; but they raised issues upon which contemporaries held strong convictions, and which dominated political debate. The first (chronologically speaking) was that of the Hapsburg Imperium. Did the dynastic inheritance of Charles V mark the first stage of an expansion of the house of Austria toward a universal monarchy, *la monarquía?* If so, then its ambitions posed a threat to the liberty of Europe and justified defensive coalitions. From the point of view of Madrid or Vienna, however, such opposition was seen as attempts by the envious to deprive the house of Austria of its legitimate possessions. It, too, was waging an essentially defensive struggle.

The Hapsburg threat was primarily a secular question: the hegemony of the house of Austria affected all regardless of confessional allegiance. Thus although it might be deliberately confused in propaganda, it was essentially distinct from the second great question (which really only emerges after 1559, though there are some elements detectable in the 1530s and 1540s) of whether a major religious struggle was about to break out. If so, then it would divide Europe into two major confessional armed camps. But religious alliances, too, were ultimately defensive in purpose; they were designed to protect one side from the threat of extermination posed by the other. The coexistence of both questions and the debates they engendered (leaving out lesser and more specific issues) made diplomacy hideously complex, but their influence over strategy was a joint one. If they provided new justifications for war, they did so in essentially defensive terms.

There were other strategic implications as well. The emergence of the confessional issue meant that all major wars between 1559 and 1648 were to some extent religious civil wars. Political boundaries became of less relevance, popular participation (particularly in the sieges of major cities) was far more extensive than in previous conflicts, and to a far greater degree the role of armies was that of crushing dissidents and controlling hostile populations. To some extent these issues had in fact emerged during the first half of the sixteenth century. If the origins of the Italian wars lay in the dynastic struggle between Hapsburg and Valois over Naples and Milan, the Hapsburg victories saw the issues at stake change. Increased Hapsburg control over the Italian peninsula inspired fears that the Imperium was becoming a reality; the French in turn began to pose as the protectors of Italian liberty. If this trend did not fully emerge until the early 1550s, it can be detected initially in Francis I's response to his defeat at Pavia.[69]

For Charles V a major strategic problem was posed. However great his apparent resources, he was faced with the need to defend his possessions (initially in Italy, but in 1552 in the Empire as well) from a combination of external invasion and popular revolt. The solution was found in a new strategy that can be legitimately termed the Spanish school. As William Maltby has shown in his biography of the duke of Alba, this strategy can first be seen at work in Alba's campaigns against the Schmalkaldic League in 1546–47 and the duke of Guise in Italy in 1557. It involved an acceptance of the tactical power of the defense, which, given the essentially defensive aims of the house of Austria's policy and its potentially superior resources, would enable it to exhaust its enemies. Hostile powers would be isolated diplomatically and swamped by overwhelming force. They would then be forced to give battle at a disadvantage. The harrying of the Elector of Saxony and the Schmalkaldic League prior to the battle of Mühlberg christened this strategy with a dramatic success.[70]

The outbreak of the Dutch Revolt saw Alba employ the same strategy against William of Orange between 1568 and 1573. The dispatch of most of the companies of the Italian tercios to the Netherlands in 1567 was on one level simply the shifting of the garrison of one part of the Spanish empire to another.[71] The Netherlands were to be dominated by garrisons and cut off from external commerce; the isolated pockets of rebellion were then to be crushed with superior force. Foreign invasions would be held off by well-manned fortifications. What has been less appreciated is how closely Alba's strategy was followed by his successors, the duke of Parma and Ambrosio de Spínola. Parma's memorandum to Philip II of January 1581 repeated Alba's earlier proposals practically item by item.[72] The rebel provinces were to be surrounded by garrisons drawn from an enormous army and then cut off from external trade and support. The army was not to be wasted in unnecessary sieges and battles; the urban centers of resistance were to be isolated and starved into submission. The difficulty lay in providing the vast military establishment that this strategy demanded. Alba went to the Netherlands with less than the number of troops he regarded as sufficient.[73] The full-scale rebellion of 1572 created an emergency that forced him to raise the Army of Flanders to its peak of 86,000 men, but it was too great a burden even for the Spanish treasury.[74] Parma's attempt in the autumn of 1583 to persuade Philip II to exploit the political chaos in the Netherlands left by the duke of Anjou with a massive military effort ran into similar financial barriers.[75] His successful reconquest of the southern provinces between the siege of Maastricht in 1579 and the siege of Antwerp in 1584 was largely a political one. However large the Army of Flanders appeared on paper, it was not sufficient to carry out its strategic purpose.

From these limitations the peculiar rhythms of the Netherlands wars— "these defensive garrison wars" as the earl of Leicester called them in his frustration—were derived.[76] It was not simply physical geography that created the patchwork of garrisons; political and military imperatives also necessitated the holding of forts that were all but isolated and the construction of the rings of blockading posts that swallowed up troops. Ironically, the very loss of the southern Netherlands in 1582–85 probably improved the strategic position of the United Provinces, for it gave them a more compact territory to hold and better interior lines.[77] The retention of Ostend, on the other hand, however politically desirable (and to some degree the result of English pressure), was a major strategic liability. The central military problem on both sides lay in scraping together enough men from the garrisons to provide an adequate field army. Of the 93 foot companies left in Parma's army after the withdrawal of the Spanish troops in 1580, 56 were employed in garrisons, leaving only 37 for a field force.[78] In 1585 the States General informed Elizabeth I that while they had 200 companies in pay, if they were to form a field army, English troops would be necessary.[79] Many of the difficulties encountered by the earl of Leicester as governor-general arose from his efforts to find the money and men for such an army.

The disparity between total and deployable effectives shaped the course of the Netherlands campaigns. The actual campaigning was undertaken by field forces rarely numbering above 10,000 to 15,000 men. In the autumn of 1586 Leicester and Parma confronted each other at Zutphen with armies numbering between only 9,000 and 10,000.[80] Moreover, battles became even less important (Turnhout and Nieuwpoort were fought almost by accident) because the elimination of a few thousand men was a waste of resources when compared to the gaining of a strategic town. In this respect the reforms of Maurice of Nassau of the 1590s—the creation of an effective field force and the employment of major concentrations of artillery in sieges—were of less significance than the Spanish intervention in France between 1590 and 1598.[81] With the departure of the Spanish field army, the garrisons could be picked off individually with minimal interference. On the other hand, once the field army returned after the Treaty of Vervins, the balance was restored, and the campaigns of 1601–9, for all the skill employed by both sides, were a strategic stalemate.

Although the Low Countries wars made the "Spanish school" the model for Europe, it did have its critics, particularly in France, where an offensive tradition survived from the Italian wars. Here the most celebrated exponent was Henry IV, who alone of all the major commanders of the later sixteenth century actually sought battle.[82] However, his reasons were primarily psychological and political, and did not involve a counterstrategy. The weakness of his strategic thinking was notorious; even his closest advisors commented on it. Indeed, insofar as there was a military art in the sixteenth century, it has no better example than Parma's brilliant outmaneuvering of Henry IV in the campaigns of 1590 and 1592.[83] Despite his doubts about the overall strategy of intervention in France, Parma was able to carry out his immediate objectives and withdraw successfully, despite all Henry's attempts to force a battle on advantageous terms. The French offensive against the Spanish Netherlands between 1594 and 1598, despite the theoretical advantages of the English and Dutch alliance, was, by contrast, a disaster.

The success of the Spanish school remained intact until the outbreak of the Thirty Years' War. Paradoxically, its repudiation came a decade before the Swedish intervention and was inspired by what was apparently a military success: Spínola's invasion of the Palatinate in August and September 1620. The circumstances deserve attention. There were obvious political and military reasons for a major strike against the Palatinate following Frederick V's acceptance of the Bohemian throne in 1619. But there were also dangers: the truce with the Netherlands would expire in 1621, and an invasion of the Palatinate might trigger intervention from Britain or even France. The operation was therefore carefully planned. Spínola was provided with a field army of 25,000 men, but he was expected to conquer the Palatinate in a single campaign in 1620. The disparity in force was considerable. The Palatinate boasted only three modern fortresses: Heidelberg, Frankenthal, and the new town of Mannheim, which together provided a central defended complex. Local troops consisted of one garrison regiment and some citizen militia. Otherwise the defense of the Palatinate rested on the demoralized army of Frederick's allies, the Protestant Union (between 10,000 and 16,000), and several thousand English and Dutch reinforcements, who arrived after the campaign had opened.

Spínola's progress was cautious in the extreme. Although he occupied a number of undefended towns on the left bank of the Rhine, he made no attempt to assault the major fortresses. Instead he confined himself to building a bridge of boats across the Rhine (in the course of which, according to one account, he delivered a suitably Caesarian oration) and then quickly placed his troops in winter quarters at Oppenheim. Bloodless the invasion might have been, but conquest it was not.[84] Even though the feared foreign intervention did not occur, it took another two years for the final reduction of the Palatinate. Simultaneously, a more dramatic military operation was taking place. In Bohemia the combined army of the Emperor and the Catholic League, commanded by the League's general, Tilly, not only shattered the new king's army at the White Mountain, but by the end of the year had occupied almost the entire kingdom. In the decade that followed Tilly went on to a number of dramatic offensive victories: Wimpfen and Höchst in 1622, Stadtlohn in 1623, and Lutter am Barenberg in 1626. Only at Breitenfeld was one of his attacks defeated decisively. Tilly's aggressive campaigning was accompanied by a barrage of complaints about the dilatoriness and caution of Spínola and the Spanish commanders.[85] Spínola's reputation never recovered from the campaign in the Palatinate.

Tilly's revival of the offensive and his repudiation of the Spanish school were inspired and supported by his patron, Maximilian, duke of Bavaria. The reasons lie in the economic demands of the Spanish strategy. Perhaps the most important aspect of the first decade of the Thirty Years' War was the abstention, neutrality, or half-hearted intervention of Britain and France. Moreover, two of the major powers involved, the United Provinces and Spain, were exceedingly cautious about the extent of their commitment. There was thus a vacuum at the international level into which a number of lesser powers stepped: the Elector Palatine, Bavaria, Denmark, and Sweden. All became involved in a war that was on rational grounds beyond their means. (Their reasons for doing so are not directly relevant here, though confessional fears and allegiances were probably decisive.) It was Maximilian who earliest and most clearly perceived the problem, not least because his father William V had more or less bankrupted Bavaria through his earlier participation in the war for Cologne of 1583–85.[86]

For smaller states with limited resources, large-scale attrition warfare of the Spanish style was not possible. A short, decisive campaign was all that could be afforded. But there were further political and economic reasons for a return to an offensive strategy in Germany: what might be termed offensive logistics. It was important at all costs to avoid the damage of campaigning on one's own territory or that of allies, thus every effort had to be made to exploit the enemy's quarter and supply troops. The race for winter quarters became a constant feature of the war. Here the League armies possessed the major advantage of operating under Imperial commissions, which gave them the power to demand supplies from neutrals. However, there remained the problem of the considerable areas over which the war was fought, the limited numbers of troops, and the existence of a large body of Protestant neutrals (Brandenburg, Saxony, Hesse-Kassel, and the numerous Free Cities) whose abstention and cooperation could not be taken for granted. As a result the aggressive use of intimidation and terrorism, though not unknown before, now became established. The widespread use of such devices as *Brandschatzung,* or the threat of quartering troops on areas that refused to make contributions, were not merely the sporadic practices of mercenary freebooters, but a deliberate system.[87] It could even be used politically, as Tilly demonstrated in 1623 when he threatened to quarter his army in the Lower Saxon Circle unless they expelled Christian of Brunswick.[88]

The Bavarian use of such methods, first in Bohemia and then in the Palatinate, inspired retaliation, such as that carried out by Christian of Brunswick in the bishopric of Paderborn in 1622. The system became institutionalized. Wallenstein's employment of these devices, for all its notoriety, was simply a somewhat idiosyncratic variant of the Bavarian practice. If he employed the Bavarian system of logistics, his strategy was, if anything, a last example of the old Spanish school. Unlike Tilly's, his campaigns were characterized by cautious and defensive tactics (Dessau Bridge or the Alte Veste), and his effort to amass large numbers was very much a revival of the attrition and saturation strategy of Alba and Parma.[89] The Danish and Swedish interventions saw further variations on this theme. Christian IV relied in the main on foreign subsidies, largely inspired by Britain, that never (or seldom) arrived. The Danish Rigsråd's opposition to the war meant that he could not support it by taxation. Instead he was forced to fall back on his private war chest, derived from the profits of the Sound Tolls. Since his army never advanced beyond the allied territories of the Lower Saxon Circle he was never able to employ more aggressive logistics. The Danish intervention remained a private war in the fullest sense of the word.[90] Gustavus Adolphus, on the other hand, developed offensive logistics in perhaps their most ruthless form. Not only did his demands for *assecuratio* and *satisfactio* resemble the Bavarian agreements with the Emperor, but his use of contributions, threats of quartering, and employment of enemy territory for winter quarters (as with the Catholic bishoprics in the winter of 1631–32) was little different to Wallenstein's.[91]

Given its purpose, the Swedish intervention had no use for a defensive strategy. The limited forces and resources at Gustavus's disposal meant that a decisive victory by battle was essential. But the Swedish strategy was no more successful than its predecessors. The significance of Breitenfeld lay in Tilly's failure to inflict a defeat on the Swedes that would drive them out of Germany. The victory of Swedish firepower over Tilly's attacking columns simply reinforced a lesson taught in a number of sixteenth-century battles. When employed offensively (as the mixed results of Gustavus's earlier Polish campaigns had already revealed), neither Swedish tactics nor Swedish resources were sufficient. Lützen was all but a draw; Nördlingen was a clear defeat.

It is from this perspective that the dramatic increases in projected armies obtain their significance. Gustavus's plan for an army of 200,000 in 1632 was intended to provide the means to force a final decisive conclusion to the war. It was not seen as a level that could be maintained indefinitely. Similarly the Spanish and French mobilizations of 1634–35 were means to the same end. The recent works of R. A. Stradling and David Parrott have revealed that both Olivares and Richelieu were planning major offensives with overwhelming strength that would achieve victory in a single campaign.[92] Neither intended to wage a defensive or attritional war. But like Gustavus, both completely overestimated the financial and military resources at their command. Not only did both offensives fail, but both countries found themselves in a war that they could only wage with forces too limited to produce more than an extended stalemate, while the expanded number of combatant powers saw a further diversion of forces to more dispersed fronts. Given the relatively small numbers engaged in the majority of the later battles, the casualties suffered were not, in themselves, sufficient to have a major strategic impact, even Rocroi.[93]

The political inspiration for this return to the offensive underlay its failure. Neither side's administrations were able to fund military expenditure at this level; both were operating on a scale beyond their means. In this respect the "greater powers" were reduced to the financial level of the lesser. Yet the fiscal irresponsibility of the Thirty Years'

War was not necessarily typical of the period as a whole. If Elizabeth I's attempt to wage war by budget, as in the Netherlands intervention in 1585–87, owed much to her general parsimony, it also reflected the response of the English political elite to the near-bankruptcy caused by the military overextension of the 1540s. Nor were the worries of Sir William Cecil in 1565 over "the uncertainty of the charge of the war, as at this day it is seen that all wars are treble more chargeable than they were wont to be," unique.[94] At the same time the Venetians also concluded that war was the quick way to economic suicide.[95] Only Spain could bear the burden of an attritional strategy, and even its success was limited. For lesser powers the temptation to risk all on a possibly decisive offensive is understandable.

The strategic significance of the political context of the Thirty Years' War is highlighted by the comparison with the later seventeenth century. Louis XIV revolutionized the international context: first, by replacing fears of a Hapsburg Imperium with fears of a French Imperium, and second, by almost single-handedly bringing the confessional wars to a close by attacking Spain and the United Provinces indiscriminately. This transformed the nature of the later seventeenth-century wars, for religious tension (though not completely eliminated) no longer inhibited the anti-French coalition in the way anti-Hapsburg coalitions had been. The real causes of the tragedy of the Thirty Years' War were diplomatic rather than military: the failure to obtain a settlement in its early years, and the failure to create a decisive anti-Hapsburg grand alliance. Both can be attributed ultimately to confessional hostility.

Any final conclusions about the military revolution must therefore take its political context into account. It was the Thirty Years' War that led to the expansion of armies, not the converse. The relatively minor advances in weaponry and tactics between the development of effective small arms fire in the early sixteenth century and the replacement of the pike by the bayonet at the end of the seventeenth meant that on the tactical level changes were largely variations on a theme. Similarly the relatively limited size of field armies gave to none of the combatants a decisive advantage. Even comparatively minor states could (temporarily) raise armies of 20,000 to 30,000. If the Spanish monarchy possessed greater resources than its rivals, it possessed greater liabilities and greater commitments. The essentially defensive strategy described here as the Spanish school was the product of the political concerns of the house of Austria. Yet the scale of resources it demanded when employed in the Netherlands (let alone the combination of the Netherlands and Germany) was too great even for Spain to provide, and effective concentration of force proved impossible. Political frustration on the part of the minor powers led to the repudiation of this strategy. The return to the offensive in the Thirty Years' War was a political rather than a military imperative. Yet even the victory of one minor power (like Bavaria) over another (the Palatinate) was insufficient to sway the wider balance. Nor did the adoption of an offensive strategy by the major powers produce a short decisive war. No state of the period possessed the ability to raise armies of the size it considered necessary. To Geoffrey Parker's observation that the states of early modern Europe had not discovered how to lead armies to victory, we can add the suggestion that behind the failure of armies in this period lay the fact that much more was expected of them than they could provide.

NOTES

1. S. R. Gardiner, *The Thirty Years' War, 1618-1648* (London, 1881), 139-40.

2. Michael Roberts, *Gustavus Adolphus* (London, 1958), 2:182. The "Military Revolution" is explored more directly in his essays "The Military Revolution, 1560-1660," and "Gustavus Adolphus and the Art of War," reprinted in *Essays in Swedish History* (London, 1967).

3. Geoffrey Parker, "The 'Military Revolution, 1560-1660' — A Myth?," *Journal of Modern History* 48 (1976): 195-214, reprinted in *Spain and the Netherlands, 1559-1569* (London, 1979), 86-103, with significant revisions. All further references are to the later version.

4. Quoted from *The Military Revolution: Military Innovation and the Rise of the West, 1500-1800* (Cambridge, 1988), 80.

5. Robert Barret, *The Theorike and Practike of Moderne Warres* (London, 1598), 75, 77, recommends its use, though with experienced men. See also John A. Lynn, "Tactical Evolution in the French Army, 1550-1660," *French Historical Studies* 14 (1985), 179-80, and David Parrott, "Strategy and Tactics in the Thirty Years' War: The 'Military Revolution,' " *Militärgeschichtliche Mitteilungen* 18 (1985): 8-9. I am most grateful to Professor Lynn and Dr. Parrott for bringing these articles to my attention, and to Dr. Parrott for permission to use his excellent dissertation "The Administration of the French Army during the Ministry of Cardinal Richelieu," D.Phil. diss., Oxford University, 1985.

6. Martin van Creveld, *Supplying War: Logistics from Wallenstein to Patton* (Cambridge, 1977), 4.

7. Roberts, "The Military Revolution," 203-4.

8. Parker, "Military Revolution — A Myth?," 95-96.

9. Creveld, 5-6.

10. The distinction is noted in Parker, "Military Revolution—A Myth?," 95, and Parrott, "Strategy and Tactics," 16-17, but overlooked in the table of army strengths in J. R. Hale's, *War and Society in Renaissance Europe, 1440-1620* (London, 1985), 62-63.

11. Ferdinand Lot, *Recherches sur les effectifs des armées françaises des Guerres d'Italie aux Guerres de Religion, 1494-1562* (Paris, 1962), the one sustained attempt to analyze sixteenth-century army strengths, takes an impressively skeptical approach toward literary sources. Cf. their uncritical employment in Charles Oman, *History of the Art of War in the XVIth Century* (London, 1937).

12. For Pavia, see R. J. Knecht, *Francis I* (Cambridge, 1982), 170-71.

13. Ibid., 164. Golo Mann, *Wallenstein: His Life Narrated* (London, 1976), 649; A. van der Essen, *Le Cardinal-Enfant et la politique européenne de l'Espagne, 1609-1641* (Brussels, 1944), 1:422.

14. See Essen, *Cardinal-Enfant*, 1:413, n. 3.

15. Geoffrey Parker, *The Army of Flanders and the Spanish Road, 1567-1659* (Cambridge, 1972), 3.

16. The Dutch *Staaten van Oorlog* are summarized in tabular form in F. T. G. Ten Raa and F. de Bas, *Het Staatsche Leger, 1598-1795* (Breda, 1911-18). For the period 1588-1609, see vol. 2 (1913), 344-69. For 1621-48 see also Jonathan I. Israel, *The Dutch Republic and the Hispanic World, 1606-1661* (Oxford, 1982), 96, 167-68, 176-77, 317. For the French, see Parrott, "Administration of the French Army," 88-89. Cf. also the comments of W. Brulez, "Het Gewicht van de Oorlog in de Nieuwe Tijden. Enkele Aspecten," *Tijdschrift voor Geschiednis* 91 (1978): 398, n. 46.

17. For examples, see Parker, *Army of Flanders*, 207-11, and Parrott, "Strategy and Tactics," 19, and "Administration of the French Army," 96.

18. Knecht, *Francis I*, 171, and Lot, *Recherches*, 56.

19. In general, see Lot, *Recherches*, 69-100, 129-61, 171, passim. C. S. L. Davies, "Provisions for Armies, 1509-50: A Study in the Effectiveness of Early Tudor Government," *Economic History Review*, 3d. ser., 17 (1964-65): 234, gives 48,000 as the size of the English army of 1544.

20. P. D. Lagomarsino, "Court Factions and the Formulation of Spanish Policy Towards the Netherlands (1559-1567)" Ph.D. diss., Cambridge University, 1973, 268, 278.

21. Léon van der Essen, *Alexandre Farnèse, Prince de Parme, Gouverneur Général des Pays-Bas (1559-1567)* (Brussels, 1933-37), 5:294-95, 333.

22. Roberts, *Gustavus Adolphus*, 2:766.

23. Essen, *Cardinal-Enfant*, 1:413, n. 3.

24. R. A. Stradling, "Olivares and the Origins of the Franco-Spanish War, 1627-1635," *English Historical Review* 101 (1986): 83.

25. Hans Wertheim, *Der Tolle Halberstädter: Herzog Christian von Braunschweig im Pfälzischen Krieg, 1621-1622* (Berlin, 1929), 2:308-11, 371-72, 494-95, gives the composition of the three armies, though some skepticism is justified.

26. Israel, *Dutch Republic*, 252. Cf. Parrott, "Administration of the French Army," 25-29, "Strategy and Tactics," 19.

27. London, Public Record Office, SP 14/119/93. In 1542 Charles V warned his brother Ferdinand that the army of 40,000 foot and 8,000 horse he was

proposing to raise for the Hungarian campaign was too large to manage. See P. S. Fichtner, *Ferdinand I of Austria: The Politics of Dynasticism in the Age of the Reformation* (New York, 1982), 128–29.

28. Quoted in Roberts, *Gustavus Adolphus*, 2:470.

29. Mark A. Kishlansky, *The Rise of the New Model Army* (Cambridge, 1979), 36–37. For Wallenstein's commission, see pages 33–34 of this essay.

30. Parker, *Army of Flanders*, 271–72. Israel, *Dutch Republic*, 162–65.

31. Parker, *Army of Flanders*, 6.

32. J. H. Elliott, *The Count-Duke of Olivares: The Statesman in an Age of Decline* (New Haven and London, 1986), 509.

33. Ibid., Stradling, "Origins," 90.

34. M. E. Mallett and J. R. Hale, *The Military Organization of a Renaissance State: Venice c. 1400 to 1617* (Cambridge, 1984), 213.

35. See n. 16 above.

36. Roberts, *Gustavus Adolphus*, 2:676–77.

37. Gerhard Benecke in Geoffrey Parker, *The Thirty Years' War* (London, 1984), 100.

38. The lists for the period 1621–34 are printed in tabular form as appendices to *Documenta Bohemica Bellum Tricennale Illustrantia*, ed. Josef Janék, et al. (Prague, 1971–77), vols. 3–5.

39. *Documenta Bohemica*, 4:51, 77.

40. Ibid., 11, 130, 137. Wallenstein did send 74 foot companies (20,000 men at full strength) to Tilly on the eve of Lutter am Barenberg. See also Mann, 289.

41. *Documenta Bohemica*, 4:204–5, 215. Wallenstein's conference with the Imperial councillor Eggenberg at Bruck an der Leitha in November 1626, in which he is said to have proposed the creation of an Imperial standing army, is discussed in Mann, 324–29.

42. Mann, 438.

43. John A. Lynn, "The Growth of the French Army during the Seventeenth Century," *Armed Forces and Society* 6 (1980): 569, 573. Parrott, "Administration of the French Army," 103.

44. Lynn, "Growth," 573. Cf. David Buissert, *Henry IV* (London, 1984), 174. The remaining 25,000 were diversionary forces deployed in Navarre and Italy.

45. Parrott, "Administration of the French Army," 103–4.

46. Ibid., 105–17 passim, and the table on page 142.

47. This point was made to me by Professor Parker in conversation.

48. See Parrott, "Strategy and Tactics," 16–21. This article draws the same distinction between the growth of field armies and overall establishments as that made above and sees logistical considerations as the central limiting factor on the size of field armies. Cf. the comments of Davies, "Provisions," 246.

49. Parker, "Military Revolution—A Myth?," 97.

50. Parrott, "Administration of the French Army," 81.

51. See the tables in Parker, *Army of Flanders*, 271–72, and *Het Staatsche Leger*, 2:344–69.

52. Roberts, *Gustavus Adolphus*, 2:203.

53. Robert Stradling, "Catastrophe and Recovery: The Defeat of Spain, 1639–43," *History* 64 (1979): 216, and, more specifically, "Spain's Military Failure and the

Supply of Horses, 1600–1660," *History* 69 (1984): 211–15. Parrott, "Administration of the French Army," 81–82.

54. Roberts, *Gustavus Adolphus*, 2:444. Parker, "Military Revolution—A Myth?," 97.

55. Simon Pepper and Nicholas Adams, *Firearms and Fortifications: Military Architecture and Siege Warfare in Sixteenth-Century Siena* (Chicago, 1986), 27–28. Judith Hook, "Fortifications and the End of the Sienese State," *History* 62 (1977): 373–74.

56. Practically all of the towns listed by Brulez, "Het Gewicht," 394, as fortified between 1529 and 1572 are southern.

57. William S. Maltby, *Alba: A Biography of Fernando Alvarez de Toledo, Third Duke of Alba, 1507–1582* (Berkeley, Calif., 1983), 81.

58. Buissert, *Henry IV*, 70–71.

59. For Wallenstein and Stalsund, see Mann, 412–15.

60. Pepper and Adams, *Firearms and Fortifications*, 31, 129–30; Mallett and Hale, *Military Organization*, 411–12; M. L. Bush, *The Government Policy of Protector Somerset* (London, 1975), 7–39 passim.

61. For Italy, see the comments of Pepper and Adams, *Firearms and Fortifications*, 27–28, 157, and Mallett and Hale, *Military Organization*, 421–23. Cf. the observations of the earl of Leicester on Ireland: "I have oft times noted in the service of that land, whensoever we have placed any garrisons to front the enemy . . . it hath fallen out to be the way to chasten and plague him." Oxford, Bodleian Library, Carte MS 56, fols. 103v-4, to Sir William Fitzwilliam, 5 Dec. 1572.

62. For the creation of the Dutch provincial regiments after 1572, see Ten Raa and de Bas, *Het Staatsche Leger*, 1:254–62. J. W. Wijn, "Het Noordhollandse Regiment in de Eerste Jaren van de Opstand tegen Spanje," *Tijdschrift voor Geschiednis* 62 (1949), 245–46, notes that only a third of the original complement of the regiment was comprised of natives of the province, though the proportion varied from company to company.

63. For the dispersal of the French *bandes* after 1559, see Lot, 188, 253 ff.

64. *War and Government in Habsburg Spain, 1560–1620* (London, 1976), 19.

65. See, for example, the instructions of Francis II to Marshal Tavannes, 12 April 1560, printed in *Négociations, lettres et pièces diverses . . . tirées du portefeuille de Sebastien de L'Aubespeine, Evêque de Limoges*, ed. Louis Paris (Paris, 1841), 341–42.

66. For the Irish stage of this process, see Brendan Bradshaw, *The Irish Constitutional Revolution of the Sixteenth Century* (Cambridge, 1979), 119–21.

67. Cf. Parrott, "Strategy and Tactics," 12–16.

68. The arguments outlined in the following paragraphs are developed more fully in my paper " 'The Catholic League' and the Emergence of Protestant Alliance Politics, 1559–1572," delivered at the Anglo-American Conference of Historians in London in July 1987, to be published in *Historical Research*.

69. Francis I justified his Turkish alliance against Charles V in 1532 as a means to "rassurer toutes autres gouvernements contre un ennemi si grand." J. Ursu, *La politique orientale de François I (1515–1547)* (Paris, 1908), 75. For the French

claim to be protecting Sienese liberty in 1552, see Pepper and Adams, *Firearms and Fortifications*, 62.

70. Maltby, esp. 60–62.

71. For the establishment of the system whereby the Italian tercios provided trained companies for use elsewhere, see Parker, *Army of Flanders*, 33.

72. Essen, *Alexandre Farnèse*, 3:53–54. Cf. Maltby, 151–52.

73. Maltby, 140.

74. Parker, *Army of Flanders*, 140–41, 233.

75. Essen, *Alexandre Farnèse*, 3:143–44.

76. *Calendar of States Papers, Foreign Series, Elizabeth I*, vol. 21, pt. 3 (London, 1929), 316, to Sir Francis Walsingham, 16 Sept. 1587.

77. As the States General informed the English in 1585; see the report of the Dutch commissioners at the making of the Treaty of Nonsuch. The Hague: Algemeen Rijksarchief, Eerste Afdeling, Staten Generaal 8299, fol. 19–v.

78. Essen, *Alexandre Farnèse*, 2: 264.

79. Algemeen Rijksarchief, Eerste Afdeling, Regeringsarchieven I-97, art. 4. Cf. Israel, *Dutch Republic*, 96–97, who claims that both the Dutch and the Spaniards were forced to deploy over 30,000 men in garrisons during the 1620s.

80. Essen, *Alexandre Farnèse*, 5:62, 65.

81. On Maurice's reforms, see B. H. Nickle, "The Military Reforms of Prince Maurice of Orange," Ph.D. diss., University of Delaware, 1975.

82. See the comments of Cardinal Bertivolio quoted in Christopher Duffy, *Siege Warfare: The Fortress in the Early Modern World, 1494-1660* (London, 1979), 63.

83. See Buissert, *Henry IV*, 36–39.

84. The best account of the invasion of the Palatinate is Anna Egler, *Die Spanier in der linksrheinischen Pfalz 1620-1632: Invasion, Verwaltung, Rekatholisierung* (Mainz, 1971). See pp. 31–51 and pp. 183–87, Archduke Albert's letter to Philip III of 14 April 1620. A contemporary translation of Spínola's oration can be found in the Henry E. Huntington Library, San Marino, Calif., MS EL 6899.

85. See M. S. Junkelmann, "Feldherr Maximilians: Johann Tserclaes, Graf von Tilly," in *Wittelsbach und Bayern. II. Um Glauben und Reich: Kurfürst Maximilian I*, ed. H. Glaser (Munich and Zurich, 1980), 2/1: 377–80. Cf. Roberts, *Gustavus Adolphus*, 2:264, and Wertheim, *Toller Halberstadter*, 1:177.

86. Dieter Albrecht, *Die auswärtige Politik Maximilians von Bayern, 1618-1635* (Göttingen, 1962), 2–3, 91.

87. Creveld, *Supplying War*, 16, describes the process as a "flight forward." Cf. Roberts, "Gustavus Adolphus and the Art of War," 73, and Wertheim, *Tolle Halberstädter*, 1:157.

88. W. Brunick, *Der Graf von Mansfeld in Ostfriesland (1622-24)* (Aurich, W. Ger., 1957), 109–11.

89. On Wallenstein's strategy, see Mann, 327, 655, 667.

90. E. Ladewig Petersen, "Defence, War and Finance: Christian IV and the Council of the Realm, 1596-1629," *Scandinavian Journal of History* 7 (1982): 277–313, esp. 280, 301–4.

91. Roberts, *Gustavus Adolphus*, 2:650–53. Creveld, *Supplying War*, 13–17.

92. Stradling, "Origins," 90–91. Parrott, "The Causes of the Franco-Spanish

War of 1635–59," in *The Origins of War in Early Modern Europe*, ed. Jeremy Black (Edinburgh, 1987), 72–111, and "Administration of the French Army," 19.

93. Stradling, "Defeat of Spain," 216–17.

94. London, British Library, Cottonian MS Caligula B X, fol. 353, "A consideration of the whole matter of Scotland" (12 Sept. 1565). For Elizabeth's attitude to the financing of the Netherlands intervention, see J. E. Neale, "Elizabeth and the Netherlands, 1586–7," in *Essays in Elizabethan History* (London, 1958), 170–201.

95. Mallett and Hale, *Military Organization*, 215–16.

Politics, Professionalism, and the Evolution of Sailing-Ship Tactics, 1650–1714

WILLIAM MALTBY

RECOGNIZABLE BROADSIDE sailing ships had evolved by the middle of the sixteenth century. Why, then, did another century and a half elapse before the supposedly natural method of fighting them in line-ahead formation became tactical doctrine in European navies? The question was of considerable interest to the great naval historians of the pre–World War I era.[1] It seemed obvious that only by bringing the maximum number of guns to bear simultaneously could a fleet realize the full potential of its armament, yet for many years admirals were apparently reluctant to adopt this principle on a consistent basis.

They certainly knew of the formation because the line ahead is probably as old as the shipboard gun. Vicente Sodré used it against an Arab fleet off the Malabar Coast in 1502,[2] and another Portuguese squadron employed it against William Towerson in 1557;[3] but many sixteenth- and seventeenth-century admirals continued to attack in line-abreast formation or in no formation whatever, thereby hoping to create a general melee. Their purpose was often to board and capture ships, though they sometimes intended only to sow confusion, break up whatever formation the enemy may have assumed, and batter their opponents into submission on a ship-by-ship basis. Such luminaries as Maarten Tromp, Prince Rupert, and George Monk, duke of Albemarle, all appear to have supported this view, though each of them used the line ahead on occasion.

It was not until the 1690s that French and English fighting instructions insisted upon the line ahead as the only acceptable formation for fleet actions. Other nations, though more flexible in theory, had

53

by this time adopted the tactic in general practice. The Dutch used it with some regularity after 1672, and the Venetians employed it in the Morean War of 1696–97.[4] The Spanish fought no independent fleet actions in the later seventeenth century; their fighting instructions have not been found, but they, too, appear to have accepted the verdict of the times.

Alfred Thayer Mahan saw this long gestation period as the product of indolence and conservatism.[5] One or two men, he said, can change technology, but to change tactics one has "to overcome the inertia of a conservative class."[6] Sailors are indeed conservative. They live and fight in an environment that does not encourage lighthearted innovation, but their reluctance to make an inviolable principle of the line ahead was not entirely mindless. There were many obstacles to its adoption. So many, in fact, that the evolution of sailing-ship tactics may be taken as a case study in the development of a naval mentalité — an international consensus on the way battles should be fought that owed as much to social, economic, and political considerations as it did to technology or tactical necessity.

Technology, though not central to the process, as Mahan apparently assumed, was hardly irrelevant. In principle the ships of the Armada were similar to those of Nelson's time; in detail they were substantially different. Rigging, for example, evolved throughout the seventeenth century in ways that directly affected tactics. Bonaventure mizzens disappeared, but the gradual addition of mizzen topsails, top gallants, staysails, studding sails, and a spritsail topmast fitted to the bowsprit greatly increased sail area and flexibility. The introduction of reef points eliminated the cumbersome bonnets and drabblers of an earlier day and greatly simplified the process of shortening sail. All of this, in theory, made ships more maneuverable, especially in the light airs that graced most seventeenth-century battles. This was important because bringing as many as one hundred ships, all of which had different sailing characteristics, into a coherent line was no small achievement. Keeping station under battle conditions was even more difficult.

Hull design also changed, primarily to accommodate more guns. The upper works fore and aft were reduced in height, and the sheer became less pronounced. The old square stern was replaced by a rounded tuck, and the long, low "galleon" bow by a more rounded configuration with a short, wide beak set at a relatively higher angle. The first three-decker, *The Sovereign of the Seas,* was built in 1637, and by mid-century most fighting ships carried their greatest beam at the waterline, giving them a pronounced tumblehome. This not only made boarding more difficult but lowered the center of gravity. With as many as 120 guns in the main battery, they needed all the stability their designers could achieve.[7]

The new ships may actually have been less seaworthy than their predecessors, but they were better suited to the line of battle. This was no accident. A chronology of changes in hull and rigging indicates that they were probably a response to tactical innovation rather than its precursors.[8] If this is true, technology was a restraining influence only in the sense that expensive ships, once built, were unlikely to be scrapped simply because they were obsolete. Until the 1690s battle fleets contained many ships that were ill suited to maintaining the line ahead and complaints about undergunned vessels or poor station keeping based on faulty design were numerous.

A possible exception to this rule involves the vexing question of outboard loading. If, as most authorities believe, shipboard guns were not permitted to recoil until about 1625, it would explain some of the more mysterious aspects of sixteenth-century tactics.[9] There is no doubt that outboard loading was a common practice. The gunner crawled out through the port and loaded his piece while sitting astride it or while standing precariously on a strake.[10] It was therefore advisable after a broadside had been delivered to fall off and return so as to present the opposite battery to the enemy, a lengthy process that at least protected gunners while they were reloading. This practice may not have been universal, especially on larger ships whose beam permitted the recoil of long guns, but while it was prevalent, line-ahead tactics were impractical.

Technology, however, was but one of many obstacles to tactical development. During much of the seventeenth century, sea officers apparently felt that tactical planning was a waste of time. In an age that produced hundreds of books on the conduct of armies, they restricted their professional reading to treatises on navigation or gunnery supplemented by accounts of voyages. The latter sometimes described sea fights, but their chief purpose was to "advance enterprise" and to prepare captains for the hazards of little-known coasts. The first French treatise on tactics, written by Père Paul Hoste at the direction of Admiral Tourville, appeared in 1697. The English saw no reason to emulate it for another century.[11]

The reasons for this indifference are clear. As Sir William Monson put it:

> Ships which must be carried by wind and sails and the sea offering them no firm and steadfast footing, cannot be commanded to take their ranks like soldiers in a battle by land. The weather at sea is never certain, the winds variable, ships unequal in sailing; and when they strictly keep their order, commonly fall foul of one another, and in such cases they are more careful to observe their directions than to offend the enemy, whereby they will be brought into disorder among themselves.[12]

A clearer statement of the problem would be hard to imagine, but Monson's is not exhaustive. Before the Dutch Wars, Nathaniel Boteler could rightly say of fleet actions, "This is a particular, touching which neither this age nor that which is past can afford any help or precedent."[13] There had been too few battles, and none were sufficiently alike to permit generalization.

Even after sea battles became common, the lessons to be drawn from them were often unclear because no one ever seemed to know precisely what had happened. War at sea took place, so to speak, on level terrain. There was no vantage point from which the entire action could be seen, and commanders, by tradition and necessity, had to be in the thick of the fight. There they were quickly immersed in a violent, smoke-shrouded world where communication with the rest of the fleet was at best sporadic.[14] Accounts of naval battles therefore tended to be even more confusing and contradictory than accounts of battles on land, and because nearly every engagement was the occasion of bitter controversy, reports were also likely to be self-serving and partisan. It was a perceptual muddle from which tactical conclusions could be drawn only with great care.

When these difficulties, experiential and otherwise, are added to the lack of adequate signals, the magnitude of the problem becomes evident. Signaling in the seventeenth century was normally a matter of firing guns, raising and lowering sails, and altering the position of a very limited number of flags.[15] As only the latter method was usable in battle, admirals tried to confer personally with their captains whenever possible. The actions of the Dutch Wars may have been leisurely by modern standards, but lowering a boat, rowing to the flagship, and then rowing back was hardly conducive to tactical precision.[16] Failure to develop a "modern" system of signal flags until the last quarter of the eighteenth century had two opposing effects: at first it discouraged the search for tactical innovation; then, when the decision was finally made to fight in line ahead, it fostered tactical rigidity. If the Fighting Instructions were followed invariably and in detail, the need for confusing signals was reduced.

The early opponents of formal tactics gave varying weight to these considerations, but they were also opposed specifically to the line ahead. In fact, much of their distaste for theorizing may have been based on its early association with what to them was a dubious practice.

The line ahead was basically a defensive tactic. If orders were followed precisely, it offered no hope of breaking the enemy's formation or of preventing his withdrawal. A fleet that took up its position to leeward of the enemy could not ordinarily be brought to battle as long as it had sea room. A fleet to windward had the initiative and could rarely be attacked at all. If on the other hand, both sides desired battle, two opposing fleets sailing on parallel courses could batter each other for hours without achieving a decision, as the fleet actions of the early eighteenth century demonstrated with tiresome regularity. This was in part because a ship of the line was remarkably sturdy; and even if one should be badly damaged it had only to drop out of line and the ships keeping station fore and aft would close the gap. This was somewhat easier in the leeward fleet, whose vessels could drift out of harm's way even if their rigging were destroyed, but a ship to windward could still escape as long as it had steerage. Boarding was obviously impossible as long as the line was maintained, a major deficiency in the eyes of those who sought a clear decision or who hoped, like sailors of all ranks, for a share of prize money.

To aggressive sea officers like Rupert, Monk, the Tromps, or de Ruyter, the line ahead was therefore a recipe for stalemate. For a while, fireships were thought to provide an offensive solution compatible with the line, but their usefulness, too, proved limited. The theory was that smaller, usually superannuated, vessels with skeleton crews would sail to windward of the line of battle. When the opportunity offered, they would move in and grapple with an enemy ship, set themselves afire, and presumably burn both the enemy and themselves to the waterline. Alternatively, they might present such a terrifying prospect by bearing down in flames upon the enemy that he would break his formation. Unfortunately, their use was largely restricted to the windward fleet. Moreover, speed in a displacement hull is largely a function of waterline length. Fireships, being smaller, could rarely keep up with ships of the line and added greatly to the already severe problems involved in station keeping. Even if they succeeded in approaching their target, they could normally be warded off by the force of a broadside fired just as they were about to attack their grappling irons. Fireships had their successes, especially when the enemy was at anchor or otherwise immobilized,[17] but by the Third Dutch War even such die-hard believers as Michel de Ruyter were beginning to lose faith.[18] By 1700 fireships had ceased to play a major part in fleet actions.

The weaknesses of the line ahead as tactical doctrine were in fact many, and they were not overcome as long as the Permanent Fighting Instructions and their French counterparts remained sacrosanct. It would therefore be wrong to stigmatize the opponents of formalism as simple reactionaries. They were right, not only in their assessment of technological reality, but in terms of the strategic objectives embraced by both England and the Netherlands. Whatever the virtues of the line ahead, it was ill suited to achieving command of the seas through offensive action. This was acknowledged by Sir Julian Corbett when he said that neither the formalists nor their opponents were right in any absolute sense.[19] It was the willingness of a Rodney or a Nelson to cast aside the rule book and "break the line" that led to the victories of the heroic age. In their desire to seek a decision by throwing the enemy into confusion they were more akin to Rupert or Monk than to Rooke and Torrington, but there was a difference. When Nelson went into battle, he did so with a fleet trained in precision maneuvers whose signals, gunnery, and ship handling were in every sense superior to those of its seventeenth-century counterparts. The improvement had been due largely to the triumph of the formalists, even if the more immediate result of their efforts had been nearly a century of tactical stalemate.

The actual sequence of events by which formalism ultimately triumphed is well known, having been described at length by Corbett, Mahan, Taylor, Lewis, and others. In England the first official mention of the line ahead was in the Commonwealth Orders of 29 March 1653. Signed by Blake, Deane, and Monk, it was apparently a reaction to Blake's defeat off Dungeness on 30 November 1652, and to a more successful, though disturbingly chaotic, bout with Tromp on 18 February. Successful actions off the Gabbard, 11 June 1653, and the Texel, 10 August, appeared to justify the new order of battle, but the Peace of Westminster ended further trials until after the Restoration.

When the Duke of York took command of the fleet in 1665, he resurrected the Commonwealth Orders in a more restrictive form.[20] The Dutch, too, had learned their lesson, and the Battle of Lowestoft, or Second Texel, 3 June 1665, was the first in which both sides maintained the line ahead. The English had the better of it, but the Dutch were able to withdraw and a number of officers, including Rupert and Monk (now Duke of Albemarle), felt that more aggressive tactics were needed. They had their opportunity in the Four Days' Fight, 1–4 June 1666. The result was a Dutch victory, though tactics were less important to the outcome than the strategic decision to divide the fleet. For the first two days Albemarle was therefore hopelessly outnumbered. He gave a good account of himself, but critics like Pepys and Sir William Penn were inclined to blame the loss on his failure to maintain the line ahead.[21] Then, on St. James' Day, both sides maintained the line and the English won. The memory of this victory caused them to begin the Third Dutch War, 1672–73, under the Duke of York's rules. At Sole Bay, 28 May 1672, York and the Earl of Sandwich were poorly supported by their French allies. The line failed, and Sandwich, a formalist, died in a desperate reversion to more old-fashioned ways. He was succeeded by Rupert, whose nonformalist ardor achieved little in the battles of 1673.[22]

This is a much-abbreviated account of a long struggle, not only between the Dutch and English but between different factions of English sea officers. It is presented only to demonstrate that the Dutch Wars offered no incontrovertible support to any tactical doctrine. A consensus in favor of the line ahead may have been developing among the English, but the issue remained very much open to debate. After maintaining the line against Rupert in the Schooneveld on 7 June 1673, de Ruyter attacked him on 21 August in what can best be described as a flying wedge.[23] He would later use the line at Alicuri, 1676,[24] but he and the other Dutch admirals evidently preferred to keep their options open. The line ahead was not mandated in their instructions or signal books until they were merged with the English fleet after the Glorious Revolution.[25]

The English eventually drew different conclusions. The period from 1673 to 1688 was one of intensive debate on naval matters, during which the views of the Duke of York, who became King James II in 1685, were eventually adopted. They survived his deposition because the officers of the new navy objected, not to his tactics, but to his religious and political views. When William III appointed the formalist Arthur Herbert, Earl of Torrington, to command both of his fleets, the triumph of the line ahead was assured. Torrington's orders of 1689 and 1690 were the basis of the Permanent Fighting Instructions issued by Lord Russell in 1691 and preserved virtually intact for more than eighty years thereafter.[26]

In France similar ideas were imposed by the leading French officer of the day, Anne Hilarion de Cotentin, comte de Tourville. A veteran of the Third Dutch War and of the successful battles of 1676 in the Mediterranean, he was appointed naval commander in chief in 1689. His ideas, developed into a lengthy treatise by his chaplain, the Jesuit Paul Hoste, became the basis of eighteenth-century French tactical thought.[27]

Like the English formalists, Tourville believed in rigid adherence to the line ahead, but he was less impressed with the advantages of fighting from the windward. Though virtually essential to taking the offensive, the windward position offered limited possibilities for withdrawal if things went wrong. Morever, it was the windward fleet that had to approach the enemy. If the approach were direct, the attackers would be exposed to raking fire, often for many minutes. The only alternative was a gradual or "lasking" approach that exposed the windward van to crippling broadsides from several enemy ships in succession. Most tacticians favored the direct approach because a ship's area of exposure, bow on, was minimal and because rates of fire were by later standards low, but either choice involved a certain loss in morale and fighting efficiency before battle could be fully joined.[28]

The French were also troubled by the fact that, in anything more than a breeze, ships in the windward position lost half their available firepower when the angle of heel put their lower gunports under water. These considerations led them to prefer the leeward position, whose defensive nature was in any case more suited to their usual strategy. Mahan was largely correct in asserting that while the English sought control of the sea through the destruction of enemy fleets, the French tended to concentrate on the limited objectives of specific mission.[29]

The ultimate triumph of formalism should not, therefore, be regarded as inevitable. The line ahead had enjoyed only partial success in the Dutch Wars. Few claimed that it offered a sure recipe for victory, yet by the end of the century it had been adopted by nearly everyone. What were the sources of this consensus?

Perhaps the most obvious was a growing sense of caution. The Dutch Wars had been a great trial of men and ships. As Michael Lewis put it, "In all ages, given a Dutch-British battle, there was a fight to the death, with little evasion and with long casualty lists."[30] Among the results of these struggles was a sobering improvement in gunnery and ship handling that made it impossible to take one's enemy for granted. Penn's early recognition of this fact is evident in his criticism of the Four Days' Fight. He knew that England's naval superiority under the Commonwealth had given way to virtual equality, but Rupert and Albemarle were apparently slower to accept reality.[31] Success in a melee depended upon superior skills. When both sides were evenly matched, the results were unpredictable and there was a corresponding need for the control provided by formal tactics. It is worth remembering that when Nelson abandoned the line at Trafalgar, he did so in the knowledge that his crews were far better trained than those of the enemy.[32]

The melee was also incompatible with strategic objectives other than the destruction of an enemy fleet. This argument weighed little with the English, who normally desired nothing else, but it appealed to the French and, on occasion, to the Dutch. The line ahead could screen a convoy or an amphibious landing, and it was the ideal formation for a strategic retreat. The French, with their preference for mission objectives, and the Dutch, with their overriding need to protect trade, could not ignore this flexibility. An orderly retreat also came to be associated with the strategic concept of a "fleet in being." The idea was first articulated by Torrington in defending his conduct at Beachy Head, 1690. Torrington, an arch-formalist, had been ordered to attack and destroy a French fleet that he knew to be superior. He engaged the fleet but soon retired to the protection of the Thames estuary on the theory that if he were destroyed, a French invasion was assured, but Tourville would not hazard a landing as long as an English fleet, however weak, was "in being."[33] The merits of his decision were hotly debated, but the argument appealed to many, especially those whose countries rarely possessed naval superiority.

These are all valid arguments for the line ahead, though it is difficult to know how widely they were accepted at the time. The absence of tactical literature other than that of Hoste and the persuasive modern formulations of Mahan and Lewis may be leading us to put thoughts in the minds of our forebears. There were clearly other reasons for the triumph of formalism; those mentioned above, however persuasive, do not account for the rigidity of the Permanent Fighting Instructions or for the determination with which they were later enforced. Lord Russell's instructions of 1691 went far beyond those of the Duke of York. The article permitting the division of the enemy from to leeward was removed and no pursuit was allowed until the main body of the enemy "was run."[34] Initiative was not only stilled, it was virtually forbidden, as Admiral Matthews learned when he was cashiered in 1744 for breaking the line in perfectly understandable circumstances.[35] The suspicion that other concerns were involved is reinforced by what little we know of the nonformalist opposition.

Few of those who campaigned for or against the new tactics did so on paper, at least in England. Richard Gibson was an exception. Born the son of a merchant captain at Great Yarmouth, he served the Commonwealth in the First Dutch War, became a purser, and then in 1665 a clerk in the Navy Office. There he remained for forty years. In his "Discourse" of 1702 and in an earlier tract apparently intended for in-house consumption, he denounced the employment of "gentleman" officers as opposed to "tarpaulins" who had been bred to the sea.[36] This had long been a divisive issue in both the French and English services, but Gibson's arguments went far beyond the usual assertion that gentlemen were incompetent in the management of their vessels. He claimed that the line ahead had been devised by and for gentleman officers in part because they did not otherwise know what to do in a sea fight, and in part because the new tactics required more and bigger ships. A larger, more expensive navy, he implied, would expand royal authority while enriching the gentlemen and their well-connected friends through new commands and more lucrative naval contracts.[37]

It is an argument worthy of an old Commonwealth man, but hardly compelling when taken at face value. The first great advocate of the line ahead had been Sir William Penn, a tarpaulin from Bristol who, like Gibson, had served the Commonwealth.[38] Prince Rupert and his entourage of cavaliers had opposed him. There were also disinterested motives for supporting a larger navy, but in spite of his prejudices and his fondness for conspiracy theories it would be unwise to dismiss Gibson altogether. By the 1690s most gentleman officers probably supported the line ahead, and some of them no doubt preferred, as Gibson claimed, to oversail, overbuild, overgun, and overman their ships without even trying to find the vessel's proper trim.[39] The task of opposing them had fallen largely to disgruntled tarpaulins. Moreover,

Pepys, who was otherwise ambivalent on the tarpaulin-versus-gentleman issue, believed that many highborn officers, including Torrington himself, did not know one line from another.[40]

Gibson was also right to discern a connection between the line ahead and a navy that was not only larger but substantively different from the fleets of the Commonwealth. As John Ehrman put it in his study of the navy under William III:

> Because her [the ship of the line's] dimensions and equipment did not alter, because they were much the same whatever her country of origin, and because her size bore a fixed relation to her fighting strength, she was effective only when used in superior force to the enemy. Victory lay not with individual performance or equipment, but with numbers. The effect upon administration was thus cumulative, for beyond a certain point an increase in the degree of organization becomes an increase in kind.[41]

Individual performance and the overall quality of equipment were not, of course, wholly irrelevant, but the overall truth of this statement would probably have been accepted by both tarpaulins and gentlemen in 1700. Even the Dutch, whose shallow harbors precluded the use of truly large ships and who in any case could ill afford the change, began decommissioning their smaller warships during this period. They were prevented from reorganizing their whole naval system not by class conflict but by the decentralized political structure of the Seven Provinces.[42]

Adoption of the line ahead required increased expenditures and the centralization of administrative control, neither of which could be achieved until the state developed the financial resources to support them. After 1650 the governments of both France and England absorbed an ever-increasing share of their subjects' wealth, often at the expense of traditional privileges. Like the effort to control the day-to-day conduct of war, this involved a self-conscious attempt to increase the authority of the crown, thereby linking military reform with royal authoritarianism in yet another way. Was "absolutist" theory the impetus behind these exactions, or was "absolutism" itself rooted in the need to provide more efficient means of organizing and financing war? In either case virtually all of the wealth that seventeenth-century states extracted from their subjects was used for war, and the enemies of royal aggrandizement were quick to perceive the connection.[43]

It is evident, then, that the tarpaulin-versus-gentleman controversy indicates the presence of larger issues. Though he did not think of it in precisely these terms, Gibson was complaining about one aspect of the transition from a navy based largely on contractual relationships with the maritime community to one more directly controlled by the crown.

As this transition has already been described by historians as part of the development of naval professionalism, a certain precision of language is required.[44] The maritime community is here defined as those people in the port towns of Europe who made their living from the sea whether in peace or in war. The degree to which they constituted a hereditary occupational class remains open to question, but landsmen in the sixteenth and seventeenth centuries tended to regard them as a separate nationality, the denizens of a world whose language and customs were almost wholly alien to normal experience.[45] In part this was a natural function of the system of apprenticeship in which they were trained. Other trades had esoteric customs and vocabularies, but the isolation of seamen and the vicissitudes of life at sea may well have intensified their deviation from land-based social norms. There was also, as in other trades, an element of family influence in their choice of occupation.

Here it may be necessary to draw social distinctions of another kind. "Tarpaulin" officers were not "gentlemen" in the courtly sense, but they tended to come from the more established port families and were often men of considerable sophistication. Seafaring dynasties like the Hawkinses or the Tromps were not uncommon. Blake, Penn, Duquesne, and many others were the sons of sea captains or merchants. Also, capable outsiders were not excluded; Drake was the son of a dockyard chaplain and de Ruyter's father had driven a beer wagon, but even these men had grown up, in a sense, on the docks. From the standpoint of their governments they were collectively a major resource, a source of ships, skills, and connections without which naval activity, prior to the 1660s, was inconceivable.[46]

The normal procedure for enlisting their services was to secure them by contract. Before approximately 1660, governments, whether French, English, Dutch, or Spanish, preferred to tie up as few of their resources as possible in ships or men when all could be hired from the maritime community. Mechanisms for administering the process had evolved over the centuries and fleets were increasingly augmented with ships built for, and often by, governmental authority, but the essentials were little changed until the middle of the seventeenth century. At that point both England and France began to centralize their navies under direct royal control. Ships were built and outfitted in royal dockyards solely for the use of the crown, and efforts were made to develop a permanent officer corps with a table of ranks determined at least in part by examinations and seniority. The chief architects of the new systems were Pepys in England and Colbert in France.

Their efforts were inspired by two beliefs. The first, an outgrowth of what is now called mercantilism, held that the power and prosperity of states rested upon seapower. Though widely held, especially in England, this idea was still thought to require vigorous advocacy. One of the reasons for preferring gentleman officers was to raise the prestige of the service, thereby making the navy and its claims more acceptable at court.[47]

The second and far more important belief was that control of the state rested ultimately on the control of warfare, the state's most important activity. The experience of the past century seemed to indicate that reliance on private contractors, whether on land or sea, had contributed to intolerably high costs and meager results. This was not because contracting was inherently more expensive. The practice had been adopted in the first place because it was thought to be cheaper,[48] but it placed the power to make military decisions in the hands of private citizens rather than in those of the king and his officials.

This was no longer considered tolerable. The Thirty Years' War and its sixteenth-century predecessors had proved that military contracting, as it was then practiced, made it virtually impossible to control either the quantity or quality of men and material. The Spanish had perhaps come closest to doing so with their system of tightly drawn and closely supervised *asientos,* but even they were often dissatisfied with the results.[49] The simplest supply contracts were difficult to administer. Contracts let for a company of soldiers or a fleet of ships were far more complicated and raised the additional issues of discipline and reliability in action. If the contractor commanded in person, as was often the case, he could be expected to pursue his own interest if it came into conflict with that of his employer. On land he could become a Wallenstein with political ambitions of his own or an uncontrollable extortionist like Christian of Brunswick, thus raising the ancient fear of "overmighty" subjects in new and acute forms. At the very least, the system bred a degree of caution and lack of discipline that virtually precluded decisive action in the field. The government was dependent upon the contractors, and each contractor was essentially the equal of any other. A command structure, if it could be established at all, was easily ignored, and disputes over precedence were universal. Moreover, the contractor's profit came from keeping his unit understrength, short-changing his men on supplies, and avoiding the kind of bold activities that might put him out of business.[50] There were honorable exceptions, but contracting was one of the reasons that, as Michael Roberts put it, war had become "eternalized."[51]

It is difficult to say how far these judgments can be applied to naval warfare. Contracts for sea service were probably harder to administer than those on land because the technology involved was more complex. Corruption was rampant, as it was on land, and it would continue to be a problem long after shipyards, manning, and provisioning were controlled directly by royal officers.

The behavior of tarpaulin officers sailing under contract or lease is even more difficult to characterize. Complaints about their independence, their "unmilitary" attitude, and their reluctance to risk their ships were numerous.[52] The Dutch, who preserved the old system longer than anyone else, were driven to distraction by arguments over the chain of command and by the accusations of cowardice and treachery that followed every battle. At one point, three members of the States General, including Pensionary Jan de Witt, found it necessary to sail with the fleet and mediate disputes between its more than twenty admirals.[53] This was an extreme case brought about in part by the fact that the Dutch navy was made up of ships owned or leased by five separate governmental authorities, but problems with seagoing contractors were universal.

The attitudes of governments may also have been affected by religious distrust. In France, Duquesne and a number of his brother officers were Huguenots. Many of them left the service in the 1680s, but even those who converted were viewed with suspicion by the government.[54] As for England, the close links between maritime interests and the Commonwealth have been thoroughly documented.[55]

A desire for independence from the maritime community is therefore understandable, but were tarpaulin officers in royal ships less reliable than their highborn counterparts? Pepys, among others, thought that they were not. Gentlemen, too, were touchy and insubordinate. They drank more, or so Pepys thought, and their endless rivalries were often prompted by factional intrigues.[56] Most, if not all, owed their commands to membership in one or another of the rival systems of clientage that were a persistent feature of English naval life until the nineteenth century. As these factions had ties to both Court and Parliament, disputes between officers not only disrupted naval operations but caused political trouble as well.[57]

The one virtue universally conceded to gentleman officers was that they had presumably studied the "art of war." They were familiar, in other words, with the great body of military theory that had developed during the late sixteenth and early seventeenth centuries.[58] It was at this point that the arguments over political control, social origins, and tactical formalism converged, though Gibson could be forgiven for having missed the connection. Control over warfare meant far more than dismantling an antiquated system of contracting. Military literature in the early modern period has not yet been analyzed to exhaustion, but the fear of chaos that inspired it is obvious. Writers saw the debacles of the age as arising from two related causes: administrative disorder and tactical stasis. A passion for regulation pervades their work and extends beyond matters of pay, rank, promotion, and logistics to the actual management of troops on the battlefield. Tactics, they thought, must be more aggressive, but they must also be more precise. Good order was often seen as the key to military success, and if some of their suggestions for achieving it are geometrically ingenious and overly optimistic about the behavior of men under fire, the impulse behind them is understandable.[59] The relative success of such innovators as Maurice of Nassau and Gustavus Adolfus seemed to confirm their views. Writings on war became extremely popular, and an acceptance of the need for tactical development along formal lines became an integral part of reform programs.

The preference for tactical formalism was necessarily influenced by the intellectual preoccupations of the age. Sixteenth-century captains like Alba and Parma had limited their use of geometry to siegecraft and relied heavily on the individual skills and initiative of their veterans. This was no longer acceptable. The increasing size of battles and armies mandated a higher degree of control,[60] and leaving matters to the initiative of private soldiers seemed almost like leaving them to chance.

The seventeenth century was an age of increasing social and economic polarization, and the implicit snobbery that underlay the tarpaulin-versus-gentleman argument may have been at work in this as well, but formal tactics were also more compatible with the political theories of the day and with the growing interest in science. The authoritarian royalism of Louis XIV, Colbert, and Louvois requires no comment. In England it was shared by Pepys, James II, and the other architects of the navy and envied by William III. A well-ordered society or a well-ordered war demanded control from the top. If formal tactics—like administrative reform, a table of ranks, and half-pay for off-duty officers—strengthened that control, it was a powerful argument in their favor. We have already seen that opposition to the new tactics was sometimes associated with a lingering attachment to the Commonwealth and with opposition to the extension of royal authority. It would be unwise to make too much of this, but Gibson's conviction that the line ahead and authoritarian government were connected was no doubt shared by others.

To the degree that seventeenth-century science gave men a vision of a coherent universe based upon mathematical principles or the belief that such principles could be applied to war, it too played a part in military reform.[61] The scientific interests of Vauban and Tourville are well known. Colbert founded the Académie des Sciences, and Pepys was a member of the Royal Society. Even Sir Robert Holmes, as crusty a commander as any, felt called upon to send back his rather dubious observations on the flora and fauna of the Guinea Coast.[62]

Absolutist theory, the hard military lessons of the Iron Age, and the first stirrings of the scientific revolution were combining to produce a mentality that valued order and control and believed that a systematic approach to war and government was a more important ingredient of victory than individual skill or valor. The evolution of these ideas among members of the educated elite has been traced by historians in various countries and for Western Europe as a whole.[63] Its extension to the world of ships was unavoidable, and it was this, even more than pure operational necessity, that produced tactical formalism and a rigid adherence to the line ahead. To quote Father Hoste, "Without the art [of naval evolutions] a fleet resembles that of the barbarians."[64]

It has been shown that the diffusion of such ideas among naval officers during the Dutch Wars was not prompted by their demonstrable success in action. This remained open to question. The definition of success, however, changed subtly as sea officers, like their counterparts on land, began to realize that victory meant little if it resulted in the loss of operational control. Gentlemen who knew military theory could perhaps be trusted to appreciate this fact, but it was feared that professional sailors who were at best military amateurs could not.

The adoption of the line ahead as tactical doctrine cannot, therefore, be regarded as a foreordained response to technological change. It was instead a deliberate step toward a new concept of naval organization based upon the extension of military values to warfare at sea. Mahan and Lewis were well aware of naval professionalism and its development but did not associate it with a specific tactical doctrine. To them, tactical development came from the application of new weapons systems rather than from the evolution of professional ideologies.

The line ahead was clearly an adaptation to the technical requirements of the broadside sailing-ship, but as its long gestation period and ultimate, if partial, rejection indicate, it was neither the only, nor the ultimate, application of that technology. Between 1690 and 1780, the line ahead was an article of faith and an affirmation of a new set of professional values. The pursuit of total victory, with all its attendant glory and risk, was subordinated to the need for discipline and operational control.[65] It was a price that captains, naval administrators, and kings were prepared, however reluctantly, to pay.

NOTES

1. Julian S. Corbett, *Fighting Instructions, 1530–1816,* Navy Records Society Publications, no. 29 (hereafter cited as NRS) (London, 1895) is largely devoted to this issue. It is also discussed in detail by Alfred Thayer Mahan, *The Influence of Seapower upon History* (Boston, 1941), first published in 1890.

2. From the account of Gaspar Correar, analyzed by Peter Padfield, *Guns at Sea* (London, 1973), 26–27.

3. There is an excellent description of this engagement in John F. Guilmartin, *Gunpowder and Galleys: Changing Technology and Mediterranean Warfare at Sea in the Sixteenth Century* (Cambridge, 1974), 85–94.

4. R. C. Anderson, *Naval Wars in the Levant* (Princeton, 1952), 223–36.

5. Mahan, 116.

6. Ibid., 10.

7. For an excellent summary of seventeenth-century changes in naval architecture, see Geoffrey Marcus, *A Naval History of England* (Boston, 1961), 180–81. For rigging, see A. Moore, "Rigging in the Seventeenth Century," *Mariner's Mirror* (hereafter cited as *MM*) 2 (1912): 267–74, 301–8; 3 (1913): 7–13. I am indebted to Professor J. F. Guilmartin for suggesting the effects of tumblehome on boarding.

8. For a discussion of this issue see A. H. Taylor, "Galleon into Ship of the Line," *MM* 44 (1958): 267–85; 45 (1959): 14–24, 100–114.

9. L. G. Carr Laughton, "Gunnery, Frigates, and the Line of Battle," *MM* 14

(1928): 339–63. The issue is also discussed by Padfield, 67–69, who agrees that inboard loading was a recent phenomenon in 1625. Geoffrey Parker and Colin Martin, however, have found evidence that the English used inboard loading as early as 1588, while the Spanish and Portuguese in all probability did not. I am indebted to Professor Parker for this communication.

10. See the drawing by Van de Velde in Padfield, 61; also C. R. Boxer, "Notes," *MM* 16 (1930): 292, and P. Holck, "Notes," *MM* 19 (1933): 282.

11. John Clerk of Eldin, *An Essay on Naval Tactics*, first published in Edinburgh in 1797; subsequent editions in 1804, 1827. As John Smith put it in 1627: "I have seene many bookes on the Art of Warre by land and never any for the Sea." *A Sea-Grammar* (New York, 1968), 59, first published in London in 1627. Smith's didactic representation of a sea fight in *A Sea-Grammar*, 60–61, reprinted with some changes from his *An Accidence or the Path-way to Experience* (London, 1626), remains the only English discussion of tactics actually printed during the seventeenth century. He advocated the Armada-era tactic of firing a broadside, then returning to fire the other side.

12. *Naval Tracts of Sir William Monson*, ed. M. Oppenheim, vol. 4, NRS, no. 45 (London, 1913), 97–98.

13. Nathaniel Boteler, *Dialogues about Sea Services*, ed. W. G. Perrin, NRS, no. 65 (London, 1929), 307.

14. The difficulty of reconciling various accounts of battles is illustrated by the masterful analyses of Lowestoft and the Schooneveld in J. C. M. Warnsinck, *Van Vlootvoogden en Zeeslagen* (Amsterdam, 1942), 270–328, 382–401. Many contemporaries did not even attempt to describe what happened. Maarten Tromp's entire description of the Battle of the Downs (1639) is as follows: "we fought him again and drove the enemy to the total of 23 ashore." *The Journal of Maarten Harpertszoon Tromp, Anno 1639*, ed. and trans. C. R. Boxer (Cambridge, 1930), 195. Tromp usually devoted more words to a sail change.

15. L. E. Holland, "The Development of Signalling in the Royal Navy," *MM* 39 (1953): 5–26. Confusion over signals could also be used as an excuse for disobeying orders. See Rupert's complaints against d'Estrées at the battle of the Texel in his "Briefe Relation," H. T. Colenbrander, *Beschieden vreemde archieven omtrent de groote Nederlandsche Zeeorlogen. 1672–1676* (The Hague, 1919), 2:306–9.

16. Monson, 4:81, held that every captain and pilot should speak to the admiral daily. As late as the battle of Alicuri (1676), Duquesne sent a boat to order one of his captains to engage more closely at the height of the action. Colenbrander, 2:365–94, is the best description of the battle.

17. Notably at Guétaria (1638) and Palermo (1676), or in the destruction of the *Royal James* at Solebay (1672). There is a lengthy discussion of fireships in Mahan, 109–14.

18. P. J. Blok, *Life of Admiral De Ruyter*, trans. G. J. Renier (London, 1933), 310.

19. Corbett, 135.

20. Orders of 10 April 1665, printed in Corbett, 126–28.

21. Corbett, 116–21. The Dutch, too, were either unable or unwilling to form

a line in this action. For English reports see *The Rupert and Monck Letter Book, 1666*, eds. J. R. Powell and E. K. Tinnings, NRS, no. 112 (London, 1969), 231–57.

22. Accounts of these actions are found in *Journals and Narratives of the Third Dutch War*, ed. R. C. Anderson, NRS, no. 86 (London, 1946), and also in Warnsinck, 270–328, 382–401.

23. Blok, 343.

24. The action is described in Colenbrander, 2:365–94.

25. For Dutch signal books, see R. E. J. Weber, *De Seinboken voor Nederlandse Oorlogsvloten en Konvooien tot 1690* (Amsterdam, 1982).

26. Michael Lewis, *The Navy of Britain: A Historical Portrait* (London, 1948), 475. Lewis regarded the instructions as "a millstone about the neck of the Navy," 471. Torrington's Instructions of 1690 were found after Corbett published *Fighting Instructions* in 1905. See R. C. Anderson, "Two New Sets of Sailing and Fighting Instructions," *MM* 6 (1920): 130–35. Russell's Instructions and the "Permanent Instructions" issued by Sir George Rooke in 1703 are in Corbett, 188–99.

27. Paul Hoste, *L'Art des armées navales au traité des evolutions navales* (Lyon, 1697).

28. There is a discussion of this problem with diagrams in John Clerk of Eldin, *An Essay on Naval Tactics* (Edinburgh, 1827), 30–40.

29. Mahan, 339. An eighteenth-century exception was Suffren's campaign in the Indian Ocean.

30. Lewis, *Navy of Britain*, 466.

31. *The Rupert and Monck Letter Book*, 212–13. Albemarle's attitude was due in part to his belief in English superiority. In the same volume, see 221, 223.

32. Corbett, 338–39.

33. Marcus, 203; Lewis, *The Navy of Britain*, 468–69. The best detailed account of the battle is Warnsinck, 426–37.

34. Lord Russell's Instructions, (1691), article 20, in Corbett, 192.

35. The best account of this affair is in Lewis, *The Navy of Britain*, 497–500.

36. Richard Gibson, "Reminiscences" and "Discourse" in *Letters and Papers Relating to the First Dutch War*, vol. 1, ed. S. R. Gardiner, NRS, no. 13 (London, 1899). The second document is in the British Museum (hereafter cited as BM), Add. 11602, fols. 37–38. Gibson's chief opponent in this debate was Sir Henry Sheere, James II's lieutenant of the ordinance and a close friend of Pepys. Sheere's naval essays, written in prison after the Revolution of 1688 are in Rawlinson MSS, D147.

37. Gibson, BM, Add. 11602, fol. 37.

38. D. Granvelle Penn, *Memorials of the Professional Life and Times of Sir William Penn, Knt.* (London, 1833), 1:1–3.

39. Gibson, "A Discourse," *Letters and Papers*, 1:45.

40. *The Tangier Papers of Samuel Pepys*, ed. E. Chappell, NRS, no. 73 (1935), 235. It should be remembered, though, that Pepys disliked Torrington for other reasons. For the great Secretary's views on the larger issue, see *Samuel Pepys' Naval Minutes*, ed. J. R. Tanner, NRS, no. 60 (1926), 52–53, 194, 230, 405.

41. John Ehrman, *The Navy in the War of William III* (Cambridge, 1953), 19.

42. J. C. de Jonge, *Geschiedenis van het Nederlandsche Zeewesen* (Haarlem, 1860), 2:73–84. The need for naval reform had been recognized since 1652. For

the problems involved, see Herbert H. Rowen, *John de Witt* (Princeton, 1978), 79-82, 574-97.

43. The issue is discussed in Michael Roberts, "The Military Revolution, 1560-1660," in *Essays in Swedish History* (London, 1967), 201, 204-5.

44. This is the approach taken by Michael Lewis, *England's Sea Officers* (London, 1939), and by Mahan, 127-29. It is inherently teleological and has tended to obscure other aspects of the transition to a more formally constituted officer corps.

45. Eugenio de Salazar, "Carta escrita al Licenciado Miranda de Ron, 1573," in C. Fernández Duro, *Disquisiciones náuticas* (Madrid, 1876-81), 2:178-200 is based upon this metaphor. See Carla Rahn Phillips, *Life at Sea in the Sixteenth Century: The Landlubber's Lament of Eugenio de Salazar*, the James Ford Bell Lectures, no. 24 (Minneapolis, 1987).

46. Though Colbert preferred to recruit among the nobility, Richelieu had relied heavily on the maritime community, as indicated by the inquest carried out by d'Infreville in the Ponant (1629). The issue is discussed by G. Lacour-Gayet, *La Marine Militaire de la France sous les règnes de Louis XIII et de Louis XIV* (Paris, 1911), 1:34-40, 86.

47. Ehrman, 140-41. For France, Lacour-Gayet, 1:86-87.

48. For a discussion of this question in Spain, see I. A. A. Thompson, *War and Government in Habsburg Spain, 1560-1620* (London, 1976). There are no comparable studies for other countries.

49. There is a detailed description of the system and its administration in Carla Rahn Phillips, *Six Galleons for the King of Spain* (Baltimore, 1986), chaps. 2-4.

50. The most useful discussion of this system remains Fritz Redlich, *The German Military Enterpriser and His Work Force*, Vierteljahrschrift für Sozial- und Wirtschaftsgeschichte, nos. 47-48 (Wiesbaden, 1964-65). See also Geoffrey Parker, *The Thirty Years' War* (London, 1984), 191-208.

51. Michael Roberts, "Gustav Adolf and the Art of War," *Essays in Swedish History* (London, 1967), 60.

52. For an example, see Anthony Deane, "Som Observation touching the Dutch warr . . . ," in Colenbrander, 1:591-94. It is fair to say, however, that "the concept of duty and obedience to the state not only was foreign to the mentality of seamen and merchants, but it was present in the minds of naval captains and admiralty lieutenants only insofar as it suited their interests and then only in direct proportion to the ability of the central power and its agents to control their actions." Eugene Asher, *The Resistance to the French Maritime Classes* (Berkeley, 1960), 30.

53. Blok, 214-15, Rowen, 578-80.

54. Geoffrey Symcox, *The Crisis of French Sea Power 1688-1697* (The Hague, 1974), 17-18, 29-30.

55. Hans-Christoph Junge, *Flottenpolitiek und Revolution*, Publications of the German Historical Institute, London, vol. 6 (Stuttgart, 1980).

56. *Letters and the Second Diary of Samuel Pepys*, ed. R. G. Howarth (London, 1932), 413.

57. Ehrman, 390. For some disturbing examples, see Richard Ollard, *Man of War: Sir Robert Holmes and the Restoration Navy* (London, 1969), 168-69.

Pepys, however, claimed that tarpaulins were not entirely free of this vice. *Letters and Second Diary*, 381.

58. Ehrman, 141. For a contemporary statement, see Sir Henry Sheere, Rawlinson MSS, D147, fols. 23-24.

59. An extreme example is Leonard and Thomas Digges, *An Arithmeticall Militare Treatise, Named Stratioticos* (London, 1590). For a discussion of English military literature, see Henry J. Webb, *Elizabethan Military Science* (Madison, Wisc., 1965). An international survey is as yet unavailable.

60. Roberts, "Military Revolution," 203-4; Geoffrey Parker, "The "Military Revolution, 1560-1660'—A Myth?," *Spain and the Netherlands, 1559-1659*, ed. Geoffrey Parker (Short Hills, N.J., 1979), 95-98. For a different view, see the essay by Simon Adams in this volume.

61. Asher, 94; Roberts, "Military Revolution," 206.

62. Ollard, 96.

63. Paul Hazard, *The European Mind, 1680-1715* (Cleveland, Ohio, 1964) remains an excellent general survey.

64. Hoste, v.

65. Lewis, *Navy of Britain*, 470.

Warfare, Changing Military Technology, and the Evolution of Muscovite Society

RICHARD HELLIE

In 1450 CAVALRYMEN, armed with bows and arrows, personified the might of Muscovy; yet by 1725 Russia had completely adopted the weapons of the gunpowder revolution, and infantryman, armed with flintlock muskets and organized in regular army units, best represented its power in battle. An equally dramatic social change accompanied this military transformation: Muscovite society evolved from a relatively unstratified society with numerous slaves to a rigidly stratified one with no slaves. This essay examines the impact of the military revolution, largely imported from the core West, on the social evolution of early modern Russia at the periphery of Europe between 1450 and 1725. This essay will outline the change in military technology, trace the social evolution, and show how both types of change interacted in the respective areas of the period under discussion.

An initial caveat: non-Russian area scholars looking for contemporary Muscovite analyses of what was occurring militarily and socially are going to be disappointed by this essay, for there were no such analyses. This lack of philosophical, or other, reflection in Muscovy was the concern of Father Georges Florovsky in a classic essay entitled "The Problem of Old Russian Culture," which I would most strongly recommend to anyone interested in such issues.[1] Moreover, inferences made here about the reasons for governmental actions are strictly circumstantial, for the deliberations of governmental bodies were not recorded (as far as is known) or ever made public.

Muscovy concluded a bitter civil war in 1453, and we have a relatively good idea of how the combatants fought: they were primarily highly mobile horsemen whose tools of war were mainly bows and arrows and perhaps included light armor and a saber. As far as one can tell, most of the military manpower was attached to princely courts; the troops were paid by the courts and also kept the booty they seized in military actions. Consequently armies were small, as were most military encounters. As for fortifications in heavily wooded Russia, most were variations on stockades that followed the landscape; some stockades were built on top of wall and moat structures. The Moscow kremlin was one of the few brick fortifications in the country. (Others were in Novgorod, Pskov, Vladimir, and Tver'.) Artillery had been introduced earlier into Rus', but was primarily still a noise machine. The military structure just sketched not only was adequate for fighting internal civil wars but was also sufficient for coping with various Turkic enemies on the steppe frontiers, where the contest was for resources, and with the Lithuanians on the western frontier, where the contest was for territory.[2]

Society in 1450 was very simple and probably highly consensual—at least in the provinces, if one judges by the dyadic (horizontal) legal relations that prevailed.[3] Government was very limited and had very little contact with most of the citizenry other than to collect an occasional tax. There were no legal strictures preventing social mobility, so that a peasant could freely move into a town, a townsman could join a military retinue, and anyone could sell himself or herself into slavery. All inhabitants were free to come and go as they wished (except for the relatively large body of slaves, ranging throughout the period from 5 to 15 percent of the population, that were a result of civil wars and self-sales).[4] Treaties between princes contained promises not to raid populations from other jurisdictions, but it is not clear that much heed was paid to them. Most of the population was rural, although perhaps 2 percent lived in towns. There were no guilds or other forms of urban organization known in the West.[5] The great Muscovite civil war introduced one discordant element into this picture: probably as a payoff for loyalty during the war, the government permitted a few monasteries to limit the mobility of peasant debtors to the period around St. George's Day (26 November)—obviously to facilitate debt collection.[6] Thus the first small step in the direction of a rigidly stratified society was taken as a consequence of military events, although not as a result of any military change.

By the 1450s the first steps had been taken, almost imperceptibly, in the gunpowder revolution and toward a rigidly stratified society— the introduction of pop-gun cannon and a few instances of selective limitation on the right of peasant debtors to move. The initiators of both actions, state figures of the Moscow elite, certainly had not the slightest idea of what they had begun. Their innovations probably were borrowed from Germany and Poland, respectively, although one cannot be sure about either.[7]

The First Service-Class Revolution and the Beginnings of Stratification, 1460–1600

The years 1460–1600 witnessed a broad-based introduction of the gunpowder revolution, the establishment of the Muscovite service-class military system, and the laying of a solid base for the rigid stratification of society. Dynastically, these years extended from the reigns of Ivan III through those of the last Riurikid, Fëdor the Bellringer. In all probability it would be wise to include Boris Godunov (r. 1598–1605) in the period, for he was the actual ruler during Fëdor's reign (1584–98) and introduced important measures in the military sphere and especially in the social sphere. Otherwise, the personal role of the monarchs in most of these developments is unknown, and reigns are mentioned only for the sake of reference.

The reign of Ivan III (1462–1505) witnessed the full-scale introduction of usable artillery that had an effect on the outcome of warfare. Technology transfer was already sufficiently rapid that Western and Central European inventions reached Muscovy within at most a few years after they were made. The new artillery forced the rebuilding of most major fortifications; walls were straightened to eliminate blinds and were thickened. The most visible figure behind both the new armaments and fortifications was Aristotle Fioravante, who had been imported from Bologna after the initial Russian attempt to build the Assumption (Uspenskii) Cathedral in the Kremlin failed when the structure collapsed. He first taught the Russians how to build large-scale vaulted structures; then he introduced the casting of bronze cannon and participated in the building of the new fortifications. The 1490s and the first years of the sixteenth century witnessed protracted wars between Muscovy and Lithuania over control of the upper Oka and Dnepr basins, resulting in Muscovy's considerable enlargement at the expense of Lithuania. Particularly noteworthy were two battles on the upper Dnepr River in 1514 in which artillery played the decisive role. One was the September battle of Orsha, which Muscovy lost and which probably halted westward expansion. More significant, perhaps, was the earlier July battle for Smolensk, in which 140 to 300 cannon participated. This Muscovite victory secured Moscow's western flank and gave Russia control of the upper Dnepr.[8]

Ivan's reign also witnessed the conquest of Novgorod (1471–78), which secured Moscow's northwestern frontier against the Swedes and surrounded its ancient rival Tver', which dropped like a ripe apple in 1485. Also associated with the conquest of Novgorod was the first service-class revolution—the creation of the middle service-class cavalry, which became the backbone of the Muscovite military establishment for more than a century and played the central role in the story of Muscovy's changing social stratification. After the annexation of Novgorod, some unknown genius (perhaps State Secretary Vasilii Dolmatov) decided that the way to garrison the vast region after the mass deportation of the native elite, and to expand the army to maximum size while removing the expense from the palace court, was to assign each plot of land to pay rent to a particular cavalryman. This came to be known as the "service land" (*pomest'e*) system, which in some ways resembled the Byzantine *pronoia,* the Persian *ikhta,* and the Ottoman *timar* systems, but also had precedent in Russian conditional land grants dating back at least to 1339. Its virtue was that it maximized the income payable to each cavalryman by short-circuiting the centralized collection/disbursement process that had often been expensive. Its ultimate vice was that it made each cavalryman interested in maintaining the presence of the peasants on his particular service landholding (*pomest'e*), which became a crucial factor in the enserfment process.

During Ivan's reign the social stratification process took one giant step forward: the St. George's Day provision, earlier applied to peasant debtors, was applied to all peasants by the *Sudebnik* (judicial handbook) of 1497.[9] No one has ever figured out why this was done, except perhaps to imitate laws in Poland and in Pskov that had restricted peasant movement to Philip's Fast Day (12 November). It seems not to have made much difference, for the post-1497 decades were the best Muscovy had known for centuries: Wars and the tax burden were comparatively less onerous, and no major pestilence or famine stalked the land. There seems to have been no perceived labor shortage as the

population expanded, and the three-field agricultural system was introduced because population pressure forced curtailment of the previous system of extensive farming. The St. George's Day provision
seems to have been largely ignored until 1560; its significance is that
it set a precedent for state regulation of peasant mobility. The provision
was repeated in the *Sudebnik* of 1550 and ammended in order to cope
with the new three-field system.[10] But in the pre-1550 era the Russian
state lacked the administrative apparatus that later proved necessary
to enforce the norms of a near-caste society.[11]

The reign of Vasilii III (1505–33) and the early years of the reign of
Ivan IV (1533–84) were more significant for Muscovy's political future
than for its military or social one. The theory of Muscovite autocracy
developed during this period as a consequence of various disputes in
the church (over the church's role in the world, church landownership,
the Judaizers, and other issues). Its chief architect was Abbot Joseph
of the monastery at Volokolamsk (a supporter of Vasilii III in the
dynastic crisis of the late fifteenth century). His theory is embodied in
the statement of the sixth-century Byzantine theologian Agapetus that
"although the ruler in body be like all other men, in the power of his
office he is like almighty God."[12] Further development of thoughts on
the divine essence of the monarch ensued and essentially culminated
in the "correspondence" between Ivan IV and Andrei Kurbskii in the
1560s and 1570s.[13] One may assume that such a development was
essential to legitimize the governmentally directed stratification of society that was to become such a pronounced feature of later sixteenth-
century Muscovy, for it is difficult to imagine that a government lacking
this legitimation could have conceived of the manipulation of the social
structure that was effected between 1580 and 1650.

Two other developments should be noted in passing that occurred
in the first two-thirds of the sixteenth century. In the military sphere,
the invention of the arquebus caused the Muscovites to create units
of foot soldiers known as the *strel'tsy*, who were recruited from commoners (probably, in Michael Howard's words, Muscovy's "adventur-
ous and desperate").[14] The military future belonged to their heirs rather
than to those of the cavalry, but this was not apparent until the mid-
seventeenth century, when the Tatar menace from the steppes finally
dissipated. Be that as it may, the Muscovites developed the "walking
fortress" (*guliai gorod*), a tactic that anticipated seventeenth-century
linear formations that maximized infantry firepower, which functioned

very well with the cavalry. The arquebusiers took log walls with them to the battle that were mounted on wheels or skis from behind which they would shoot at the enemy. The cavalry, while protecting the flanks of the infantry, waited behind the *guliai gorod* until the arquebuses had been discharged and then moved in with sabers for the kill. Thus the invention of the arquebus brought participation in warfare to Muscovite commoners, who previously had been used only in engineering battalions. Cannon founders trained in Germany brought the latest in Western cannon technology to Muscovy in the second half of the sixteenth century.[15]

In the social sphere, one major development was the collapse of the medieval consensual society that had found juridical expression in Muscovy's dyadic system of law. This collapse, which may have been accelerated by rapid population growth, was epitomized by a wave of lawlessness in the 1520s and 1530s that resulted in a radical alteration through decentralization of the governance of the Muscovite countryside.[16] Another major development in this period concerned the institution of slavery. Although self-sale into slavery apparently had always been a feature of the institution of slavery in Russia, the form of self-sale known as "limited service contract slavery" (*kabal'noe kholopstvo*) was perfected in the first two-thirds of the sixteenth century and replaced "full slavery" (*polnoe kholopstvo*) as the major form of slavery. The relative attractiveness of limited service contract slavery may have induced more self-sales. Initially the transaction looked like a loan for a year; only upon default did the borrower and his or her offspring become permanent slaves. Whether limited service contract slavery was more popular than full slavery is unknown, but since repayment of the "loan" proved to be impossible, the consequence of self-sale into both institutions was the same: perpetual, hereditary slavery. The Muscovite institution of slavery must be noted here because it is the precursor of serfdom, which borrowed most of its features from slavery and ultimately replaced it.[17]

It also is likely that significant changes were occurring in the service classes in these years. The lower service class, which included the *strel'tsy*, artillerymen, gatekeepers, and other salaried (not landed) servicemen, was created from townsmen and peasants. The middle service class continued to grow in size to about 17,500 by 1550 as the *pomest'e* system spread throughout Muscovy.[18] Service was for life: when the servicemen were too old or decrepit to serve in the field and on campaigns, they were required to render "siege service"—to defend Muscovy from inside its many fortifications. The provincial cavalry, also recruited from diverse social elements, was totally the creature of the state in the first century of its existence, as far as is known, and exhibited no independent strivings. Nevertheless, the groundwork was laid for that group to make demands (in the direction of becoming a gentry) upon its master, the state, which the latter only conceded most unwillingly.

The upper service class—the Moscow-based boyar oligarchy and lesser palace and military servitors—also went through significant change in this period. That development was probably not in response to technological change or significant expansion, but rather to the development of the conception of autocracy outlined earlier. Although the boyars and others never had been independent agents, or anything like a Western aristocracy, it is fairly certain that the adoption of the Agapetus formula, combined with accelerated recruitment of newcomers, turned the elite into more obsequious functionaries than they had been previously.

The years of the most dramatic social change were the 1580s and 1590s. Before they are discussed, however, a few preliminary facts must be presented. With the aid of foreign mining engineers, the Muscovites captured Kazan' on the Middle Volga in 1552, and followed that up by annexing Astrakhan' on the Lower Volga in 1556. That was crucial militarily because it weakened the steppe peoples by permanently cutting the Turkic world in two and thus prepared the way for the diminution and ultimate extinction of the Crimean Khanate by Catherine the Great. It was crucial socially because, first, it opened the Middle Volga to Slavic settlement (migration was encouraged by state recruiters) and, second, it prepared the way for even more extensive population migration out of the podzolic Volga-Oka mesopotamia into the more fertile chernozem steppe. Both movements contributed to the increasing sense of population shortage in the Muscovite heartland that so stimulated the enserfment process. Moreover, not only did the magnet of better land, the prospect of lower rent, and the absence of landlords draw the peasants out of the heartland, where the *pomest'e* cavalry was based, but the peasants were being "pushed out" as well by the Livonian War (1558–83) and excessive taxation, Ivan's mad *Oprichnina* (1565–72) and excessive rent collection, the famines of 1569–70, and other misfortunes. The consequence was massive depopulation of certain heartland areas of Muscovy, especially around Moscow and Novgorod.[19]

The second development occurred in the central government. In order to run and finance its military establishment more effectively, the government developed its chancellery (*prikaz*) system. The very names tell what the majority of the chancelleries were all about: the Service Land Chancellery, the Military Chancellery, the Arquebusiers/Musketeers Chancellery, the Gun Barrel Chancellery, the Fortifications Chancellery, the Troop Mobilization Chancellery, the Foreign Mercenaries Chancellery, the Grand Revenue Chancellery, the Dvina Tax Collection Chancellery, Excise Tax Chancellery, Grain Collection Chancellery, Kostroma Tax Collection Chancellery, and a host of others. The origins of the government apparatus in the princely household have been debated for years, but suffice it to say that great strides were made in creating a relatively rational bureaucracy in the 1550s and that it was largely in place by the 1570s.[20] That was crucial both for movement beyond the *pomest'e*-based army and for the management (or at least control) of a stratified society. Unlike its European counterparts, however, government in Muscovy was a lean and efficient operation (probably thanks to the medieval heritage of slavery ministers running the royal household). Thus the Muscovite bureaucracy cannot be blamed for whatever manifestations of "the seventeenth-century crisis" occurred in Russia. Moreover, unlike elsewhere in Europe, the development of the chancellery system meant that Muscovite military planners were not hamstrung by bankers or private industrialists; instead they were free to extract resources directly from the populace and use them as wages paid to military men or as subventions for state-produced or imported military supplies. Whether command mobilization was "efficient" remains to be determined, but one can be sure that it seemed rational to those directly involved, for when that crucial instrument of war—money—was needed, the Muscovites often had enough.[21]

The most dramatic social change involved the peasantry. Beginning in the 1580s, the law granting the right of certain peasants to move on St. George's Day was "temporarily" repealed.[22] The process behind this change seems to have been similar to that behind the introduction of the St. George's Day restrictions on movement in the mid-fifteenth century. In the 1580s, however, it was members of the middle-service-class provincial cavalry, rather than the monasteries, who perceived a labor shortage and asked the government to "temporarily" forbid their peasants from moving away. This the government did for a number of landholders, who were thereby converted into serfholders as well. In another parallel, for unknown reasons the so-called "Forbidden Years" were universalized in 1592 for all peasants.[23] This meant that the peasants were bound to the land wherever they happened to be registered (in written documents) or otherwise claimed by a lord. They were not bound to their lords, and lords had no right to move, sell, or otherwise dispose of their peasants. Again, it should be stressed that the Forbidden Years were supposed to be temporary (*do gosudareva ukazu*), and obviously no one had the slightest idea that they would endure until 1906. It is assumed that the Forbidden Years and subsequent enserfment edicts were enacted at the behest of members of the middle service class, which was the foundation of the first service-class revolution. The members of this class only had an average of about 5.6 peasant households apiece paying them rent/dues that enabled them to provide military service. It is clear that peasant mobility, on balance, was advantageous to the larger landowners, the monasteries, and members of the upper service class. The institution of the Forbidden Years also proved to be contagious: in 1590 it was applied to the townsmen of Toropets, who had been fleeing their communally assessed tax obligations.[24]

The enserfment of the peasantry was not yet complete with the universalization of the Forbidden Years in 1592 because of another measure, which was enacted simultaneously, perhaps to assuage the large landowners. A five-year statute of limitations was imposed on the recovery of fugitive peasants.[25] Thus a landholder/owner had only five years to locate and file suit to recover a fugitive peasant. If he could not do this, he lost all claim to the fugitive. The process for recovering fugitive slaves, like that for recovering fugitive serfs, was still a dyadic process; the government only offered the services of its judicial mediators to resolve ownership disputes but did not itself attempt to locate and return fugitives. This made it difficult for members of the middle service class to locate their fugitive serfs, for they had to spend half the year in cavalry service, were not at home to prevent flights, and had no surplus manpower to locate fugitives and sit out the court process for their recovery. (Finding fugitive slaves, on which there never had been a statute of limitations, often took decades, when the slaves could be located in the vast expanses of Rus' at all.) The large landowners, on the other hand, had stewards (usually slaves) who ran their estates full time; they also had the manpower (again, usually slaves) to look for fugitives and to tend to the judicial process governing their return. For these reasons the enserfment is not considered to have been completed until the repeal of the statute of limitations in 1649.

The 1580s and 1590s also witnessed intense legislative activity on the institution of slavery, which often coincided chronologically with the enserfment legislation. As a result, it is often assumed that the two were somehow linked in the minds of the legislators; no scholar, however, has been able to determine precisely what those links were, other than the obvious one that binding the peasants to the land made them much more like slaves. In the seventeenth century this linkage became even more obvious as the government not only resolved trouble cases involving serfs by making analogies with slaves but also mentioned peasants and slaves together in most decrees. Be that as it may, the institution of limited service contract slavery came into its own in the last third of the sixteenth century as the same forces which depopulated the heartland of the Muscovite state also drove larger numbers of people to sell themselves into slavery. The binding of the peasants to the land through the evolving enserfment process may have contributed to the attractiveness of slavery, for it was probably not perceived as being significantly different from being bound to the lord as a slave, and peasants had to pay taxes, whereas slaves as a rule did not.

Whatever the motivation of the legislators, they could see that slavery was likely to encompass an ever-larger portion of the population because it was permanent and heritable upon the default on the "loan" after the first year. Thus they decided to alter the essence of limited service contract slavery: initially the "limitation" had been for the first year of the "loan," but this was changed to the life of the owner. Since this form of slavery now ended with the death of the owner, the loan could not be collected; and although the owner could no longer will the "defaulted borrower" to his heirs, the slave could not escape slavery except by manumission or the owner's death. This remained the premier form of slavery until its abolition in the 1720s. Whether the institution of slavery would have been altered so dramatically in the absence of the first service-class revolution and the catastrophes of Ivan's reign is a counterfactual question that cannot be answered, but it would seem unlikely.[26]

The stratification of society also made headway during these decades, especially in the middle service class. The first steps leading to this class's "gentrification" were taken when the law limited access to the provincial cavalry to the heirs of those who were already in its ranks and decreed that service landholdings be transmitted directly to heirs.[27]

In summary, both changing military technology and warfare itself had significant impacts on Russian society by the end of the sixteenth century. Handguns began the popularization of warfare in the persons of the arquebusiers, and warfare combined with other developments to cause so much dislocation that the peasants became enserfed and the creation of a rigid, caste-like society was well advanced.

The Time of Troubles

There has been much historiographic debate over the role of the Time of Troubles in Russian history, and particularly its impact on subsequent events. The dates of the Time of Troubles depend on how one defines the phenomenon, but suffice it to say here that they range from the broadest, 1582 to 1618, to the narrowest, 1605 to 1613. Its three major elements were a dynastic crisis (the end of the seven-century-old Riurikid dynasty and the inauguration of the Romanovs for a three-century reign), civil war, and foreign intervention by the Poles (who occupied Moscow) and the Swedes (who occupied Novgorod). Militarily, the most important innovation was the introduction of linear tactics, in a 1605 battle at Dobrinichie, only five years after they had been "invented" by Maurice of Orange to maximize fire power.[28] (This disregards the fact that the arquebusiers had used linear tactics with their movable fortress, the *guliai gorod*.)

The revolving-door governments during the Time of Troubles waffled on the Forbidden Years, but in 1607 Vasilii Shuiskii's administration confirmed them, along with a fifteen-year statute of limitations on the recovery of fugitive serfs. More ominous for the long term was Shuiskii's regular linkage of slaves and serfs in his social legislation, which, inter alia, made government much more concerned with society than it had been customarily.[29]

The impact of the Bolotnikov rebellion (1606–7) on the enserfment process has been heatedly debated in Soviet historiography; scholars such as L. V. Cherepnin, V. I. Koretskii, and A. A. Zimin alleged that the affair so frightened the government that it forced a four-decade delay in the completion of the enserfment.[30] Their position is based on two assumptions that to me seem spurious: (1) that the Bolotnikov uprising was a "peasant war" and (2) that the government and/or the oligarchs running it rabidly desired the peasants' complete enserfment. Both of those assumptions, in my view, are in fact contrary to the historical reality. Bolotnikov, a former elite slave, was not himself a peasant, and the peasants were only the fourth largest social contingent among his forces. Thus he did not lead a peasant war (a concept borrowed from Engels), and the government had no particular reason to fear the peasantry. Equally to the point, as we shall see in what follows, it is almost certain that "the government" did not want to see the peasants definitively enserfed. The Bolotnikov uprising did have one major impact on warfare, however: a significant portion of the rebels were elite combat cavalry slaves who had learned how to fight earlier under the supervision of their owners. The uprising taught the government that it could be dangerous to train slaves how to fight, with the result that slaves were relegated to the role of body servants in the baggage train as rapidly as practicable. This development became especially prominent as the utility of the cavalry declined with the advance of the gunpowder revolution and the introduction of the new formation regiments beginning in the 1630s.[31]

From the Time of Troubles to the Ulozhenie of 1649

The Time of Troubles left Muscovy in ruins, and the treaties with Sweden (Stolbovo, 1617) and Poland (Deulino, 1618) failed to resolve Muscovy's problematic international relations. Most troubling were relations with Rzeczpospolita, which had seized the great fortress of Smolensk (in the sixteenth century, one of the largest construction projects in the world) by treasonous stealth in 1611. (A traitor, Dedushkin, had informed the Poles where the mortar was weak because it had been spread in the winter time, whereupon they blasted a hole through the wall and took the citadel by storm.) The Rzeczpospolita also continued to claim the Muscovite throne. Muscovy's recovery began in 1619 with the return of Patriarch Filaret (Tsar Mikhail's father) from Polish captivity. A devout (perhaps "rabid" might be more accurate) polonophobe, Filaret turned to the problem of gaining revenge against the Rzeczpospolita as soon as the material means could be found to do so. He resolved that this meant reforming the Muscovite army as thoroughly as possible.

Beginning in 1630 the Muscovites began to recruit entire companies of officers and men in Central and Western Europe to form the so-called "new formation regiments," units of regularly trained and salaried troops that came to comprise approximately one-half of the Russian forces that fought in the Smolensk War (1632–34).[32] Those forces, just over 34,000 strong, approximated in number the 40,000 that were later discovered to be the maximum number of forces which could be controlled in a European battle. The Smolensk War proved to be an event of classic siege warfare, for the Muscovites were able to control much of the territory around the city but could not seize the fortress itself. Muscovy half-won the Smolensk War: neither the fortress itself nor any territory was recovered, but the Poles gave up their claims to the Russian throne. The foreign mercenaries proved to be inordinately expensive and consequently were dismissed and sent back to their places of origin soon after the war was over. Regardless, the government concluded that the days of the *pomest'e* cavalry and the musketeers were limited because they were obsolescent.

Revanchism was part of the international order, and Muscovy was determined to recover Smolensk and its environs. Filaret had died in 1633, and his successors, who ran the government for Tsar Mikhail, resolved that the Tatar menace had to be resolved before initiating further action on the western front. Therefore in 1636 they initiated the ambitious 800-mile Belgorod fortified line project, reminiscent of the old Roman lines, which essentially walled off (and secured) the southern frontier. This, along with continuing high taxation despite the end of the Smolensk War, precipitated massive peasant flight once again from the central heartland to the southern chernozem. Although the Belgorod *zasechnaia cherta,* built with the aid of French Huguenot fortification specialists and Dutch engineers, was not completed until 1653, it was well under way by Tsar Mikhail's death in 1645 and proved its effectiveness in sealing off the southern frontier.

Tsar Aleksei was only sixteen when he came to the throne, and his government was run by his tutor, Boris Ivanovich Morozov, one of the most remarkable individuals in Muscovite history. Morozov soon resolved that it was time to begin preparing once again for war with the Rzeczpospolita to recover Smolensk, and sent recruiters west to recreate the new formation army that had been disbanded after the Smolensk War. The recruiting was more leisurely and selective than it had been in 1630–32, with attention more to officers who could train

Russians than to men who could bring entire units with them. The consequence was that in the summer of 1648 the new formation army was in the process of being created, but the fundamental military force of the Muscovite state still consisted of the middle-service-class cavalry, primarily armed with bows, arrows, and sabers, and the musketeers. The obsolescence of this cavalry was epitomized by the fact that it was no longer summoned annually to meet the Crimean Tatar threat because the new frontier (south of the Belgorod fortified line) was so far away from the heartland and the *cherta* was doing its job. On the western front, the cavalry was of little use in the siege warfare for the control of fortresses that was becoming Russia's concern vis-à-vis the Poles and Swedes. As for the musketeers, they already were being converted from a military force into a constabulary body.[33]

The rush toward a caste society became a rout between 1613 and 1649. The major issues involving the peasantry were the repeal of the statute of limitations on the recovery of fugitives and the legal treatment accorded to peasants bound to the land. Lengthy documents survive from a middle-service-class petition campaign of 1637, 1641, 1645, and 1648 to repeal the legislation and are as revealing as any documents of early modern Russian history.[34] The obsolescent provincial cavalrymen never, to my knowledge, formally expressed the lament of the Turkish cavalrymen that "manliness died when firearms were invented" (*tüfeng boldu, mertlik öldü*), but many of them acted, and probably felt, that way. In their petitions the Muscovites concentrated on other concerns. They narrated in considerable detail that their peasants were fleeing and stressed that peasant flight was often to the estates of great magnates, who then moved them for purposes of concealment to distant estates until the statute of limitations had expired. As a result of the campaign, the five-year limit (the fifteen-year limit of Shuiskii had been forgotten) was extended to nine years in 1637, then to fifteen years in 1641; in 1645 the government promised that it would be repealed once a census had been taken. Although the census was taken in 1646–47, the promise was "forgotten." Morozov's correspondence with his steward reveals why: he himself was receiving fugitives and telling his stewards how to conceal them from investigators. This issue finally was forced by riots in June of 1648, after which the government promised to convoke an Assembly of the Land (a *zemskii sobor*, a temporary elected representative parliamentary body) and set up a commission headed by N. I. Odoevskii to compile a new law code.[35]

Although no minutes are extant from the sessions of the *zemskii sobor* (1 October 1648 to 29 January 1649), some of that body's activities can be followed in the trail of legislation issued during those four months. Moreover, scholars have been studying the law code (the *Ulozhenie* of 1649) produced by the Odoevskii commission together with the Assembly for nearly two centuries and have calculated that approximately 7 percent of the 967 articles in the document are there because of demands made by the elected representatives.[36] Among those demands were those of the obsolescent middle-service-class cavalrymen that the statute of limitations on the recovery of fugitive serfs be annulled, which it was. This change was to definitively bind the Russian peasants to the land until 1906.[37] (Counterfactually again, one can ask whether the peasants would have remained enserfed until 1906 had the middle-service-class cavalry not forced the issue in the summer of 1648 and instead had simply faded out of existence in the 1660s. My answer would be no.) The *Ulozhenie* also contained additional provisions on the serfs, such as what should be done in the case of fugitives who married while in flight; these provisons were usually borrowed from legislation regarding slavery. (As for the institution of slavery itself, perhaps as much as 15 percent of the *Ulozhenie*'s articles dealt with it — by far the largest concentration on any topic. Fundamentally, however, it only codified refinements of the 1597 legislation, particularly on the issue of compulsory manumission on the death of the slave-owner, and introduced nothing new.)[38]

The *Ulozhenie* codified a near-caste society, and this obviously involved more than the peasants; the townsmen also became bound to the towns, as the peasants became bound to the land, but with the difference that "the townsmen" (not all of them, obviously) asked that it be done as a favor to them. This request was essentially a response to the government's tax policy for raising revenues to pay for the army: the government insisted on assessing taxes on collectives rather than on individuals (demographically, not a bad system, in stable times) and was unable to make regular or frequent reassessments. The chaotic post-1613 years found the government trying to collect taxes from the urban population on the basis of cadastres that were hopelessly irrelevant to the contemporary reality. This tax pressure caused more people to flee the towns. Those who remained began to demand that the Forbidden Years be applied to towns as well, and they were. Logically, the issue of a statute of limitations arose as well, and the government, whose controlling oligarchs had little personal interest in the townsmen, simply used 1613 as the reference point for binding townsmen to their towns. Thus in 1638 the statute of limitations for returning fugitive townsmen was already twenty-five years.

Perhaps more ominous, because of its implications for the rest of society, at the end of the 1630s the government agreed to get into the business of hunting down and returning fugitive townsmen, something it had never done for fugitive peasants (with the paper exception of Shuiskii's 1607 edict). Fugitive townsmen were still an issue at the Assembly of the Land of 1648–49, and the *Ulozhenie* of 1649 bound them and their offspring to the towns. Townsmen, however, were bound to where they resided at the time of the legislation (probably as recorded in the 1646–47 census), unlike the peasant serfs, for whom the statute of limitations was anulled. The difference in treatement may have been due to the realization that returning townsmen were more disruptive than returning fugitive serfs. Also, the issue was the assessment of taxes based on a census, not the livelihoods of those relying on the presence of the townsmen's labor (unlike the case of the provincial cavalrymen demanding the peasants' enserfment).

Geographic immobility was not all there was to the townsmen's demands. In 1613 much town property had been taken over by non-taxpaying institutions and individuals ranging from monasteries to provincial cavalrymen and musketeers. Even worse, those institutions and individuals encroached on the townsmen's livelihoods by engaging in tax-exempt trade and handicraft. Major planks in the townsmen's political platform in the years 1613–48 were monopolies on ownership of urban land and structures, as well as on trade and handicraft. The government was reluctant to concede to those demands because the oligarchs were urban property owners, and also because military compensation was so low that to no one's surprise, musketeers, for example, tried to supplement their pay by running shops. Despite this fact, though, after the disorders of 1648, the government conceded to all the townsmen's demands. The *Ulozhenie* of 1649 granted them near-monopolies on trade and manufacturing (nothing was said, however, about government trade and manufacturing) as well as a near-monopoly on the ownership of urban real estate (the provincial cavalrymen were permitted to own one townhouse and keep one slave caretaker in it). The musketeers also were granted certain concessions denied to other members of the lower service class.[39] As if to show the world its seriousness about creating a caste society, in 1654 the Muscovite government ordered all foreigners to reside in the Northern European Settlement (*Nemetskaia sloboda*). After that, the only free people in Muscovy were manumitted slaves, but even that was chimerical, for given the fact that they were propertyless, most freedmen had little option but to sell themselves right back into slavery.[40]

The big winners in terms of the *Ulozhenie* were the obsolescent provincial cavalrymen. Not only did they force the peasants' enserfment, but their ranks were relatively closed to outsiders, their members were forbidden to sell themselves into slavery, and they were granted privileges with their *pomest'e* land that would have been unthinkable in the reign of Ivan IV.

Renewal of the Army and Consolidation of a Caste Society, 1649–1700

The gunpowder revolution finally triumphed in Muscovy during the Thirteen Years' War (1654–67). The recruitment of foreign mercenaries initiated prior to 1648 continued after the fall of Morozov in June of that year, with the consequence that when the war began in 1654, Muscovy was well on its way to a full reinstitution of the new formation regiments that had been dismissed after the Smolensk War two decades earlier. That round the Muscovite approach was, if not more rational, at least more experienced than had been the case under Filaret. After the end of the Thirty Years' War, mercenaries were in good supply at lower prices than previously, so the Muscovites were able to hire them much more cheaply than before. Of greater import, the Muscovites in the 1650s preferred to hire only officers, rather than complete companies, and required them to train Muscovites as rank-and-file recruits. During the Thirteen Years' War, over 80 percent of the command positions in the Muscovite army were held by non-Russians. More than 100,000 men were drafted during the war, a fact which brought the reality of war directly to the common people. (Incidentally, the fact that recruiting was done on a household basis, one man per 10.0 to 95.5 households, unquestionably accelerated the creation of the extended family in Russia, which was primarily the product of household-based taxation. Per capita, the burdens of recruiting and of taxes assessed on households diminished as households increased in size to three-generational extended households.) The majority of the new formation regiments were infantry rather than cavalry.

The extent of the Muscovite commitment to the new army can be judged partially by the fact that time, effort, and expense were invested in translating and publishing a German manual on warfare, Johann Jacob von Wallhausen's 1615 *Kriegskunst zu Fuss*. Under the Russian title, *The Drill and Art of the Military Administration of Infantry* (*Uchen'e i khitrost' ratnogo stroeniia pekhotnykh liudei*), the manual enjoys the distinction of competing with the *Ulozhenie* of 1649 for the honor of being the second civil book published in Muscovy. (The military manual was printed first but had to wait for plates made in Western Europe, so that the law code was actually available first.) The German manual was probably obsolete, and there is some question about how many copies of the Russian-language edition were actually sold and read, but nevertheless, symbolically it was a very significant gesture.[41]

Very meaningful steps were taken to add to the ranks of the new formation regiments such as sending to them all recruits produced by the draft. Moreover, every attempt was made to direct personnel from the old army into the new one. For example, as children sired by the traditional cavalrymen matured, they were directed into the new formation regiments, as were cavalrymen who did not have sufficient land or peasants to support themselves. Several battles of the Thirteen Years' War (especially at Konotop and Chudnovo) resulted in the near-extermination of the old middle-service-class cavalry, and after the disorders of 1648 most of the musketeers were directed into constabulary service.[42]

Russia confined to the area west of the Urals lacked the necessary mineral base for any kind of military autarky or independence. Although bog iron existed in the Tula region, and relatively insignificant deposits of better iron ore and copper ore were discovered in the North after 1650, Muscovy was still dependent on imports for its higher-grade iron and for most of its handguns. Domestically produced artillery were satisfactory, scientifically manufactured in large numbers during the Thirteen Years' War, and continually improved throughout the period, but most muskets, pistols, and similar ordnance were considered acceptable only if imported. This situation was not to change until after the opening of the Urals metallurgical industry during the reign of Peter the Great.

Although Russia seems to have ended the Thirteen Years' War with primarily the new formation regiments (a semi-standing, semi-regular army) as its military base, the obsolescent provincial middle service class refused to die. The first service-class revolution had done its job and then decayed. In spite of significant contests with the Ottoman Empire and its client state the Crimean Khanate in 1687, 1689, 1695, and 1696, comparatively little seems to be known about the army in the decades at the end of the seventeenth century. Probably for cost reasons, the new formation regiments apparently were not maintained, and the obsolescent provincial cavalry remained on the books. It is also relatively clear that it was not a very useful military force. Not only were the bow and arrow of little utility, but apparently the members of the middle service class did not even report for service if they did not feel so inclined. One must also note that in the 1680s Peter began to create regiments (the Preobrazhenskii, Semenovskii, Lefortovskii, and Gordonovskii) commanded primarily by foreigners that later served as the nucleus of his post-1700 army.[43] All of this, however, is greatly in need of further study.

The post-1649 years witnessed the consolidation of the Muscovite caste society. It was soon discovered that, because of the intense competition for labor, the mere returning of fugitive peasants (and slaves) was insufficient to discourage runaways. What proved to be necessary was sanctions that would inhibit landlords from receiving (or recruiting) runaways. [This reminds one of the contemporary U.S. debate about what can be done to inhibit illegal immigration and the current best solution: fine employers who hire illegal aliens.] The Muscovites tried government fines and compensation to the lords who had suffered the labor loss charged against those who had caused it, but these measures had little impact. Then the government prescribed that one additional peasant, as well as the fugitive, be returned to the rightful lord. This, too, did no good, so the number was raised to two plus the fugitive, without results. When the penalty number was raised to four extra (with their families), though, apparently the harborers of fugitive serfs drove them out en masse. (Peter the Great in 1704 even prescribed capital punishment, confiscation of landed property, and damnation for receiving and concealing fugitives, but it is not known whether his edict had any impact or was ever enforced.)[44]

Just as important as the sanctions was the move to involve governmental agents in the search for runaways. This had been initiated at the end of the 1630s for townsmen, and after the *Ulozhenie* of 1649 was extended to fugitive serfs and slaves. Central agents were sent to the provinces and they interviewed everyone. Their principle was: if you cannot prove you belong here, then you must belong somewhere else and we will send you there. Tens of thousands of fugitives were returned to former places of residence as a result of such dragnets.[45]

Almost all edicts of the post-1649 era mentioned serfs and slaves together. The social condition of the serfs continued to deteriorate as they were increasingly equated with slaves in almost every dimension, except that they could not yet be sold without land. The distinction remained, however, that slaves did not pay taxes. Not surprisingly, when the government took the great census of 1678, it discovered that the number of slaves had increased enormously. In response, the government in 1679 decreed that all slaves engaged in agriculture henceforth had to pay taxes equally with the serfs. That essentially abolished the institution of agricultural slavery.[46]

The townsmen used the *Ulozhenie* of 1649 to great advantage and strengthened their control over urban property and occupations. Non-townsmen were forced to surrender their urban enclaves and most of their town lots and houses. They also were compelled to vacate green belts around many of the urban concentrations, where the townsmen were allowed to keep livestock and gardens. The townsmen also were granted their prescribed monopolies on urban handicraft and trading activities. The issue of whether "town air made one free" became a real one after 1649. The government insisted that it did not and ran its dragnets through the towns as well as through the countryside. In spite of that fact, however, a form of a statute of limitation was imposed on returning fugitives from urban areas to the effect that all those who had been in the town since a certain date were allowed to remain there. The result was that the urban population increased slowly in the second half of the seventeenth century.[47]

As already mentioned, after the townsmen, the big winners of 1648–49 were the middle-service-class cavalrymen. In addition to the enserfment of the peasantry, their big push was to monopolize enrollment in their caste while gaining ownership-like control over their service landholdings, that is, to convert the *pomest'e* into a *votchina* (a hereditary estate). Although the latter goal was not completely realized until the 1730s, the conversion process was very far advanced by 1700. Except for the musketeers, all the other members of the lower service class (cossacks, artillerymen, fortifications masons) suffered at the expense of the townsmen's monopolies after 1649. Their ultimate destinies were to be replaced, by and large, by the new formation regiments.[48]

The last half of the seventeenth century did not witness any great military or social innovations, but merely saw the working out of the technologies and social policies that were in process prior to 1649. These were sufficient, however, to serve as a solid base for the transition to the reign of Peter the Great.

Peter's New Regular Army and Society, 1700–25

The seventeenth century ended with a great loss for Russia: its defeat by the Swedes at Narva in 1700 was hardly an unexpected event to anyone aware of the relaxed slide the Muscovites had been on since 1667. Peter had raced home from his European junket in 1699 after the revolt by the *strel'tsy,* whom he ordered hanged, and began to institute a standing regular army by raising three divisions of nine regiments each.[49] The Narva defeat at the opening of the Northern War (1700–21) was a failed artillery siege operation that turned into a major Russian catastrophe. When Charles XII lifted the siege by defeating Peter's forces, he revealed that they were totally inadequate; Peter responded to the challenge. Again, mercenary officers were hired, and, again, levies of men followed one after another. In the seventeenth century slaves were essentially immune from the draft (as though confiscation of private property were illegal or immoral in Rus'!), but Peter turned to them first when he desired to add to his new formation cannon fodder; townsmen and serfs were drafted later. Recruiting levies between 1705 and 1713 drafted 337,196 men (out of a total population of roughly fifteen million). Just before the great 1709 Poltava battle, in which Russia triumphed over the arrogant Swedes in a brilliantly commanded field battle, the infantrymen were equipped with flintlock muskets and the new bayonet, which permitted them to go on the offensive and thus greatly increased the importance of shock combat in addition to fire (shot, projectile) combat. Linear tactics were perfected further, with the cavalry, when used in combat at all, relegated to defending the flanks, primarily with cold weapons. In July 1711 Peter was defeated ingloriously on the Pruth by the Ottomans because the subject Christian Moldavian population unexpectedly failed to rebel or otherwise assist the Russians. Also, because his parched and hungry forces were outnumbered four to five times by the Turks and Crimean Tatars they could not employ their linear tactics. However, Moscow went on to build a military establishment of enormous size — 265,000 men in all land and sea branches, one of the largest in Europe — and to win the Northern War.[50]

By 1725 a solid Russian new formation officer corps was constructed, and the law was able to stipulate that no more than one-third of any cadre of officers could be foreigners. The officers were of relatively diverse social origins; first they followed Austrian and Swedish manuals, later, domestically produced ones. Much to his credit, Peter broke the slothful habits of the middle-service-class gentry and put them "back in harness" by forcing all of them to serve when and where ordered. Immediately after Narva, ten regiments of dragoons were created from these men. Others were converted into new-style cavalrymen (reitary, first introduced for the Smolensk War) and lancers. Because the bayonet allowed the infantry to protect itself, the cavalry's primary role was altered to that of scouting, sudden attack, and pursuit. In the early years of the eighteenth century the cavalry was nearly worthless, and only in 1709 did it become effective. Decrees of 1714 and 1723 required that gentry officers know military affairs well. Toward that end, Petrine military schools turned out three to four hundred officers per year, and his military education effort is regarded as among his most important military contributions. The professionalization of the Petrine army was most evident in its adoption of the tactic of pursuing a defeated enemy to destroy it for political reasons, rather than the traditional Muscovite practice of remaining on the battlefield to loot the fallen enemy for economic reasons.[51]

Some of the Petrine response to the Narva defeat was technological, in accord with Peter's personal preferences. The first response was to upgrade manufacturing facilities to the best European standards and to lessen reliance on imported ordnance and metal. This was particularly imperative because Sweden, one of Russia's prime suppliers, was its major adversary in the Northern War. Although 25,000 handguns were imported during the first decade of the Northern War, more important was the fact that 125,000 were manufactured in Russia in that time. Artillery became a special branch of service early in the Northern War, and Peter restored his country's ordnance to world-class status. The second response was to develop domestic sources of minerals to cut reliance on imports, and this led to the opening of the Urals metallurgical industry. By the time of Peter's death, Russia was nearly independent in the metallurgical sphere. Moveover, under Peter a woolens industry was established for the first time. Its purpose was to manufacture uniforms for the new regular army; before that time, nearly all troops had made their own uniforms.[52] Only in Peter's time did the state cede to a handful of private entrepreneurs a small portion of the military industry, which before that time always had been a matter of exclusive state concern.

Social changes followed upon the Petrine military ones. The reharnessing of the middle-service-class gentry was only one aspect of the militarization of society that ultimately came to be epitomized in the 1721 Table of Ranks. Little happened to the townsmen, but the juridical condition of the peasants continued to deteriorate as they became nearly bound to the person of the lord by the tax system and by developing reality. The Petrine legislation forbidding the use of the gavel in serf auctions epitomized the slave-like condition of the serfs. As for the slaves, their numbers were diminished by army recruiting, but slavery continued to persist because of its attractiveness as a tax dodge, if only for house slaves. Again, the precipitating development was a census, of 1719, which revealed that the number of house slaves was much larger than should have been the case. In response, the government decreed in 1723 that house slaves had to pay the soul tax (inaugurated to replace the household tax, which had been "dodged" by the creation of extended families), which effectively converted them into house serfs and put an end to the institution of slavery.[53]

The requirements of warfare—keeping up with the Swedes—forced the Russians to rationalize the service state in order to put all estates in harness.[54] If the military emergency did not actually "force" Peter to regiment society, it certainly served as his excuse for doing so. An attempt was even made to cut down on superfluous priests and monks by drafting them into the army. No one can dispute that the second service-class revolution was effective, that the Petrine system not only was rational but also worked[55]—the clergy prayed while the townsmen and peasant-serfs paid. The enormous army was the largest in Eastern Europe (and, with the possible exception of France's army, the largest in all of Europe), the terror of all countries from Sweden to the Ottoman Empire. In legislation the estates were rigidly prescribed and caste-like, but the nature of the Russian autocracy was such that rigid legislation could be ignored for any *raison d'état*.

Once the military pressure was off, however, the rationality of the system began to collapse. In nearly a "rerun" of the seventeenth century, the landholding gentry quickly became the major pressure group and in the 1725–62 era undid the Petrine requirements, ranging from the principle that service had to be rendered in order to hold/own land to the principle that service had to be rendered at all. After 1762, when compulsory state service for all landowners was abolished, serfdom became a grotesque anachronism, but this fact failed to penetrate the minds of any but a handful of radicals until the Crimean War in the mid-1850s, which revealed that the Petrine system was no longer relevant either to the requirements of new conceptions of human dignity or the requirements of warfare. The Great Reforms of Alexander II began a new chapter in the Russian social response to the technology of war.[56]

Conclusion

The centuries 1450–1725 witnessed two service-class revolutions in Russia that were direct responses to military threats. The first was a response to the Tatar light cavalry threat, the second to the Swedish infantry threat. Similarly, the light bow and arrow yielded to the musket; warfare changed from a contest over the control of resources to a contest over the control of territory. The Russians—pushed by, as well as utilizing, military changes originating in the West—coped with both threats by legislating the creation of highly stratified, rigid social estates that were near-castes. The human cost was enormous, but the Tatars, Lithuanians, Poles, and Swedes all failed to deprive Russia of its independence.

NOTES

1. Georges Florovsky, "The Problem of Old Russian Culture," *Slavic Review* 21, no. 1 (1962): 1–15.

2. Richard Hellie, *Enserfment and Military Change in Muscovy* (Chicago, 1971), 25–26, 152–53, 157. Much of this essay is a synthesis of my own previous work. Therefore I shall cite other works only in cases when they have appeared since my own on a particular topic.

3. Daniel H. Kaiser, *The Growth of the Law in Medieval Russia* (Princeton, 1980), 7, 15–17.

4. Hellie, *Enserfment,* 78; idem, "Muscovite Slavery in Comparative Perspective," *Russian History* 6, pt. 2 (1979), 140–42; idem, *Slavery in Russia, 1450–1725* (Chicago, 1982), 496–98, 681–89.

5. Richard Hellie, "The Stratification of Muscovite Society: The Townsmen," *Russian History* 5, pt. 2 (1978), 121–22.

6. Richard Hellie, *Muscovite Society* (Chicago, 1967), 94-104.

7. Hellie, *Enserfment*, 152.

8. Ibid., 153-56; S. M. Zemtsov and V. L. Glazychev, *Aristotel' Foravanti* (Moscow, 1985).

9. Hellie, *Muscovite Society*, 104-5.

10. Ibid., 105-6.

11. Peter Bowman Brown, "Early Modern Russian Bureaucracy: The Evolution of the Chancellery System from Ivan III to Peter the Great 1478-1717," 2 vols., Ph.D. diss., University of Chicago, 1978.

12. Iosif Volotskii, *Poslaniia Iosifa Volotskogo*, ed. by A. A. Zimin and Ia. S. Lur'e (Moscow-Leningrad, 1959), 90.

13. J. L. I. Fennell, *The Correspondence Between Prince A. M. Kurbsky and Tsar Ivan IV of Russia, 1564-1579* (Cambridge, 1955).

14. Michael Howard, *War in European History* (Oxford, 1976), 28.

15. Hellie, *Enserfment*, 160-64; G. M. Zakharikov, "O boevom naznachenii Tsar'-pushki," *Pamiatniki nauki i tekhniki 1984* (1986), 31-46.

16. Kaiser, *Growth of the Law*, 188.

17. Hellie, *Slavery*, 48-56.

18. Hellie, *Enserfment*, 267. The numbers I presented on pp. 267-73 for the size of the Muscovite total military forces at various times and on different major campaigns have not been challenged.

19. Ibid., 94-95, 157, 159; idem, "What Happened? How Did He Get Away With It? Ivan Groznyi's Paranoia and the Problem of Institutional Restraints," *Russian History* 14, nos. 1-4 (1987), 199-224. This journal volume was also published as Richard Hellie, ed., *Ivan the Terrible: A Quarcentenary Celebration of His Death* (Irvine, 1987).

20. Brown, "Early Modern Russian Bureaucracy."

21. For a discussion of these issues in the Eurasian context, see William H. McNeill, *The Pursuit of Power* (Chicago, 1982), 111-12. I myself doubt that it was efficient, for, inter alia, Russia never developed (and, as First Secretary Mikhail Gorbachev would probably be the first to say, has not yet developed) the "self-sustaining feedback loop" that raised the West's wealth and power above that of other civilizations (ibid., 117).

22. Hellie, *Enserfment*, 96; idem, *Slavery*, 671-73.

23. Hellie, *Muscovite Society*, 116-18; idem, *Enserfment*, 101; idem, *Slavery*, 671.

24. Hellie, *Muscovite Society*, 47.

25. Ibid., 123; idem, *Enserfment*, 105.

26. Hellie, *Muscovite Society*, 137-41, 247-54; idem, *Slavery*, 52-56.

27. Hellie, *Enserfment*, 45.

28. Ibid., 165.

29. Ibid., 108-9; idem, *Muscovite Society*, 137-41.

30. Hellie, *Enserfment*, 107; idem, "A. A. Zimin," in *The Modern Encyclopaedia of Russian and Soviet History* 46 (October, 1987): 76-83; V. I. Koretskii, *Istoriia russkogo letopisaniia vtoroi poloviny XVI-nachala XVII v.* (Moscow, 1986), 269.

31. Hellie, *Enserfment*, 220, 271; idem, *Slavery*, 473, 574-75.

32. Hellie, *Enserfment,* 271.

33. Ibid., 178–79, 186–90, 204–7.

34. Hellie, *Muscovite Society,* 167–75, 178–96, 198–205.

35. Hellie, *Enserfment,* 135–39; idem, "Zemskii Sobor," in *The Modern Encyclopaedia of Russian and Soviet History* 45 (August 1987): 226–34.

36. Richard Hellie, "Muscovite Law and Society: The Ulozhenie of 1649 as a Reflection of the Political and Social Development of Russia Since the Sudebnik of 1589," Ph.D. diss., University of Chicago, 1965), 444–68; idem, "The Ulozhenie of 1649," in *The Modern Encyclopaedia of Russian and Soviet History* 40 (1985), 193.

37. Hellie, "Muscovite Law and Society," 50; idem, *Enserfment;* idem, *The Muscovite Law Code (Ulozhenie) of 1649* (Irvine, 1988), 85–86.

38. Hellie, *Slavery,* 31; idem, *The Muscovite Law Code,* 161–94.

39. Hellie, "Townsmen," 119–75; idem, *The Muscovite Law Code,* 152–61.

40. Hellie, "Townsmen," 164; idem, *Slavery,* 46, 133–34, 382–83, 520–22.

41. Hellie, *Enserfment,* 188. William McNeill has pointed out that Wallhausen pirated the book from a 1607 Dutch volume by Jacob de Gheyn (*The Pursuit of Power,* 134).

42. Hellie, *Enserfment,* 188–95, 356–57.

43. Richard Hellie, "The Petrine Army: Continuity, Change, and Impact," *Canadian-American Slavic Studies* 8, no. 2 (Summer 1974), 237–39.

44. Hellie, *Slavery,* 567–71.

45. Hellie, *Enserfment,* 250–53; idem, "Townsmen," 138–40.

46. Hellie, *Slavery,* 697.

47. Hellie, "Townsmen," 140, 144–51, 159–63.

48. Hellie, *Enserfment,* 214, 217; idem, *The Muscovite Law Code,* 153, 155.

49. M. D. Rabinovich, *Polki petrovskoi armii 1698–1725. Kratkii spravochnik* (Moscow, 1977).

50. N. N. Molchanov, *Diplomatiia Petra Pervogo* (Moscow, 1986), 279–83; Hellie, "Petrine Army," 245–47; idem, *Slavery,* 699–702. On the Pruth Campaign, Peter lost 27,285 men, but only 4,800 of them in battle; the rest died of hunger, thirst, and disease. The Molchanov volume is an interesting xenophobic period piece, with its attack on foreign mercenaries, who communicated with the Russians in Latin (280), and its claim that the merit of Foreign Minister P. P. Shafirov (of Jewish origin), who negotiated Peter out of the Pruth disaster, is "exaggerated in Russian and especially foreign literature" (283).

51. Hellie, "Petrine Army," 245–52.

52. Ibid., 240; Arcadius Kahan, *The Plow, The Hammer, and the Knout. An Economic History of Eighteenth-Century Russia,* ed. Richard Hellie (Chicago, 1985), 97–98, 101, 190–91.

53. Hellie, *Slavery,* 698–99.

54. John L. H. Keep, *Soldiers of the Tsar. Army and Society in Russia 1462–1874* (Oxford, 1985), 118. Part 2 of Keep's volume, "The Warrior Tsar, 1689–1725," is most highly recommended to anyone interested in Petrine military affairs.

55. Richard Hellie, "The Structure of Modern Russian History: Toward a Dynamic Model," *Russian History* 4, pt. 1 (1977), 5.

56. Hellie, *Enserfment,* 261–62.

The Transition to European Military Ascendancy in India, 1600–1800

BRUCE P. LENMAN

THE CORE OF THIS ESSAY consists of an analysis of the eighteenth-century military events that laid the foundations of the British Raj in the Indian subcontinent. Within that analysis there is considerable emphasis on the well-trodden, but perhaps less well-understood, field of Plassey, where in 1757, at a cost of fewer than twenty English lives, Robert Clive won control of Bengal. In itself, this is a theme not unworthy of attention, and even now is of some contemporary relevance. The empire of the East India Company which Clive served is still with us, lightly disguised and somewhat reduced on the periphery; it is called the Republic of India. Furthermore, the spirit of the bureaucratic imperial executive, bred by the British Raj in India, flourishes today, as much in New Delhi as at Westminster. Nevertheless, the theme also has the virtue of forcing us back in time to the seventeenth and, indeed, the sixteenth centuries, and toward aspects of the history of European commercial and political expansion in Asia which are not triumphally Anglo-centric. To understand the victorious British of the second half of the eighteenth century, it is necessary to look at English defeats in India in the late seventeenth century. To understand the role of Europeans in seventeenth-century India, scholarship must encompass the Portuguese and Dutch experience, as well as that of the English.

Lurking below these somewhat surface events lie even deeper questions. One which must be examined is the military capability of the Mughal Empire, not least in order to explain its apparently rapid later decline. A connected question, which may be partially ducked but cannot be totally ignored, is whether certain areas of the world are particularly prone to foreign domination. South Italy and Sicily were colonized by Carthaginians, Greeks, Byzantines, Arabs, the Hohenstaufen, the Aragonese, and the Bourbons, as well as by the Normans, before they were colonized by Northern Italians; and Hindustan has a surprisingly similar tendency, historically, to succumb to predation.[1] However, at this point it is surely imperative to find a point of departure for what is bound to be a complex web of argument.

No discussion of the fate of European arms in the Indian subcontinent in the seventeenth and eighteenth centuries can avoid starting with some examination of the Portuguese experience. By 1600, the intricate structure of fortified ports, trade, and protection rackets which the Portuguese called their *Estado da India* was undoubtedly past its peak of vigor and achievement, but that achievement had been both early and great. Much of the activity conducted under the aegis of the *Estado da India* lay beyond the bounds of India as we understand it, but, of course, the unchallenged capital of the whole complex, and seat of the Viceroy, was "Golden Goa" on the Malabar Coast, and events in the Persian gulf in the early seventeenth century cannot be understood without reference to the Portuguese response to the arrival of the English East India Company on the Malabar Coast. Above all, Portuguese activities are important for present purposes because of the pervasive streak of violence which was always present in them — either openly or by menacing implication. In a sense, violence was inescapable, for, as C. R. Boxer has convincingly demonstrated, Portuguese officials were so conscious of the adverse balance-of-payments situation implicit in their desire to purchase pepper and spices with gold and silver bullion that they bandied around as a platitude the old saw that when Vasco da Gama reached Calicut, a major port on India's southwest coast, in May 1498, "it was India which discovered Portugal."[2]

It was the use of force, to exclude rival European powers and to levy protection money from local shipping, which was always meant to turn the *Estado da India* into an inherently self-financing operation. Of course, in practice there were long periods when it failed to be any such thing, being upheld mainly by the vested interests of those who held office in it, but even then it is clear that the incomes of these men depended significantly on the control of local distribution networks, ultimately by force. Nor were there lacking the sort of gangster personalities needed to act as "enforcers." Seventeenth-century Englishmen, like Captain Downton of the East India Company, were liable to sneer at the Portuguese Papists. "Who so cowardly as a Portuguese?" asked Downton before the fight in Swalley Hole in January 1615, but he admitted in his journal afterward that he had never seen better fighters than the Portuguese who boarded his ship, the *Merchant's Hope*. The Anglo-Portuguese struggle in the Persian Gulf, which came to an end with the truce of 1635, threw up Portuguese commanders like Nuño Alvarez Botelho and Ruy Freyre, who combined great courage with absolute savagery. Freyre was particularly noted for his success in recruiting and training native troops from India's western seaboard and from among the Gulf Arabs. The expeditionary force he led out of Ormuz in 1621 for Kishm, for example, carried on thirty-three sail 2,000 Portuguese soldiers and 1,000 Arab auxiliaries.[3]

Yet the Portuguese capacity for extensive conquest of land in India proved small. For this there are several explanations, but not the least of them is the very small margin of superiority in weaponry the Portuguese enjoyed (if they enjoyed any at all) once they left their ships. Contemporary Portuguese chroniclers like Antonio de Sousa de Macedo or Diogo do Couto (whose intimate friend João Freyre d'Andrade was chancellor of India and father of Ruy Freyre, the Gulf warrior) repeatedly stressed that the Castilian *conquistadores* of the Aztecs and Incas had crushed Amerindians innocent of any knowledge of metallurgy and only equipped with weapons of wood and stone, whereas in Asia the Portuguese had to fight sophisticated opponents who were familiar with firearms and cannon. This was certainly true of India when the Portuguese reached it.

The Deccan states had plenty of cannon. When Albuquerque captured Goa in 1510, he found its arsenal full of small-caliber cannon, of which its Bijapur garrison had made rather ineffective use. Gunners from Arabia, Persia, and Turkey were common as mercenaries in the Deccan, as were *Firingi*, or European mercenaries. The last were, of course, very common in Hindustan proper, in the domains of the Mughal emperors. Jean Baptiste Tavernier, the Huguenot jeweler and traveler, who visited the realm of the Great Mughal in the period 1645–53, remarked that there were "numerous fine cannon and the gunners are generally English or Dutch." The Dutch East India Company curried favor with Mughal generals in the seventeenth century by giving them presents of bronze field guns. The bronze and iron cannon cast in the Portuguese foundries at Goa and (after 1623) Macao were as eagerly sought after by Oriental rulers as Portuguese gunners were, and though cannon were not sold indiscriminately, the Portuguese made no effort to respect papal bans on trading firearms or munitions with infidels or Muslims. In the early seventeenth century, João Rubeiro reckoned that there were at least five thousand Portuguese renegades serving Asian rulers between Bengal and Makassar.[4]

There were, of course, many other reasons for the limited impact made by the Portuguese on the Indian subcontinent. Their militant official Counter-Reformation creed, though it gave them a tight grip on the substantial proportion of the heterogeneous population of their bases who embraced it, made the extension of their authority over large Hindu or Muslim communities difficult, despite very real pragmatism in its exercise. When a reputation for cruelty and treachery is added to this, outstanding even by the standards of sixteenth- and seventeenth-century India, it is clear that the Portuguese could never hope to slip into the position of a de facto supercaste, tolerated by a divided Indian society beneath them. An additional factor was the decidedly unsophisticated nature of Portuguese military tactics. Even great leaders like Albuquerque, who created Portuguese India, or the brave and scholarly viceroy João de Castro, who preserved it, showed little tactical subtlety. On the battlefield their standard gambit was a volley followed by a rush with cold steel. Where they did show considerable science was in the art of creating the artillery-proof walls and bastions that made it so difficult for local rulers to expel the Portuguese once they seized a port. Albuquerque became a stonemason almost as soon as his final seizure of Goa was complete, while Diu's quite exceptionally massive fortifications baffled the rulers of Gujerat as much as Goa's did the Adil Shahis of Bijapur. There was a price to pay for this, of course, and nobody said louder than João de Castro that the Portuguese were by the 1540s overextended, with too many expensive, crumbling port fortifications to upkeep. The *Estado da India* never had more than an inadequate fleet and a thousand or two regular troops available for action. Its aristocratic fortress-captains, who were the core of the whole operation, probably resisted unavoidable long-term decline as well as any other conceivable managerial class could have done.[5]

None of these arguments is meant to suggest that the territorial and population resources of the Portuguese on the Malabar Coast were insignificant from a Portuguese point of view. After all, as well as the 220 or so square miles around Goa, the Portuguese also controlled, at maximum extent, over 1,000 square miles in the *"Governo do Norte,"* which stretched along sixty miles of coast well north of Goa. There may have been a quarter to half a million people in all these territories. Indigenous manpower drawn especially from the reliable Lusitanized elements in the population was an important supplement to seventeenth-century Portuguese military and, be it said, naval power in India, at least as long as the main challenge came from Islam. Faced with religious and military resurgence among the vast Hindu majority in the Deccan, the Portuguese did less well. The Bassein district, which comprised the bulk of the *Governo do Norte,* was lost to the Marathas in 1738–39.[6]

Sir Thomas Roe, ambassador of James VI and I to the court of Emperor Jahangir between 1615 and 1619, necessarily looked with some care at the nature of the physical force available to both the Portuguese and the Mughals. He already knew that on the high seas the big well-gunned ships of the East India Company were more than a match for the Portuguese. The "frigates" with which the Portuguese tried to maintain a reign of terror on the ten miles of the River Tapti between the anchorage of Swally Hole and Surat were shallow, undecked boats with one gun in the bow. Roe reckoned that an eighty-ton pinnace with twelve guns could not only carry goods over the bar at Swally, but also treat the Portuguese "frigates" with contempt.[7] At an early stage in his stay in India, Roe saw the Mughal governors of both Surat and the province of Gujerat at their military exercises, which consisted of shooting from horseback with bow and matchlock musket at a mark set up on a pole (an ostrich egg, in one case). This is interesting and important because it underlines the extent to which the Mughals, like the Muscovite state with its vulnerable steppe frontier, were militarily rooted in the tradition of the skilled horse archer. Exercises such as these could be seen anywhere from Egypt to Delhi, at any time between the fourteenth and seventeenth centuries.[8] The Mughal forces also included many footslogging musketeers; Roe refers to "horse and shott." On his journey toward the court he paused at Burhanpur, then the advance base for imperial armies operating in the Deccan under the nominal command of Jahangir's son, Prince Parwiz. At Bahadarpur, four miles west of Burhanpur, he inspected "the stoor house of Ordinance," of which he remarked casually, "I saw divers of brasse, but generally to shortt and too wyde bored."[9] Though Roe was convinced that the domains and revenues of the Mughal Emperor were greater than those of the Shah of Persia, and not much inferior to those of the Grand Turk, he was clearly not impressed by the Mughal military establishment.

He was contemptuous of the army deployed in the conquest of the northern Deccan, describing it as "an effeminat army, fitter to be a spoyle then a terror to enemyes," and he told the English ambassador to Constantinople that Jahangir was with "what they call an Army; but I see no souldiers, though multitudes entertained in the qualety."[10] Perhaps the most impressive aspect of these comments is that they were disinterested. Roe was deeply opposed to the idea of conquest. He pointed out that the Portuguese, whose ascendancy in the East he could see rested on rotten foundations, had beggared themselves by a policy of aggression and fortification, and he was shrewd enough to see that the great united VOC, the Dutch East India Company, was rapidly going down the same slippery slope by abandoning the policy of concentrating on simple trade which had been followed by the Voorcompagniën, the several Dutch companies which preceded it in Asiatic trade and which were not much inferior to it in total size.[11] Roe did not rule out vigorous self-defense at sea but he told the East India Company that "if you will Profitt, seeke it at Sea, and in quiett trade; for without controversey it is an error to affect Garrisons and Land wars in India. . . . one disaster would eyther discreditt You, or interest you in a warr of extreame Chardge and doubtful event."[12]

To that honorable and sensible position—that the English sought in India only free access to trade for all nations—the English East India Company clung until the end of the century. With characteristic stupidity and stubbornness, Charles I sponsored rival English companies in the Orient, in defiance of his own charters, on the grounds that he was being cheated by an East India Company which he would wish to see pursue the high-handed Luso-Hispanic style of conquest and fortification. Then he, in his turn, became a victim of the changeable fortunes of war.[13] There is no reason to doubt that the consequences of land war in India on any scale for any of the interloping bodies supported by that monarch, such as Sir William Courteen's Association, would have been catastrophic. Courteen's large-scale enterprise went bankrupt fast enough as it was.

Yet there is every reason to pay more than passing attention to Roe's acerbic comments on the Mughal armies. His criticisms were certainly exaggerated, but they were not baseless. What were the salient features of the Mughal military tradition? How had it evolved since the epic days of the early sixteenth century when Babur, the founder of the dynasty, led a series of invasions between 1517 and 1525 (each, in the last analysis, a swoop from the Afghan plateau onto the plains of Hindustan)? The first point which has to be made is that the Mughals stood at the end of a very long tradition of cavalry warfare. Turkish in speech, Islamic in religion, and Persian in administrative culture, they were curiously similar to the very first Islamic warrior dynasty to erupt into the vast spaces of northern India—the Ghaznavids. From 1000 A.D. to his death in 1030, Mahmud of Ghazni made annual, devastating raids down from the Hindu Kush, replenishing his treasury by targeting wealthy temple cities, and laying the foundations of Islamic ascendancy in Hindustan, albeit in the form of an eastern extension of his own central Asian realms, and an extension scarcely secure beyond the Punjab. His armies were professional, perhaps never more than 30,000 to 40,000, all told. Two-thirds of the fighting troops were cavalry. His was a multinational army, which rapidly incorporated Indian weapons, fighting elephants, and Hindu troops, acquiring also a very heavy supply and administrative "tail" which proved its downfall in later wars with the more mobile Seljuk Turkmen bands.[14]

Babur was a Timurid, a descendant of Tamerlane, and therefore, by definition, more distantly of Genghis Khan and the Mongol armies which had carved out the greatest of all land empires. Their outstanding tactical achievement had been to show that a well-organized and ferociously disciplined cavalry army could fight set-piece battles successfully without having an infantry "core" on which to base bold enveloping maneuvers. Babur was very consciously the heir of this tradition. The early part of his *Memoirs* show him as a cavalry archer, fighting endless skirmishes at bow-shot range, and capable of recalling, long after the event, a particularly good shot, even if it did not quite bring his target down. Like his Mongol ancestors, he had to change and develop his techniques for siege warfare, but he remained a marksman. At an individual level, sieges were when the crossbow came into its own. He admired a good crossbowman shooting from inside a besieged town, and when his turn came to be besieged, he used a crossbow from the ramparts. The cavalry exercises that Roe witnessed in the early seventeenth century were part of a living tradition of mounted missile warfare.[15]

There is irritatingly little contemporary comment on the reasons why the transfer of this particular style of warfare to the plains of Hindustan proved so spectacularly successful. Mahmud of Ghazni employed one of the finest minds of central Asia, the scholar from Khvarazm known as Alberuni, to write a survey of India, but the resulting work of genius is an analysis of Hindu civilization. Its sole contribution to the analysis of the first wave of Muslim conquest is a throwaway remark that Mahmud owed a lot to the work of his father in improving the approach routes that made the invasion of India possible.[16] Babur was convinced that his achievement was greater than that of Mahmud of Ghazni because he started from a much weaker, poorer power base in the hills of the Hindu Kush. What is clear from his incomparable *Memoirs* is that he owed much in his Indian campaigns to the firepower of his cannon and matchlock men, both supervised by his cherished and much-rewarded master gunner, Ustad Ali Kuli. That the cannon were unwieldy monsters with a slow rate of fire and useful mainly for sieges is clear; but chained together, they and the massed matchlock men under Ustad Ali Kuli did form the imperial center on the decisive field of Panipat, so Babur, unlike Genghis Khan, could maneuver his cavalry as wings to a stable, if not static, infantry body. Furthermore, he was willing to pay stiffly for firepower. Thus in 1528, after the treasures looted out of Delhi and Agra had been expended, and "at this crisis . . . it being necessary to furnish equipments for the army, gunpowder for the service of the guns, and pay for the artillery and matchlockmen, on Thursday the 8th of Safir, I gave orders, that in all departments, every man having an office, should bring a hundred and thirty instead of a hundred, to the Diwan, to be applied to the procuring and fitting out the proper arms and supplies."[17] A 30 percent increase in regular taxation is tribute indeed.

Obviously, the Mughal Empire was not entirely immune from the general military and political malaise that affected the Islamic world and subjected it to graver and graver humiliation at the hands of Europeans from the late seventeenth century onward. Yet it will not do to accept a simplified version of Carlo M. Cipolla's argument that Oriental societies were not capable of modifying their military techniques to cope with the European challenge because military change would have involved unacceptable social, political or ideological change. Although such a thesis contains a measure of truth — broadly valid in Confucian China,[18] where the whole ideology of the scholar-bureaucrat militated against militarization of a European kind — Mughal India was not like that. Its ruling class set as high a value on the warrior virtues as contemporary Europe did. Nor was Mughal India a society comparable to, say, Mameluke Egypt at the end of the eighteenth century, where political and economic power, as well as military clout, were monopolized by a few thousand aristocratic cavalrymen of alien origin. Long before Napoleon's invasion of 1798, indeed long before the French Revolution, the government in Paris had marked out Egypt as a potential field of conquest, on the ground that it hardly had a serious defense force. Irresponsible and unsuccessful though it was, Napoleon's brief adventure did demonstrate how totally ineffective the Mamelukes were against the musketry of disciplined French infantry squares.[19] Although Mughal India could put much larger forces into the field than ever the Mamelukes dared, and though under Aurangzeb (1658–1707) the imperial dynasty retreated from the heroic heights of ideological syncretism scaled by Akbar (1555–1605), the empire, for all its Islamic cavalry core, was from the start doomed to an empirical and syncretist approach to the ethnic structure and physical equipment of its forces.

It will not do to suggest that Islamic-ruled states in India were inherently incapable of rapidly modifying their political and military structures. Many of the successor states in the eighteenth-century — in the military sphere, most strikingly, the Mysore of Hyder Ali and Tipu — were notable examples of flexible adaptation. It might be more useful to see the Mughal empire under Aurangzeb as an extreme example of elephantiasis (a disease marked by pathological enlargement of the limbs and thickening of the skin). If the American scholar Jane Jacobs should be right,[20] this is the inevitable fate of overcentralized, militarized superstates. They all end up spending too much on defense forces which become less and less cost-effective. Their central bureaucracies proliferate, with effects of a paralytic kind, and they invariably end up having to bribe or beat peripheral provinces into loyalty at disproportionate cost to loyal taxpayers. All these traits are econocidal. To them must be added a point which Jacobs does not make: centralized autocracies are all inherently centrifugal, especially when the autocrat is too lazy or ineffective to check private empire-building by his effectively irresponsible henchmen. Soviet Russia in the late twentieth century shows some of these traits, often described as "imperial overreach," as does the United States, and, more remarkably, the United Kingdom. The United Kingdom is an unusual case of an imperial power that kept only unprofitable parts of its global empire, like Ulster and the Falklands, and actually increased its financial and political commitments, not only in these marchlands, but also in structures such as NATO and the Common Agricultural Policy of the Common Market. The Mughals had neither the strong bureaucracies nor the technological facilities that enable the USSR or the United Kingdom to stagger on, let alone the devolved and democratic checks to central executive power characteristic of the United States.

In many ways, it was the absence of a potentially decisive military challenge which enabled the Mughal empire to slowly disintegrate. The loss of Kandahar to the Persian army of Shah Abbas II in 1649, and the failure of the Mughal forces under the princes Aurangzeb and Dara Shikoh to recover it in the campaigns of 1649–53, seems in retrospect something of a military watershed, but only in retrospect. The Emperor Shah Jahan (1628–58) certainly did not perceive it as such at the time. He and his sons had tried preliminary heavy bombardment, "human wave" assault, and bribery. The imperial family's view of their failure is summed up by Dara Shikoh's comment on the ineffectiveness of his bribes: "Perhaps we did not approach the right men at the right time."[21] The long reign of Aurangzeb left the empire, at its maximum extent, prey to internal faction, but not to external assault, least of all from Europeans.

Europeans themselves tended to think little of Indian rulers—they also tended to come disastrously unstuck. When in the 1620s Abraham van Uffelen, the governor of the Dutch factories on the Coromandel Coast, started to throw his weight around and tried to bully the local ruler, he died in the prisons of the Sultan of Golconda. In 1638, only intervention by the English and the Mughal Emperor saved Goa from the Marathas.[22] Most instructive of all was the debacle that ensued when the English East India Company in the late seventeenth century abandoned its long-standing policy of avoiding conflict in India and sought armed confrontation.

The East India Company's conscious aim is probably fairly stated in the State Papers Domestic of England in 1685, the first year of the brief and disastrous reign of James II. There the monarch is recorded as looking with favor on a petition from the East India Company that it be allowed to coin in its forts in India any kind of foreign money there current. Previously it had always done this by permission of local rulers. However, having gone to great charges to develop its fortifications so as to gain increased independence from Indian princes, the

East India Company now asked permission from James II alone. The East India Company also gained royal approval for an extension of its power to exercise martial law (hitherto a power available only in the case of company forts and plantations) to its ships on the far side of the Cape of Good Hope whenever the company was in a state of war with some other nation.[23] Written across the face of such requests was a challenge to the authority of the Mughal Empire, and a policy of coercing the empire by amphibious operations.

The central figure on the English side is usually taken to have been Sir Josiah Child, though it would be quite wrong to shift on to his shoulders total responsibility for what happened; he could not possibly have pushed through the policies he followed without the general support of both the Court of Directors of the East India Company, and indeed within the royal court of James VII and II. Child's great achievement was to tie the East India Company firmly to the chariot of late Stuart absolutism and imperialism. This was all the more remarkable because he was himself an old Cromwellian who had made his fortune as a victualler and deputy naval treasurer to the Protectorate's fleet in Portsmouth. He does not, apart from a distaste for high-flying Anglicanism, appear to have been very ideologically motivated; when he moved back to London after the Restoration, he steadily bought his way into the East India Company, and into royal favor, not least by arranging for the East India Company to make a regular Christmas present of ten thousand guineas to Charles II, as well as an appropriately smaller one to his brother and heir, James, duke of York. These Stuart brothers may have been inclined to cultivate good relations with the great Counter-Reformation absolutisms of Europe which they admired so much, but elsewhere they were exponents of an extremely aggressive naval imperialism, of a kind congenial to Child.

Sir Thomas Grantham, the arrival of whose frigate had been the first symbol of royal determination to discipline Virginia after the chaos of Bacon's Rebellion in 1676, was also the commander of a royal task force of ten ships which reached Bombay in late 1684, with a view to disciplining the mutinous garrison there. Handed over by Charles II to the East India Company because it was seen as just another encumbrance acquired by Charles as part of Catherine of Braganza's dowry, Bombay had been starved of funds by Sir Josiah's namesake (but not a relative) Sir John Child, the president of the old East India Company center on the Malabar Coast—Surat. Once Keigwin's Rebellion was suppressed, Sir John was appointed by commission under the great seal of Charles II, captain general and admiral of all East India Company forces, with Sir Thomas Grantham as his vice admiral. None of this could make Sir John a soldier; it was, however, the prelude to an attempt to refuse to pay duties on company trade to Mughal officials. Charles II had already tried this gambit on the Tsar of all the Russias, who, in refusing, had patiently explained the importance of the ready cash supplied by customs dues for the usually starved treasuries of contemporary monarchs.

That Bengal would be the flash point was determined by two factors. The more significant one was the economic importance of the province to European trading companies, and not just to the English East India Company. Due to the inherent wealth of the province and the relative cheapness of its trade goods, Bengal had become as vital to the Dutch as it was to the British. By the early 1700s, Bengal supplied nearly 40 percent of the value of Asian goods sent to Holland, and over half of all the textiles (mostly the highly colored cotton piece goods known as calicoes) exported by the Dutch East India Company from Asia.[24] The English East India Company was equally dependent on, and involved with, Bengal. Indeed, as early as 1660–63, when the imperial general Mir Jumla held the *subahship* (or governorship) of Bengal, the East India Company became involved in a clash with Mughal authority. Mir Jumla used East Indian Company shipping to carry on an extensive private trade with Persia on his own account. When English factors at the town of Hooghly seized a local boat as security for Mir Jumla's debts to them, the future of the English in Bengal was saved only by an apology and the restoration of the ship.[25] In 1686 apology was not something characteristic of the new chief of the English council in the Bay of Bengal, Job Charnock. He had recently removed from Kasimbazar to Hooghly with some difficulty, due to allegations of unpaid debts in the former place, and he was already locked in a quarrel with the *foujdar,* or Mughal criminal law magistrate, in Hooghly, a quarrel which he was delighted to settle with force when the Court of Directors sent out unexpected troop reinforcements.

The Mughal regime in Bengal had already had to deal with a Portuguese threat in the form of slave raiding by Portuguese renegades based in Arakan and attempts by official Portuguese elements based in Hooghly to set up their usual protection racket, with tolls on all non-Portuguese shipping. In 1632, after three months of stiff fighting, the

Portuguese abandoned Hooghly. The new conflict in Bengal was not very different, despite the arrival of a flotilla from England carrying six companies of infantry to reinforce the few hundred European and mixed-bloods (mostly "Topazes," i.e., part-Portuguese) whom the East India Company employed to police, rather than defend, its settlements. The river system allowed the Mughal authorities to bring down reinforcements, artillery, and munitions without difficulty. The regular English infantry lacked easily maneuverable field guns like the six-pounders Clive was to deploy at Plassey. They had no cavalry. More seriously, they could only protect themselves against horse by having a fair proportion (at least one third) of their ranks armed with the pike—the musketeers had a slowish rate of fire in an era when the more efficient flintlock was just beginning to replace the matchlock in the English service. Charnock was driven back. Naval reinforcements mounted a bombardment of Balasore before evacuating Charnock and his men to Madras. An enraged Emperor Aurangzeb declared war. His admiral, Sidi Yakub Khan, landed on Bombay with 20,000 men, chased Sir John Child into Bombay Castle, and bombarded him and the East India Company into a humiliating surrender and apology, which alone enabled the English to go on trading in India. Sir John conveniently died soon after.[26]

There is, of course, no reason to doubt the truth of the view advanced by so many commentators in seventeenth- and early eighteenth-century India, that the armies of the Mughal Empire compared poorly, in terms of cost-effectiveness, with those of European military monarchies. The classic example is Niccolao Manucci, the Venetian adventurer who served as an artillery officer in the Mughal and other Indian armies before spending a lengthy period at the Mughal court itself as physician to Shah Alam, a future emperor. Manucci was in Goa in the summer of 1683 when the governor, the Conde de Alvor, was heavily defeated by the Marathas in battle at Ponda, and he subsequently lived in Madras, with trips to the French settlement at Pondicherry. A friend of Governor Pitt of Madras (the father of the Elder Pitt), Manucci knew the realities of his India better than most, but he stated quite bluntly in his *Storia Do Mogor* that the grandeur of the Mughal empire was hollow: "to sweep it entirely away and occupy the whole empire nothing is required beyond a corps of thirty thousand trusty European soldiers, led by competent commanders, who would thereby easily acquire the glory of great conquerors."[27]

Even if, however, we were to accept Manucci's jaundiced comment as totally valid, two qualifications of some importance remain. His contempt is directed, in this quotation, at the Timurid emperors in Delhi. He knew the Marathas were a tougher proposition. Then there is the fact that he suggests an expeditionary force of 30,000 men—an awesome force for any European power around 1700 even to think of supplying over many thousands of miles. Logistically, never mind politically, it was just not on. No European government in the early modern period ever contemplated a systematic conquest of India, but these governments were willing to fight one another on an increasingly massive scale for control of the lucrative Asian trade that they saw as a vital contribution to the war chest of any maritime power. The Portuguese came to terms with the English at an early stage, and by the end of the seventeenth century were even at peace with the Dutch; but in 1693, Pondicherry, the fishing hamlet that the French had turned into an important trade center, was besieged and taken by a formidable Dutch force. At its core, the Dutch striking force had several companies of veteran Dutch troops, but much of its strength derived from Asian sources. The fleet sailed originally from Batavia, and it picked up reinforcements and supplies from Dutch settlements in the Bay of Bengal and Ceylon.[28]

Though the English East India Company's war with the Mughals does seem to have been triggered by a mixture of miscalculation and arrogance, Sir Josiah Child in 1686 was also obsessed with what he saw as a French threat in the Bay of Bengal. By a bizarre sequence of events a Greek called Phaulkion had emerged as the first minister of Siam. To buttress his position, he entered into close relations with the France of Louis XIV, from which he hoped to draw troops and missionaries on a large scale. Phaulkion's satrap at Mergui, then the Siamese outlet on the Bay (though subsequently seized by Burma), was an East Indian Company renegade known to history as "Siamese White." This man embarked on a quite irresponsible piratical campaign in the Bay of Bengal, inflicting losses on English shipping. In October 1686 Child ordered the Madras council of the East India Company to send a force to seize and occupy Mergui, for fear that White and Phaulkion meant to hand it over to the French.[29] The Madras council had the wit to want to end one war rather than start another. Phaulkion's regime collapsed.

Nevertheless, Anglo-French rivalry in Asian waters had reared its ugly head. Very sensible neutrality agreements between the Compagnie des Indes and its English counterpart kept both of them out of the terrible cycle of Anglo-French wars that occupied most of the period between 1688 and 1713. Then after 1744 the Westminster government refused to accept a renewal of neutrality agreements in Asian waters that favored the French, who were at sea undoubtedly the weaker of the two combatants in the newly declared Anglo-French war. This is often seen as the decisive turning point in the history of European arms in India, for the resulting Anglo-French struggle in the Deccan precipitated intervention by French and British royal forces, both naval and military. That struggle also saw an unprecedented extension of European control over native powers, in the first instance by that remarkable Frenchman, Joseph François Dupleix, governor of Pondicherry.

He may have stumbled on the key to military success by accident on the Adyar River in October 1746, when the Swiss Paradis, commanding a force of 300 French and 700 sepoy soldiers (the latter raised locally but trained and equipped like their European comrades) routed the vastly superior army of Mafuz Khan, son of Anwar-ud-din, Nawab of the Carnatic. It was not even Dupleix's idea to raise sepoys—the idea had been conceived and implemented by his predecessor, Governor Dumas. At this point, the English East India Company forces still consisted of inadequate guards and garrisons scarcely trained for field operations. In 1742, for example, the Bombay garrison consisted of 1,593 men, of which only 346 were European, and these were scattered through all the companies. Most of the rest of the men were Topazes, cheaper by half, drawn from racially part-Portuguese, mixed-blood coastal communities. After such traumas as the capture of Madras by the French, however, the East India Company introduced hard-bitten former royal officers like Stringer Lawrence, and both he and his protégé Robert Clive adopted the sepoy system.[30] The foundations of empire were thus laid.

The snags in this beautifully overly simple model were pointed out long ago by Henry Dodwell, author of a classic study of the subject. Dupleix founded no empire, being incapable of administering one, and European troops always bore the brunt of the decisive Anglo-French battles in the south of India.[31] Besides, the military technology used by the East India Company and native armies in India was comparatively simple and relatively easy to transfer from one side to another. A disciplined infantry firing volleys, capable of maneuver and of cooperating with fast-firing, mobile field guns, was a formidable weapon; but this was no more mysterious than the bayonets the men attached to their flintlocks, and country powers were capable of developing such an infantry force just as well as the East India Company, or perhaps one should say capable in theory of incorporating such units into their armies. They did so, though never quite fast enough. This military transition in India is all the more fascinating because it preceded those technological breakthroughs in transportation, communication, and weaponry that made European imperialism in Africa and Asia so cheap and irresistible after 1850.[32] Nor can it truly be said that the professional mentality or tactics of the unsuccessful British military officers before Pondicherry in 1748 was of a different nature from those of the victors of Plassey in 1757 or of Buxar in 1764.

It is true that the first half of the eighteenth century saw a radical change in the spirit of the officer corps of the East India Company toward a competent professionalism and a willingness to accept losses as the price of success in any serious action in the field. That was a revolution compared with the mentality observed by the remarkable Scots interloper Alexander Hamilton, author of *A New Account of the East Indies,* published first in Edinburgh in 1727. He came out to India just in time for the tail end of Sir Josiah's war, and painted a picture of Sir John Child as a cowardly braggard that has stuck ever since. Hamilton did not regard the East India Company military as serious soldiers. Of Calcutta he said:

> The Garison of Fort William generally consists of 2 or 300 Soldiers, more for to convey their fleet from Patana, with the Company's Saltpetre, and Piece Goods, raw Silk and some Ophium belonging to other Merchants than for the Defence of the Fort, for, as the Company holds their Colony in fie Tail of the Mogul, they need not be afraid of any Enemies coming to disposses them. And if they should, at any Time, quarrel again with the Mogul, his prohibiting his subjects to trade with the Company, would soon end the Quarrel.

Himself a doughty fighter, as he proved against Maratha pirates on the Malabar Coast, Hamilton was made head of the East India Company's Bombay Marine in 1717, and thereafter learned—in the course of a couple of attempts in that year to relieve the East India Company's factory at Kawar, which was besieged by the Sonda Raja—that the company land forces were cowardly, ineffective, and incompetent. Hamilton and his sailors had, for example, to land from small boats to recover loaded muskets thrown away on the battlefield by fleeing so-called soldiers.[33]

The effectiveness of East India Company forces in India was not really significantly greater in 1748–49 than it had been in 1718, as the journal of a Lieutenant John Grant, who served in the expedition commanded by Admiral Boscawen, shows. Boscawen's considerable flotilla carried six Scottish and six Irish companies of foot raised for East India Company service, and at the Cape it was joined by 600 Dutch soldiers. It had a look at the French naval base of Mauritius, but decided "that our landing in this place must be attended with considerable Loss," and it sheered off. After reaching the Coromandel Coast at Fort St. David, the expedition's troops were brigaded with company units to make up a force of 2,500 European infantry, plus 100 artillerists, to which were added "about fifteen hundred Punes, a name they give to . . . Black soldiers in this Country." The ensueing siege of Pondicherry proved a fiasco, despite the deployment of twenty-four-pounders in the siege batteries. Actually, the bombardment from landward proved ineffective, especially on the part of the mortar batteries, whose shells mostly fell short. The fleet tried to warp in to bombard from the seaward, firing in all sixteen thousand rounds, to so little effect that the French hardly bothered to reply.

After the siege had been given up as hopeless, the troops were used in a campaign against Tanjore, which Grant deemed a scandal, for it was little more than an attempt by the Madras council of the East India Company to extort money from a former ally against the French. Grant was clear that the armies of the country powers, "having no regularity or Discipline amongst them," could probably be routed by European troops a tenth of their numbers, not least because of the dominance of the cavalry spirit in Indian armies and the despised and neglected state of their infantry. However, it is clear that John Grant returned to Strathspey to report to his chief, Grant of Grant, with relief. No constructive opportunity seemed to beckon him back to India.[34]

The Maratha admiral, Kanhoji Angria, appears to have been left with a profound contempt for the East India Company after the rout of its troops during the amphibious operations of 1717, a rout only halted by covering fire from Alexander Hamilton's ships. The introduction of a specialist shore-bombardment vessel by the Company in the form of a bomb-ketch in 1719 seems to have had little effect on Angria and less on his port base of Gheria. Nor did Anglo-Portuguese combined operations against him in the 1720s yield much concrete result.[35] It has been argued very cogently that it was the arrival of royal ships and regiments in India in the 1750s which allowed the "sub-imperialism" of East India Company servants, and especially their Madras officials, to cut loose, turning from the declining profits of trade to the much more lucrative business of using unprecedented military and naval power to loot the treasuries of country powers, but this rather misses the point. There was nothing unprecedented about the availability of royal ships of war, or even of royal troops. What was different was the impact they had.

The conflict in the Deccan, which ground to an effective halt with the replacement of Dupleix by Godeheu in 1754, settled very little. The French gave up nothing that they actually held in 1754, and the able de Bussy was left in a key position in Hyderabad. It was the sudden change that marked the arrival of Admiral Watson and Colonel Clive as an amphibious combination on the Indian scene, which proved truly significant. Fortunately, Admiral Watson's letter book survives, and from it we can tell what a curious mixture of accident and calculation lay behind the formation of the Watson-Clive partnership.[36] Watson originally was destined to succor Madras. A letter he wrote to Lord Holderness from Fort St. David Road on 10 October 1754 makes it clear that he believed Godeheu was full of plans for further aggression. However, by 10 March 1755, when he was lying off Madras, Watson had knowledge of a formal cessation of arms between the rival companies. Faced with the impending arrival of the monsoon on the Coromandel Coast, Watson decided to take his squadron first to Ceylon, and then, if there was no sign of Anglo-French war, "I shall proceed with the squadron to Bombay, and there consult with the Governor what Service can be done for the advantage of the East India Company on that side of India."

In the event, Watson was sent against the reigning Angria, Tulaji Angria, with Clive in command of the land forces. Admiral Watson, in a letter of 7 October 1755, neatly summed up the whole operation before it occurred: "if I can come near enough to batter . . . I shall make no doubt of success, but if by shoal water the large ships cannot come within distance to do execution, it will be doing of nothing, and consequently it will be to no purpose to make an attempt."

That was it. Where Europeans were far ahead of country powers was in the construction of big specialist warships with broadsides mounting guns of formidable size, such as thirty-pounders. Watson had been at some pains to show the Nawab of the Carnatic over his flagship. Now he was to blast Angria's base at Gheria into submission at trifling cost, and to his own and Clive's great gain (for they captured a small fortune in the assault). This was a different story from Boscawen's sixteen thousand wasted rounds at Pondicherry. In all fairness, the British needed better coastal charts; Watson hastened the process for he carried first-class marine surveyors—for example, Sir William Hewett, whose survey of Gheria was accepted as satisfactory by no less an authority than Alexander Dalrymple, father of the British admiralty chart and first official hydrographer to the East India Company and the Royal Navy. It must never be forgotten that the serious and bloody fighting that marked the campaign culminating in Plassey was all done by Watson and his sailors, in the course of a protracted and vicious artillery battle to subdue the French fortifications at Chandernagore. Plassey was a skirmish complicated by political intrigue: Watson's account of it fails to mention Clive. Watson's early death deprived him of the credit for his achievements, but it is significant that when the French dreamed of revenge in India, they followed his lead and prepared for amphibious operations with superior charts.[37]

The spectacular improvement in British fortunes in India in 1756–57 was therefore primarily due to a combination of naval gunnery with superior inshore navigation, and in Bengal with Clive's political flair. Since the East India Company was going rapidly bankrupt, and since it provided those areas around Madras and Calcutta where it had direct or indirect responsibility with truly dismal government, the next question is not so much why the company seized a temporary advantage, but why its landward power survived at all. One school of thought in effect denies the need to pose this question. I can only very partially accept that school's argument. Although all political change in eighteenth-century India occurred within the nominal framework of Timurid imperial sovereignty, and although everyone accepted the inevitability of shifting local factions at the level of the *zamindars*, Indians then, as now, could distinguish between appearance and reality. Everyone knows there is little relationship between the neo-Gandhian hot air that tends to dominate public pronouncements on foreign policy by modern Indian governments and the ruthless *realpolitik* that governs their actions.[38] Even if Mughal administrators like Reza Khan originally thought of Clive and his cronies by their Mughal Persian titles, they knew there was a new and alien regime in Bengal before they died.[39] Furthermore, it survived by the use and abuse of brute force.

The actions that ensured the survival of the East India Company raj in Bengal, Bihar, and Orissa were those which culminated in the Battle of Buxar on 23 October 1764, where Hector Munro defeated a triple alliance of the Nawab of Bengal, Mir Kasim; the Nawab Vizier of Oudh, Shuja-ud-daulah; and Emperor Shah Alam. Buxar was a dramatic, sustained, and bitterly contested action in which the company's forces suffered heavy casualties. It was a pure company victory: by definition, the Royal Navy played no part, nor were there any units of the British Army present. Company European troops were there, but as a minority. This was a sepoy army. By 1770 the East India Company's Bengal Army comprised 4,000 Europeans and no less than 26,000 sepoys. In the decade to that date, in Bengal the company had spent £8 million on the army, compared to only £5,300,000 on trade. The Nawabs of Bengal were destroyed by insatiable demands for revenue to maintain the company's forces, and Oudh was being pulled into the same trap, for its ruler was already assigning revenue to the company to sustain two of its brigades in his realm.[40]

In 1778 the secretary to the company military committee in Bengal wrote a memorandum in which he ascribed the outstanding successes of British arms in India primarily to a superior field artillery. There is little doubt that in the eighteenth century such an edge of superiority did exist, though it must not be exaggerated. European artillery was evolving very rapidly in the 1740s, not least because of the stimulus provided by the wars of Frederick the Great. That monarch developed his artillery vigorously in the aftermath of the Silesian War, mounting ammunition boxes on his gun limbers in 1742 and replacing the traditional system of elevating guns by means of a wedge with one employing a screw in 1747. Austria adopted the elevating screw in 1748.[41] Very significantly, Admiral Watson, in his letter to the earl of Holderness (in which he reported his capture of Gheria and the forwarding of Sir William Hewett's survey of the port), reported capturing Tulaji Angria's park of artillery, "six of them New Field Pieces with elevating Screws." The emperor's guns captured at Buxar included a fair number of British pieces, showing that he was imitating British carriages for all his ordnance. Arthur Wellesley, a representative of a much later kind of self-conscious British imperialism in India, said that Maratha field artillery around 1800 was good enough to be incorporated into the British ordnance as soon as it was seized, though he had found that the cannon captured from Tipu in the Mysore wars left a good deal to be desired.[42] By the time of the Sikh wars of the 1840s, the British were facing guns as good as theirs in the hands of brave and skillful Sikh gunners. The ultimate answer, at the final Battle of Gujerat in February 1849, was to beat down the Sikh batteries with a decisively superior number of British ones.[43]

Nor can it be convincingly argued that the flintlock musket and bayonet in the hands of a well-drilled infantry gave the British a permanent technological lead in Indian warfare. It certainly worked wonders in the 1750s and 1760s against hordes of undisciplined horse or matchlock men, but country powers quite rapidly learned the need for new infantry tactics. The Marathas were particularly forward in this. The Peshwa was experimenting with drilled infantry units of the European kind as early as the 1750s, but it was Sindia who, with the help of the Savoyard de Boigne and the Frenchman Perron, built up formidable flintlock-armed infantry battalions designed, in the French tradition, to operate in close cooperation with his massed field guns. Despite his reputation for conservative cavalry tactics, Holkar did the same. He had to. The British were developing their cavalry as rapidly as the Marathas were their infantry, and the communication lines of the East India Company armies were just not as vulnerable in the final Anglo-Maratha contest of 1803–5 as they had been before.[44]

Thus the real key to the subsequent military successes of the East India Company after Plassey was fairly crude: it was the sheer size of the sepoy infantry forces it raised and then funded off the territorial revenues of Bengal, Bihar and Orissa. After all, these provinces constituted much of the richest of the regional successor states into which the top-heavy Mughal structure was disintegrating. The process was natural, and indeed very healthy, but it involved several decades of instability, debatable legitimacy, and vulnerability, especially in an economy like Bengal's which was so deeply penetrated by European trading companies. Hindu and Armenian bankers, men crucial to the smooth operation of government and war, were liable to find their European clients less unpalatable than the yoke of their own Muslim Nawabs, whose ability to maintain an army, the key to any real power base, was being corroded relentlessly by the ruthless demands of the East

India Company representatives for the money needed to line their own pockets and pay their sepoys. When the British were, in 1760–61, experimenting with raising their first troops of horse in Bihar, the Nawabs' cavalrymen, whose wages were preposterously in arrears, were complaining that they dare not move out of the small area where they were known and had credit for fear that they and their horses might starve.[45] It was not the excellence of British overlordship that explains the destruction of native administration in Bengal and the Carnatic, but its corruption and vicious unfairness. Under this system, Bengal became a reservoir of force and supplies, which Clive used early to crush the French in the Northern Circars, and which Warren Hastings was to use to rescue the Madras presidency from well-deserved defeat and humiliation at the hands of the Marathas, and later to dredge that sorry clique of gangsters and con men which constituted the Council of the Madras presidency from the slough of despair into which it sank after a thrashing at the hands of Hyder Ali, Sultan of Mysore.

There was little understanding on the part of the immediate heirs of Clive in Bengal of the revolutionary military implications of what they were doing. They thought in terms of establishing and maintaining a lucrative company "interest" in India, not an empire. Harry Verelst, who succeeded Clive as governor of Bengal in 1767 after serving as his loyal lieutenant in administrative reform, told General Carnac in that year: "The Empire in its torn and divided state serves to insure the stability of the Company's Interest and affords the best expedient for the support of our Name."[46] Meantime, the company's officials busied themselves with military policies that would probably have occurred fifty years earlier had they then been feasible. Verelst recorded with zest in 1761: "The Portuguese for a repeated Disobedience of Orders, I have dismissed from every service—We are recruiting sea-poys."[47] The Counter-Reformation religious culture of the Portuguese and part-Portuguese Topazes in the East India Company service had always created problems. Their attitude toward their English employers was admirably detached, and their priests had repeatedly acted as French spies during the Anglo-French wars in the Deccan. By comparison, East India Company officers were delighted with the quality and reliability of the predominantly Hindu Bengal sepoy, whom they trained and dressed in European fashion, whose availablity was apparently unlimited, restricted only by the company's need to build up a cadre of "Black Officers."[48] General officers like John Carnac and Hector

Monro were very generous indeed in their praises of the new sepoy infantry, whom Carnac in 1764 described as bearing the brunt of the fighting and whom Munro subsumed into what he called "a glorious small army for this part of the World."[49]

The East India Company had, by the 1780s, identified two special recruiting centers for its Bengal army. One was the fort of Bijaigarth, which had once belonged to the Rajah of Benares but was taken over by the company on the grounds that it was "a proper place for a nursery of sepoy recruits to be raised and distributed to the regiments." Another was the province of Orissa, long a debatable marchland between the company and the Marathas but a splendid area for emergency recruitment. In 1782, for example, the commander in chief of the Bengal Army called for the immediate enlistment of five hundred sepoys from Orissa when he felt that his ranks needed speedy reinforcement.[50] Such recruits were numerous, and they were cheap compared with the motley crew of Englishmen, Scotsmen, Irishmen, and Germans with which the company tried to fill the ranks of its European regiments. Nor did sepoy regiments require as many expensive (and often troublesome) European officers as a European regiment. Of course, the senior positions in sepoy regiments were held by Europeans, but the bulk of the regimental officers were Indians. In a letter to "Our President and Council at Fort William in Bengal" dated 11 November 1768, the Court of Directors of the East India Company in London said it had consulted Lord Clive and agreed with him that European officers were "essential to the establishing Discipline and Subordination" among the sepoy brigades, but the court then went on to suggest, as a target, "an European Commissioned Officer to each Company will be necessary" and added that "no Officer should rise to the Command of a Battalion until he has made himself sufficiently Master of the Language to acquit himself in his Duty without the Assistance of an Interpreter."[51]

This last point was a completely reasonable one, for a battalion commander who could not speak the appropriate Indian language would not be capable of conversing with his junior officers. Nor were the services of native officers undervalued by the company. On the contrary, the Governor General remarked in 1784 that "the faithful and approved services" of native officers and sepoys "merited every mark of favour and encouragement that we could devise" consistent with the company's interest, and the court of the company approved, in 1785, the idea of rewarding "such native officers and sepoys as have been invalided in the service" by allotting them portions of waste lands "agreeably to their respective ranks."[52] The central importance of Indian junior officers in the creation of the Bengal Army has never really been appreciated in recent writings on the Indian Army. Philip Mason's "account of the Indian Army, its officers and men" is a good example. It is totally slanted toward the post-Mutiny world and, indeed, largely framed in terms of relations between British officers and faithful sepoys. In a sense, it is very like his two-volume study of the British administrators of India, which was penned immediately after the end of the Raj and which, with its huge dose of sentimental good will toward both India and the men who had ruled it, can be seen in retrospect as overobsessed with a comparatively short and very odd episode in Indian history that had its hey-day between 1860 and 1914. What Mason does spot in a brief but perceptive aside is that when a significant proportion of the Bengal native officers mutinied in 1857, they were gravely handicapped by lack of experience of field command of any unit above a company.[53]

Before the greatest of the company armies turned in 1857 against a British Raj effectively controlled from Westminster, partnership between the company and the Hindu communities of Bengal, Bihar, and Orissa was the keystone of the structure of company conquest in India. Bengal was also a vital source of financial succor for the other two presidencies. Indian armies were as efficient as their pay was regular, and the directors of the East India Company commended the prompt dispatch of ample funds from Bengal to Madras during the war between the Madras presidency and Hyder Ali of Mysore.[54] Such large flows of credit from Bengal to Madras or Bombay saved the British in the 1780s, when Madras and Bombay showed themselves militarily and financially barely superior to other Mughal successor states. Without active support from Armenian and Hindu bankers, the credit transfers could not have been made safely and easily on an adequate scale. That cooperation and support from the bankers or *banyans* was, however, pretty well guaranteed by the nature of the original British coup in Bengal in 1757, which was an Anglo-Banyan plot to exploit splits in the ruling Muslim ascendancy in such a way as to fatally undermine the ascendancy itself.

The attempt of three Muslim princes to reimpose it in 1764 was crushed primarily by the Bengal sepoy—the second great manifestation of long-term Hindu military revival after the rise of the Marathas. To answer, tentatively, a question posed at the start of this essay: no, Hindu India is not especially prone to predation. It has been experiencing active military revival since the seventeenth century. As it happens, the British emerged as managers of the second wave of that revival. When they had entrenched themselves as the entrepreneurs behind the Bengal Army, they found that they had at their disposal a potential instrument of imperial ascendancy. It was really only consciously used as such after authority in British India fell into the hands of two members of the authoritarian right wing of the Westminster-based political class: Cornwallis, an Englishman fresh from failing to crush the liberties of Englishmen in America, and the Irishman Mornington (the elder and, in the long run, the less distinguished of the two Wellesley brothers). Mornington finally smashed Mysore, bullied Hyderabad into puppet-state status, and engaged in the decisive struggle with the Marathas, perhaps a deal too confidently, for it is now clear that he could easily have lost. Yet although his margin of success was narrow, it sufficed to let both Wellesley and the private trading interests behind much of the thrust for territorial expansion on the West coast continue the game of seizing commercial assets under the guise of resisting the French "menace."[55]

There never was a transition to European military ascendancy similar to the transition that occurred in America from the sixteenth century on, or in Africa from the nineteenth. That is not to say that there was no margin of technical superiority available to the two or three Western European powers that had a significant presence in India and whose professional forces had remained in the forefront of contemporary military developments. By 1700 the French, Dutch, and English did have a significant battlefield edge, if they had cared to make an adequate effort to use it. However, this technical margin was small and it was comparatively easily transferable. Indeed, it was being transferred almost from the moment it was created in the forcing house of the vicious interstate wars of the late sixteenth and early seventeenth centuries. To describe these wars as "European civil wars," as some well-meaning but deeply misleading twentieth-century historians would like us to do, is to miss the whole point. They were wars, not civil wars, and wars within a complex of sovereign states—some of which, like Spain and Turkey (that major European power) were, by the eighteenth century, clearly failing to absorb current best battlefield and organizational practice fast enough to remain viable as great powers, and some of which, like Russia, were by heroic and ruthless measures succeeding in keeping up with the military rat race. Much the same situation existed in the complex of competing successor states to the Mughal Empire. Just as the Tsar of Muscovy hired a professional Scots soldier like General Tam Dalziel of Binns in the seventeenth century to bring the battlefield skills of the German wars to his own forces, so Indian rulers in the eighteenth century could hire the modernizing skills of a wide range of mercenaries—Scots, Welsh, Irish, English, French, Dutch, Italian, Savoyard, and so on.[56]

In this military forcing house of competing Indian regional states in the eighteenth century, three of the competitors—the Madras, Bombay, and Bengal presidencies of the East India Company—happened to be peripheral members of the British state complex. Madras and Bombay proved only marginally more formidable than other Mughal conquest states, if that. It was with Bengal money, and the Bengal Army, that the company rose to the heights of imperial power. That army was, of course, one of the many British armies of the eighteenth century. We speak too easily of the "British Army," meaning the one controlled by Westminster. There were, in fact, many more armies than that one in the planetary British state complex, nor was Westminster's army always the most cost-effective. In 1744–45, the two outstanding British armies were the New England army, which Governor William Shirley of Massachusetts launched so successfully under the command of William Pepperell against the French fortress of Louisbourg on Cape Breton Island at the mouth of the St. Lawrence, and the Jacobite army, which reached Derby and, perhaps more remarkably, contrived to retreat to Scotland in the face of vastly superior cavalry. Both are best described as semi-professional forces.

The case for regarding provincial American armies, and officers in them like George Washington, as semi-professional is argued conclusively elsewhere in this book. The Jacobite army, too, though traduced in Hanoverian propaganda as a horde of "bare-arsed banditti," was a regimented force organized in two divisions, Lowland and Highland, and commanded very expertly by ex-regulars like Lord George Murray. Its discipline was milder and more effective than that of Westminster's troops, just as its behavior toward civilians was vastly more civilized than that of its opponents.[57] The Bengal Army, therefore, takes its place as a British regional army based on a regional implied contract between the company, non-Muslim bankers and predominantly Hindu sepoys. Muslims were predominant only in its cavalry, of which it had little at first. Inevitably, Westminster assaulted the political autonomy of the company. Then, with steamships and telegraphy technology at the disposal of English and Scots bankers moving into India, it kicked away the ladder of Indian bankers up which the British had climbed. Finally came the showdown with the regional army. In America, Westminster lost; in the very different circumstances of mid-nineteenth-century India, it won and finally abolished the shadow regime of the East India Company, replacing it with acknowledged direct rule.

When the Bengal Army — the weapon the British had forged — turned against them in the Indian Mutiny, it proved possible not only to defeat it but also, for fifty years, to hold India with a much higher proportion of British troops and an implicit deal with the so-called "martial races" on the periphery of Hindu India. In the long run, the Hindu revival, strengthened by access to Western education, resumed its momentum. It used a pacifist Hindu saint, Gandhi, to mobilize massive peasant pressure on the British, though other leading Indian politicians did not really accept his pacifist principles. The pressured British first grudgingly accepted, and then could not reverse, such decisive events as the progressive Indianization of the Indian Army officer corps.[58] Militarily, there was a strong case for it after World War I. The Indian Army of 1914, already reformed backward by such reactionary exponents of the cavalry spirit as the future Field Marshal Haig, had shown the same sclerotic tendencies as the late Mughal army, which it much ressembled. After a poor performance in East Africa, its troops had gone on to shattering defeat in Mesopotamia at the hands of the more effectively modernized Turkish forces. The Indian Army of World War II performed far better in North Africa and Burma, and after 1947 the Indian government spent a very large proportion of its revenues, especially after losing a border war with China, on building up and modernizing its already large army. Thus the government of the Republic of India, a rich government ruling a poor population and spending too much on huge armed forces, stands in direct line of succession to Sivaji and to the managers of the great sepoy army of the Bengal presidency. *Plus ça change.* . . .

NOTES

1. A point made in a perceptive review by R. H. C. Davis (complete with the analogy of the Raj) in *History* 56 (1971): 86 (a review of Lord Norwich's *The Kingdom in the Sun*).

2. Cited from an official dispatch written at Cannanore in 1534 by C. R. Boxer in the preface to *Portuguese Conquest and Commerce in Southern Asia, 1500-1750* (London, 1985), ix.

3. Boxer, "Anglo-Portuguese Rivalry in the Persian Gulf, 1615-1635," in *Portuguese Conquest,* 46-129.

4. Boxer, "Asian Potentates and European Artillery in the 16th-18th Centuries: A Footnote to Gibson-Hill," in *Portuguese Conquest,* 156-72; M. A. L. Cruz, "Exiles and Renegades in Early Sixteenth-Century Portuguese India," *The Indian Economic and Social History Review* 23 (1986): 249-62.

5. Elaine Sanceau, *Indies Adventure: The Amazing Career of Alfonso de Albuquerque* (London and Glasgow, 1936) and *Knight of the Renaissance: D. João de Castro, Soldier, Sailor, Scientist, and Viceroy of India, 1500-1548* (London: n.d.). George Davison Winius, *The Black Legend of Portuguese India* (New Delhi, 1985), disposes of charges of "decadence." For the practical compromises involved in ruling multicultural Indian dependencies, see Luis Filipe Ferreira Reis Thomaz, "Estratura Polititica e Administriva do Estado da India no Sàculo XVI," *II Seminario Internacional de Historia Indo-Portuguesa* (Lisbon, 1985), 513-40.

6. Anthony Disney, "The Portuguese Empire in India c. 1550-1650: Some Suggestions for a Less Seaborne, More Landbound Approach to Its Socio-economic History, in *Indo-Portuguese History: Sources and Problems,* ed. John Correia-Alfonso (Bombay, 1981), 148-62.

7. Roe to the East India Company, Brampore, 24 November 1615, printed in *The Embassy of Sir Thomas Roe to the Court of the Great Mogul 1615-19,* ed. W. Foster, Hakluyt Society, 2d ser., vols. 1 and 2, 1899, 1:93-100.

8. G. Rex Smith, *Medieval Muslim Horsemanship: A Fourteenth-Century Arabic Cavalry Manual* (London, 1979); Norah M. Titley, *Sports and Pastimes: Scenes from Turkish, Persian and Mughal Paintings* (London, 1979), has a section, pp. 8-11, on archery which underlines this. Richard Hellie, *Enserfment and Military Change in Muscovy* (Chicago, 1971), 164-66, explains the importance of the steppe frontier as an influence on Russian military tradition.

9. *Embassy of Sir Thomas Roe,* 1:89-90.

10. Ibid., 2:357, 419n.

11. A point established in Peter Willman, "The Dutch in Asia 1595-1610," M.A. thesis, University of St. Andrews, 1986. For the titanic scale of Dutch fortification in the East (matched only at Diu by the Portuguese), see W. A. Nelson, *The Dutch Forts of Sri Lanka: The Military Monuments of Ceylon* (Edinburgh, 1984).

12. Roe to East India Company, 24 November 1616, printed in *Embassy of Sir Thomas Roe,* 2:342-62. The quote is from pp. 344-45.

13. *A Calendar of the Court Minutes Etc. of the East India Company 1635-1639,* ed. E. B. Sainsbury, with an introduction by W. Foster (Oxford, 1907).

14. C. E. Bosworth, *The Ghaznavids* (Edinburgh, 1963), is thin on the Indian provinces, concentrating on Afghanistan and eastern Iran, but excellent on the army and its Indian component. Romila Thapar, *A History of India,* vol. 1 (London, 1966) is, in the relevant chapters on the Muslim invasions, a classic example of a most competent historian skillfully sidestepping the admittedly very difficult question raised by the invasions' success.

15. *Memoirs of Zehir-Ed-Din Muhammed Babur,* trans. J. Leyden and W. Erskine, ed. Sir Lucas King, 2 vols. (London, 1921). For Babur's formative military experiences, see vol. 1.

16. *Alberuni's India: An Account of the Religion, Philosophy, Literature, Geography, Chronology, Astronomy, Customs, Laws and Astrology of India,* ed. E. C. Sachau, 2 vols. (London, 1910), 1:22.

17. The second volume of the Leyden and Erskine translation of the *Memoirs of Babur* provides an insight into his Indian campaigns. The quotation is from p. 345.

18. Carlo M. Cipolla, *European Culture and Overseas Expansion* (London, 1970). In its section on "Guns and Sails," pp. 31–109, it reprints Cipolla's major essay on this theme, originally published separately.

19. J. Christopher Herold, *Bonaparte in Egypt* (London, 1963).

20. Jane Jacobs, *Cities and the Wealth of Nations* (London, 1986).

21. Muni Lal, *Shah Jahan* (New Delhi, 1986), 268.

22. Cipolla, "Guns and Sails," 103–4.

23. *Calendar of State Papers Preserved in the Public Record Office, Domestic Series: James II,* vol. 1, February–December, 1685 (London, 1960), entries 1956 and 1957, p. 394.

24. Om Prakash, *The Dutch East India Company and the Economy of Bengal, 1630–1720* (Princeton, 1985).

25. S. Bhattacharya, *The East India Company and the Economy of Bengal from 1704 to 1740* (London, 1954), 21.

26. B. P. Lenman, "The East India Company and the Emperor Aurangazeb," *History Today* 37 (1987): 23–29.

27. Niccolao Manucci, *Storia Do Mogor,* trans. W. Irvine, 4 vols. (London, 1906–1908), 2:441.

28. *India in the 17th Century: Memoirs of François Martin (1670–1694),* trans. Lotika Varadarajan, vol. 2, part 2 (1688–1694), (New Delhi, 1985), 1542–76.

29. Maurice Collis, *Siamese White* (London, 1936), 197–221; Robert Bruce, "Constantine Phaulkion: The Greek Dictator of Siam," *History Today* 33 (1982): 36–42.

30. J. P. Lawford, *Britain's Army in India: From Its Origins to the Conquest of Bengal* (London, 1978), chaps. 1–9.

31. Henry Dodwell, *Dupleix and Clive: The Beginning of Empire* (1st ed., London, 1920; Arehon Books reprint, Connecticut, 1968), part 1.

32. Daniel R. Headrick, *The Tools of Empire: Technology and European Imperialism in the Nineteenth Century* (Oxford, 1981).

33. Alexander Hamilton, *A New Account of the East Indies,* ed. Sir William Foster, 2 vols. (London, 1930), 2:8.

34. "Journal of Lieutenant John Grant from 25 August 1748 During the East India Expedition under the Command of Rear Admiral Edward Boscawen," Scottish Record Office, GD248/413, Seafield Papers.

35. Clement Downing, *A History of the Indian Wars,* ed. William Foster (Oxford, 1924), vi–xiv.

36. Admiral Watson's letter book is MS Eur. D 1079 in the India Office Library. It is unpaginated, and the copies of Watson's correspondence are in two series,

written from opposite ends. One is a run of Royal Commissions and official letters from Holderness and Pitt; the other is a chronological sequence of letters from Watson to Holderness.

37. *Vide*, Alexander Dalrymple, *A Collection of Plans of Ports in the East Indies Published by Dalrymple in 1774 and 1775*, 3d ed. (London, 1787), 5: Gariah, Malabar Coast, by Sir William Hewett. There is a letter from Watson to Holderness from HMS *Kent*, "Off Gheria Harbour, 10 March 1756," saying that Hewett has been ordered personally to present his survey to Holderness. There is extant a superb MS French chart of the "Entrée du Gange et son cours en remontant jusqu'à Chandernagor," which is accompanied by a fine MS "Routier du Gange," and which appears to have been prepared for Choiseul in the 1760s when he was contemplating a return match in Bengal. See the scholarly entry in *Weinreb and Douwma, Ltd., Catalogue 20: Manuscript Maps and Charts* (London, 1978), 18–19, item 73. The text was compiled by Tony Campbell. I owe this last reference to the kindness of Mr. Andrew Cook of the India Office Library and Records.

38. André Wink, *Land and Sovereignty in India: Agrarian Society and Politics under the Eighteenth-Century Maratha Svarajya* (Cambridge, 1986).

39. Abdul Majid Khan, *The Transition in Bengal 1756–1775: A Study of Saiyid Muhammed Reza Khan* (Cambridge, 1969).

40. P. J. Marshall, "British Expansion in India in the Eighteenth Century: A Historical Revision," *History* 60 (1975): 28–43. There is a good description of Buxar in Lawford, *Britain's Army in India*, chap. 18.

41. Hew Strachan, *European Armies and the Conduct of War* (London, 1983), 33.

42. B. P. Lenman, "The Weapons of War in Eighteenth-Century India," *Journal of the Society for Army Historical Research* 36 (1968): 33–43.

43. H. C. B. Cook, *The Sikh Wars 1845–46, 1848–49* (London, 1975), 199.

44. John Pemble, "Resources and Techniques in the Second Maratha War," *The Historical Journal* 19 (1976): 375–404.

45. These remarks summarize letters from Colonel Caillaud to Governor Henry Vansittart, dated 16 December 1760, 1 January 1761, and 5 January 1761, written from field headquarters in Bihar, in India Office Library MS Eur. F128/1.

46. Copy, Henry Verelst to General John Carnac, 13 April 1767, fol. 4a, in uncatalogued Verelst Papers in the India Office Library. For access to this material, I am deeply indebted to Dr. Richard Bingle of the India Office Library and Records.

47. Copy, Henry Verelst to Lt. John Mathews, 23 February 1761, fol. 1v, Verelst Papers.

48. See the small bundle of copied correspondence in the Verelst Papers between Verelst and Mathews, written while Mathews was in the field in eastern Bengal, and full of confidence in the ability of sepoy troops to defeat many times their number of irregulars.

49. General John Carnac to Henry Vansittart, 4 May 1764, and Hector Munro to the Council of the Bengal Presidency, from "Camp at Buxar," 23 October 1764, both the in Verelst Papers, show this deep pride in the discipline and fighting effectiveness of the sepoys.

50. *Fort William-India House Correspondence*, vol. 9, Public Series 1782–85, ed. B. A. Saletore, Indian Records Series (Delhi, 1959), xx–xxi.

51. Court to President and Council at Fort William in Bengal, 11 November 1768, printed in *Fort William-India House Correspondence*, vol. 5, *1767–1769*, ed. Narendra K. Sinha, Indian Records Series (Delhi, 1949), 153.

52. Court to President and Council, 21 September 1785, printed in *Fort William-India House Correspondence*, 9:247. The remarks of the Governor General are cited in the introduction to the same volume, xxiii–xxiv.

53. P. Woodruff, *The Men Who Ruled India*, vol. 1: *The Founders* (London, 1953), vol. 2: *The Guardians* (London, 1954). Under his own name, Philip Mason, he also authored *A Matter of Honour: An Account of the Indian Army, Its Officers and Men* (London, 1974). The comment on the limited command experience of Indian officers in the mutineer ranks is on p. 284 of the book club edition.

54. *Fort William-India House Correspondence*, 5:11.

55. Iris Butler, *The Eldest Brother: The Marquess Wellesley 1760–1842* (London, 1973) brings out well the character of the man, remarking in the preface, p. 8, that "Richard Wellesley's sensitive, graceful verses on their marble tablet in Eton College Chapel are his best memorial. Everything else he strove for has passed away." Edward Ingram, *Commitment to Empire: Prophecies of the Great Game in Asia, 1797–1800* (Oxford, 1981), 119–24, shows how cynical was Mornington's use of "the threat" of French intrigue to justify his own naked aggression. Pamela Nightingale, *Trade and Empire in Western India 1784–1806* (Cambridge, 1970), shows equal cynicism among the private traders who called the tune in the Bombay presidency.

56. Shelford Bidwell, *Swords for Hire: European Mercenaries in Eighteenth-Century India* (London, 1971). Those skeptical of the inclusion of the Welsh on the list should read especially closely chap. 6, "The Adventures of George Thomas."

57. The case for the semi-professional status of the Jacobite army in 1745 is argued in my introduction to *The Muster Roll of Prince Charles Edward Stuart's Army 1745–46*, ed. Alastair Livingstone of Bachuil, Christian W. H. Aikman, and Betty Stuart Hart (Aberdeen, 1984), 1–5.

58. Andrew Sharpe, "The Indianisation of the Indian Army," *History Today* 36 (1986): 47–52 is a far more realistic account than that in Philip Mason, *A Matter of Honour* (London, 1974), part 5.

The Military Institutions of Colonial America: The Rhetoric and the Reality

DON HIGGINBOTHAM

THIS ESSAY SEEKS to explore the manner in which Americans moved from amateurism to professionalism in the conduct of warfare. The change was not as dramatic and sudden as has usually been contended. It was not simply the replacing of the colonial militia system with a professional or standing army under George Washington in the Revolution. Rather, the change was evolutionary and subtle in nature, involving as it did the gradual appearance and development of semi-professional military forces, which provided a transitional link between the seventeenth-century militia and the Revolutionary Continental Army. The point serves as a reminder that wars and their consequences provide us with maximum historical light when they are studied as part of an ongoing process rather than as episodic occurrences. But if the complexity of early American military history has only recently been recognized by scholars, and if it likewise went unacknowledged by many eighteenth-century Americans as well, there is at least one very important reason—both then and later—for this omission. And that has to do with the power and persistence of myth.

It has scarcely been unique for peoples or nations to employ a distinctive and exaggerated rhetoric about their military prowess. Colonial Americans boasted of human tools of war—of minds and bodies: minds that acted out of disinterested patriotism, which were attached to bodies of upstanding citizens. As fighters they were infinitely superior to the riffraff thought to be the mainstay of European professional armies. American rhetoric almost wholly eschewed references to sophisticated weapons and other equipment of war and to formal training.

All citizens were capable of service in defense of their communities and often were called to do so, declared the Reverend Ebenezer Gay in 1738. There were "no Exemptions . . . for the High, nor the Low; for the Rich, nor the Poor; for the Strong, nor the Weak; for the Old, nor the Young; for the most buisy; the new-married, nor the faint-hearted."[1] During the American Revolution both Thomas Jefferson and General Charles Lee, a veteran of two European armies, gave voice to similar sentiments. Jefferson boasted that "every soldier in our army" had "been intimate with his gun from his infancy"; and Lee, who expressed the same opinion, contrasted Americans very favorably with "the lower and middle people of England," since the latter were "almost as ignorant in the use of a musket, as they are of the ancient Catapulta."[2]

For want of a better name, we may designate this cluster of ideas about military character the militia myth. It contains untruths that are not unlike certain distorted or exaggerated notions about martial prowess found in early Russian history and French history. The middle service class in Muscovite Russia was itself a mounted militia, created from men who received land grants from the government in return for their role as the first line of defense against the Swedes, Poles, Turks, Tartars, and other enemies. Ironically, at the very time the state provided more favors to the middle service class, which culminated in the enserfment of the peasants on the lands of this military segment of society, the middle service class had outlived its wartime effectiveness. As Richard Hellie has demonstrated, it became technologically obsolete; its volleys of arrows and swinging sabers were no match for infantrymen with muskets supported by heavy artillery. Even so, this two-hundred-year-old force was not officially abolished until 1682, although the middle service class survived and prospered—without its military obligation—as a privileged gentry.[3]

In Revolutionary France, as in colonial America and Muscovite Russia, the belief that commitment and tradition took precedence over systematic training and innovation in the art of war had a tenacious life. John A. Lynn informs us that in France it took the form of the cult of the bayonet, which was grounded in an idealization of pre-1789 French national character as heroic and fearless, and which was strongly reinforced by an infusion of republican ideology during the Revolution. Seizing "the imagination of the French people and their civil and military leaders," this cult significantly influenced French military doctrine in the initial years of Revolutionary warfare in Europe.

It stressed the necessity of linking motivation and tactics so that brave republican soldiers could draw upon their great enthusiasm to make maximum use of the bayonet and other edged weapons in mass charges. Yet, as Lynn shows, the cult was simplistic and dangerous. One French general asserted that the nation had concluded "that fusils and cannon had lost their value, and that all was taken with the bayonet." In time, less was heard of the cult of the bayonet, especially from professional soldiers, for it conflicted with the realities of modern warfare.[4]

Because the task of separating history from myth can be so difficult, it is often said that they are two sides of the same coin. The most persistent myths usually appear to have their origins in some measure of truth, however distant and distorted. People have the ability to recall and reorder happenings to meet their unique needs. Few human drives equal the will to believe what we want to believe.[5] Lynn probes these components of myth in dealing with the cult of the bayonet. What he calls "the rhetoric of élan" sustained morale, holding up expectations in spite of shortages and reverses. "It served as propaganda to boost the self-confidence of officers and men who often fought at a disadvantage in conventional terms of equipment and skill." Even more significant, "leaders themselves *needed* to believe in the superior spiritual qualities of republican soldiers."[6]

Colonial Americans also had their unique needs that contributed to the growth of the militia myth. The militia was an imported English institution, which reminded the settlers not only of the mother country but of the nature of English life at the time of colony founding—a time when, in theory at any rate, the kingdom still relied on its sturdy yeomen rather than a mercenary army for protection. Later, as England turned more demonstrably to a standing army, the colonial militia served to show the superior human qualities of the provincials since they fought their own battles rather than employing people outside the mainstream of colonial life. Thomas Nairne, a South Carolina planter, exulted that "most People delight" in militia service, "and think no body so fit to defend their Properties as themselves. . . . And as we have no regular Troops, for many reasons we desire none. A planter who keeps his Body fit . . . is doubtless a better Soldier . . . than a Company of raw Fellows raised in England."[7]

In fact, because of its longevity and because of its inclusiveness, the militia was viewed as one of the most vibrant and vital of colonial institutions. Like the county court, the town meeting, and the church, the militia consisted of local people meeting local objectives. The militia, according to John Adams, was one of the cornerstones of New England society and a source of "the Virtues and talents of the People"—"Temperance, Patience, Fortitude, Prudence, . . . Justice, . . . Sagacity, Knowledge, Judgment, Taste, Skill, Ingenuity, Dexterity, and Industry."[8] Thus, to deny the credibility of the militia was to deny the worthiness of the people collectively.

We must look more closely at the militia, to see what it was initially and to determine what it became later. Then we can endeavor to separate the myth from the history of that institution and to explain the development of semiprofessional military forces. Up to a point the seventeenth-century militia resembled what publicists always claimed. In most colonies, membership was nearly universal, consisting of able-bodied men between the ages of sixteen and sixty, who were required to possess their own firearms and other military paraphernalia and to assemble a certain number of times a year for drill and instruction. As a 1634 law in the Plymouth colony expressed it, all inhabitants were "subject to such military order for trayning and exercise of armes as shall be thought meet, agreed on, and prescribed by the Governor and Assistants."[9] Everywhere the basic unit was the company—sometimes called the train band—which was part of a county regiment. The statutes brim with rules and regulations for organizing, administering, supplying, and calling out men who were truly citizen soldiers.

There were, however, discrepancies between the theory and the practice of the seventeenth-century militia. Rarely did regular companies of militia take the field except in cases of emergency involving the protection of the immediate community. For service in the major Indian conflicts of the century such as the Pequot War and King Philip's War the militia served as the military body from which volunteers and draftees were secured for more extended duty in reconstituted militia companies and regiments. But then, too, draftees were usually spared if they hired a substitute or paid a fine. What Harold E. Selesky observes for Connecticut came increasingly to apply throughout England's New World dependencies: namely, that "only in [the] early years of settlement and on the frontier were universal military obligation and universal military service the same thing."[10]

As society became more stratified and as threats to the eastern, most densely populated regions receded in the late seventeenth century, we find that the militia eligible for combat were less a reflection of society than had been the case in the years of early settlement. Transients, paupers, and generally "loose, idle, dissolute persons"—along with blacks, Indians, and indentured servants—usually fell outside the militia system; and even some respectable elements of the population were excused from active participation. In Massachusetts, for example, magistrates, legislators, Harvard educators, schoolteachers, church leaders, physicians, ship captains, fishermen, and certain kinds of artisans fell into the exempted category.[11]

All the same, if the militia no longer reflected society as it once did, its duty-eligible ranks still contained the vast majority of the freeholders, who were citizens with the vote. And their ballot power was never forgotten by the elites, whose domination of the provincial political scene rested more on responsible government than on habits of deference on the part of the public. This political fact explains why colonial assemblies were hesitant to call out the militia in behalf of unpopular or difficult and distant wars and why, if they did assemble this home guard, they did so for short periods (normally three months), with service confined to their respective colonies—and, almost always, with the opportunity for the militiamen to buy their way out of actual participation by one means or another.

But the heterogeneity of society and the political clout of the freeholders were not the only reasons for the decline of the militia as the premier war-making institution in colonial America. The militia, both in the mother country and her colonies, had always been primarily a defensive arm, infinitely more effective on its own turf than on distant offensive fields.[12] Indeed, the home front aspects of its responsibilities cannot be too strongly emphasized. For one of its local functions had been, and continued to be in the eighteenth century, to serve as an instrument of social control, as one can see from examining its assignment as a slave patrol in the Southern colonies, its role in Bacon's Rebellion in Virginia in 1676, and its part in the War of the Regulation in North Carolina in 1771. This domestic dimension of militia activity gave that body new life throughout America in the Revolution as these local forces played a crucial role behind the lines in putting down the Loyalists and giving sinews to the Revolutionary infrastructures at the colony-state levels; and, of course, a forward glance at post-Revolutionary history shows that the militia remained valuable for purposes of social control—its contributions in suppressing Shays' Rebellion in Massachusetts in 1786 and in terminating the Whiskey Rebellion in Pennsylvania in 1794 are well known.

Prior to the Revolution the militia could be an instrument of social control with only minimal training, and surely its training and military effectiveness declined in the eighteenth century. Training days, if held at all, were often more social than military. People joked about its sloppiness, its ineffectiveness, and its antiquated weaponry. When called to action against Indians or Frenchmen, its members must have displayed attitudes and behavior not wholly unlike that of the Russian middle service class. "In peace time," reported the historian N. G. Ustrialov, those "who were not on official duty calmly lived in their own villages, engaging in law suits, their economies, trade, and hunting, and least of all thinking about military matters. When the musketeer messenger arrived from the general with a decree from the Tsar, 'Prepare for service, get ready supplies to feed the horses,' they reached for their grandfathers' rusty armor, got ready a bag of food for the trip, and loaded up several wagons. . . . Many showed up late, or not at all."[13]

One must not be too critical of the Anglo-American militia, for changes in the nature of warfare and the onset of the imperial wars after 1688 provide us with additional reasons why this imported institution from England could scarcely function any longer except as a defense force, as a tool for social control, and as a recruiting and drafting agency for semiprofessional colonial military forces.

Even before King Philip's War in 1675–77, the Indians of New England demonstrated that they had become increasingly dangerous opponents by having learned to cope with the technological superiority of the colonists. First they turned from their rather limited, ritualistic style of intertribal combat to guerrilla tactics in order to counteract the settlers' superior weaponry. They also fairly quickly became proficient with firearms, a fact which serves as a reminder that technological advantage in military matters is rarely permanent and, in reality, is often short-lived. The tribesmen, notes Patrick M. Malone, "exercised careful judgment by choosing weapons with a firing mechanism suited for their environment and their methods of warfare. They rejected the inexpensive matchlocks carried by . . . most of the militiamen in the first New England military units," which were useless in bad weather and adopted instead the self-igniting flintlock.[14]

The combining of firearms with their superior knowledge of the land made the Indians formidable adversaries in King Philip's War: the colonies suffered roughly a thousand deaths and saw many towns and farms of western New England reduced to rubble. The forces of Massachusetts Bay, Plymouth, and Connecticut—raised from the militia—often fought poorly, repeatedly falling prey to Indian ambushes, and eventually prevailed only because of their superiority in numbers and material resources and because of their effective use of Indian auxiliaries. One result of the war was the discrediting of the pike as a military weapon. Pikemen had often preferred their position in the Massachusetts Bay militia to that of the musketeers—they constituted a third of the membership of each company—because they received colorful attire and did not need to own firearms. Contrary to the militia myth, some not only failed to possess muskets but did not know how to use them. Young John Dunton was not alone in conceding that he "knew not how to shoot off a musket" and that his fellow militiamen "knew it well enough by my awkward handling" of one.[15]

If King Philip's War brought the departure of the pike from the militia scene, and if, more important, that conflict forever ended the New England Indians' ability to launch a lengthy unilateral offensive, the tribesmen continued to pose a sizable threat when allied with Britain's European adversaries. And increasingly that was the case, just as the colonists, especially in the northern and lower southern tiers of North American settlement, became participants in the mother country's imperial wars. Those conflicts involved the colonists' sending larger numbers of men than ever before into military service and requiring them to serve great distances from their own communities. At one time or another between 1690 and 1760, they helped attack French posts at Port Royal, Louisbourg, Ticonderoga, Duquesne, Quebec, and Montreal, and Spanish positions at St. Augustine, Cartagena, and elsewhere. Sometimes those provincial forces performed as intercolonial armies operating independently, while on other occasions American contingents served alongside or in conjunction with British military and naval commands.

As for the British government, it confronted imperial defense only on an ad hoc basis. It periodically asked the colonies to raise forces as best they could and without any plan of integrating them into a larger imperial military structure. Nothing better illustrates Britain's poor example than the London ministry's string of broken promises between 1706 and 1746 to contribute substantially to colonial military expeditions against Canada.

Left to their own devices, the colonies, because of the defects in the militia system and because of the lack of imperial direction, adopted semiprofessional forces that were actually a hybrid between the militia and a standing army. The term semiprofessional requires a definition, one that is employed strictly within an eighteenth-century context. We are usually speaking of fairly large numbers of men—several hundred to several thousand—who in return for a bounty enlisted for a year or more, who often reenlisted, who served if required outside the boundaries of their own colonies, who were subject to a stricter form of military law than applied to the militia, and who served under officers not infrequently possessed of a strong tinge of military professionalism (they read military literature and relished the opportunity to learn more about European methods from observing British forces in America). Generally, it was only in emergencies that these semiprofessional forces employed militia drafts and other kinds of compulsory service.

Needless to say, some colonies turned to this form of military arrangement before others. Massachusetts and Connecticut were among the earliest to do so because of their proximity to French Canada. Colonies that faced a Bourbon threat only in the middle of the eighteenth century, such as Virginia, did so much later; and Pennsylvania, which was plagued by divisive internal politics and Quaker reluctance to bear arms, was the last of the North American colonies to take any kind of meaningful military measures. Let us look more closely at these semiprofessional forces in certain individual colonies, particularly in Massachusetts and Virginia and, to a lesser extent, in Connecticut and South Carolina.

Because of its strategic location, Massachusetts was better acquainted with war than any other British North American dependency. There semiprofessionalism, as John M. Murrin has demonstrated, meant that "in the military sphere . . . the trend was towards English models"— "the adoption of European institutions and European ideas." It was the failure of the Massachusetts militia to repel French and Indian thrusts against the frontier in King William's War that led to the creation of a different kind of military organization. Governor Richard Coote, earl of Bellomont, initiated the change when he coaxed the legislature to raise forces distinct from the militia and to begin the practice of subjecting those troops to martial law based on variations of Parliament's Mutiny Act (to say nothing of the governor's also obtaining funds to construct Castle William in Boston Harbor, "the first Vaubanesque fortress in English America"). Since this was to be a "marching army"—designed to serve wherever needed—Bellomont gained approval to send his colonial soldiers outside the province on his own initiative when the General Court was not in session.[16]

There were further signs of the growth of military semiprofessionalism in Queen Anne's War and the years immediately thereafter. Between 1707 and 1711 Massachusetts forces participated in five expeditions against French outposts to the north. During the summer months of those four years, the colony always had one-sixth or more of its eligible males in service. A result of the increased size of the provincial army was the importation of the British office of commissary general. Moreover, during Queen Anne's War, Massachusetts units were in the field alongside British regulars, and Bay Colony officers were receiving instructions in the military art from their experienced royal counterparts. Their drill procedures seemingly followed regular army practice, as is evidenced by the printing and reprinting of several standard English military manuals. Even after hostilities ended, Massachusetts maintained a small permanent military establishment, which occupied frontier posts in Maine and garrisoned Castle William. And some of its officers revealed certain unsavory practices associated with European professionals—treating their commissions as personal property available for sale and inflating their muster rolls.[17]

By the final imperial wars of the 1740s and 1750s, Massachusetts was far removed from whatever lessons it had learned in wilderness warfare. Consequently, the colony's military leaders drew "upon imported manuals composed for European armies and European wars. They then applied this information indiscriminately to American Indians or French soldiery, to a forest ambush or the fortress of Louisbourg."[18] But they were chiefly involved in offensive operations against Gallic citadels in Canada. Massachusetts provided the lion's share of the 1745 New England expeditionary force that employed European siege tactics to capture Louisbourg—"the Gibraltar of the New World"—on Cape Breton Island. Britain rewarded the Massachusetts military commanders, William Shirley and William Pepperell, for their achievement by appointing them colonels of two American regiments created for the British regular establishment.[19]

Massachusetts made even greater, if less spectacular, martial contributions to the empire in the Seven Years' War. The province called to arms about one-third of its service-eligible males, a record that was quite likely unmatched by any European country at that time.[20] Countless recruits served more than a single-year term. Many officers were clearly enamored of military life. One officer, William Williams of Pittsfield, could boast of seventeen years of active duty, which included both King George's War and the Seven Years' War. Such families as the Winslows, Prescotts, Gorhams, and Bournes could point to a tradition of their members securing commissions in threatening times. More than a few of these semiprofessional officers in Massachusetts and elsewhere dreamed of climbing through the royal establishment as Shirley and Pepperrell had done; but, over the eighteenth century, only a relative handful achieved that goal. They did, however, endeavor to uphold some standards of professionalism in their own provincial establishments.

Although the Massachusetts army lacked the structural complexity of the British establishment—it had no cavalry, grenadier, and light infantry contingents—its organization was a modified version of its royal counterpart. The army consisted of companies, battalions, and regiments. Each regiment had a prescribed complement of field and staff officers, which included, in the latter category, the adjutant, the commissary, the quartermaster, the chaplain, and the surgeon and the surgeon's mate. As the war lengthened, the provincial military structure became more complex. The colony's lone general officer, Major General John Winslow, was relieved of some of his burdensome responsibilities in 1758 when Timothy Ruggles and Jedediah Preble were promoted to brigadier general, the same year that Winslow formed a light infantry battalion under Lieutenant Colonel Oliver Partridge. The Massachusetts army, writes Murrin, "unquestionably resembled its British counterpart more exactly by 1760 than it had ever done before."[21]

Connecticut, like its neighbor Massachusetts, felt heavy imperial demands for manpower in the struggles with France, and it also switched from militia drafts and other compulsory steps to enlistment bounties as early as 1710. By King George's War, it had become a "paramount desire" of ambitious Connecticut officers to gain British epaulets; and David Wooster, a future American general in the Revolution, and Nathan Whiting realized their objectives. In all this, observes Selesky, there was proof "of the colony's continuing integration into the empire." During the Seven Years' War about 40 percent of all provincial officers put in at least one campaign as enlisted men before receiving commissions. Demonstrated leadership abilities enabled them to attract hosts of recruits; in 1757 alone 13 percent of the province's population performed some type of military service. Indeed, so many officers and enlisted men served in the Seven Years' War that "Connecticut's military system [turned] into a colonial American version of a mercenary professional army." British subsidies to Connecticut and the other colonies explained this remarkable phenomenon; it was truly "an abberation which Connecticut society was neither sufficiently wealthy nor stratified to have developed on its own."[22]

South Carolina and Virginia, in contrast to the Puritan settlements, faced fewer demands for their military cooperation from the mother country before the mid-eighteenth century. But Indian threats were always of grave concern to South Carolinians, as were fears of Spanish attacks from Florida.

As early as the 1670s, its founding decade, South Carolina sometimes assembled specially recruited soldiers in preference to its militia, and it always did so in its attempts to capture the Spanish equivalent of Louisbourg, the formidable Castillo de San Marcos at St. Augustine. The colony periodically resorted to semiprofessionals throughout its pre-independence years in manning frontier forts, coastal watch houses and beacon lights, and scout boats.[23] These forces were reduced in size and quality in the early eighteenth century as provincial leaders relied on their elaborate network of Indian alliances to shield them from external danger. The collapse of the alliance system led to the disastrous Yamassee War of 1715–17—South Carolina's version of King Philip's War—in which few sections of the colony were spared wholesale death and devastation. In the initial onslaught, the militia turned out in its traditional units, the first time it had done so in over thirty years. Its performance fell far short of the optimistic prediction for it by the previously mentioned planter Thomas Nairne, who, ironically, was one of the first fatalities in the conflict. In time, an army of volunteers turned the tide in favor of the whites.[24]

Following the Yamassee War, South Carolina embraced a new military policy, which included heavy outlays for defense: between 30 and 50 percent of the colony's budget during the years 1721–33. It also provided for what Theodore H. Jabbs describes as "a mixed [military] system composed of professionals who guarded the frontiers; volunteers who invaded foreign territory; and militia who provided purely local defense." During the last external threat to the colony, the Cherokee War of 1759–61, a provincial army in combination with British regulars proved effective in defeating their Indian adversaries and bringing peace to the backcountry.[25]

Virginia merits attention for reasons other than those expressed for Massachusetts, Connecticut, and South Carolina. While its mid-seventeenth-century militia was reasonably well organized and sometimes victorious in combat, it declined dramatically following Bacon's Rebellion, and its exclusionary practices—a reflection of planter fears of poor and landless inhabitants—reduced it to the status of a "bourgeois militia."[26] In 1712 Governor Alexander Spotswood asserted that Virginia's militia was "the worst in the King's Dominions," an opinion echoed four decades later by Governor Robert Dinwiddie, who discovered the militia to be "in very bad Order."[27] If the above-mentioned provinces to the north and south of Virginia shifted almost exclusively to semiprofessional forces in the early eighteenth century, the Old Dominion did not since it felt relatively secure from both native American and foreign threats. The colony's only manpower contribution in King George's War was to dispatch 136 volunteers to join an intercolonial expedition against Montreal in 1746.[28]

But the Seven Years' War was a very different matter to Virginia's leadership, which had western land claims to protect and whose frontier settlements were exposed to French and Indian raids. At last Virginia adopted a semiprofessional military organization, and soon afterward it placed its troops under the command of George Washington, who sought not only to make his regiment the equal of any in the British army but to put it on the royal establishment as well. It is this *obsession*—there is no other word for it—with professionalism that sets Washington apart from most if not all the ranking provincial officers in the other colonies.[29]

Not yet twenty-four years of age, Washington had already received a broad military education for a provincial, seizing every opportunity to acquire "knowledge in the Military Art." He obtained that education by the tutorial method, which was not unlike the way officers in Europe gained professional know-how. The tutorial approach meant discussions with battle-seasoned veterans, independent reading, firsthand observation, and actual military experience. Washington had learned about the Cartagena campaign of 1741 from his brother Lawrence and about European continental warfare from his friend and relative by marriage William Fairfax, both of whom had held British commissions. He had read Caesar's *Commentaries;* a translated version of *A Panegyrick to the Memory of Frederick, Late Duke of Schomberg,* an acknowledged master of the art of European warfare (a book he purchased from a cousin at a cost of two shillings sixpence); and Humphrey Bland's *Treatise of Military Discipline,* the best-known manual in the British army.

Observation and experience for the young Virginian began on a trip to Barbados with Lawrence when he visited and recorded his impressions of Fort James, which he described as a "pretty strongly fortified" structure. His first memorable experience came in 1754. Leading a small contingent of men, he tasted the joy of victory over French Ensign Jumonville at the Battle of the Meadows and soon afterward felt the pain of defeat when he surrendered Fort Necessity to a superior enemy party in July of that year. His service as a volunteer aide during the Braddock campaign of the following year not only afforded Washington further experience on the battlefield but also gave him the chance to witness the daily routine of a professional army. That he was a conscientious observer is indicated by his copying in a small notebook the army's daily general orders for his own edification and future study. Interestingly, he did not join other colonials in casting aspersions on Braddock's performance before and during the crushing British defeat at the Battle of the Monongahela. He admired the king's army and had made close friendships with some of its officers. His thirst for a royal commission would influence his subsequent actions, large and small — even to taking up fencing, still one of the officers' social graces.

During his three years as Virginia's military commander, Washington believed that the key to creating and maintaining a first-rate regiment lay in the quality of his officers. In his first surviving written address to his subordinates, he assured them that he would judge them by their "merit and reward the brave and deserving"; "partiality" would "never biass my conduct, nor shall prejudice injure any."[30] His field officers and company captains, in turn, should be proper and correct in relating to their own officers and men. Likewise they were to practice efficient administrative procedures and display high ethical standards, and they were to protect and establish cordial relations with the civilian population, not only for reasons of humanity but also because his regiment needed various forms of assistance from fellow Virginians.

Washington's pronouncements on tactics and discipline scarcely set him off from those regular commanders he sought to emulate. If he stressed the value of teaching "bush" tactics, so did British officers such as Henry Bouquet and John Forbes — after 1755 they emphasized that regulars should practice aimed fire and movement through wooded terrain. As for military literature, Washington instructed his officers to begin with Bland's treatise and then turn to other works with "the wished-for information." He ordered that his soldiers be taught "the New platoon way of Exercising," which was authored by the Duke of Cumberland, the British army's captain general. Washington insisted that specified drill and ceremonial procedures be followed "even in the most minute punctilio's." To that end, he ordered the captain of every frontier fort to dispatch a small detail to his headquarters to receive proper training, which it would subsequently impart to its own garrison. In these and all other measures, he admonished his subordinates, they should never forget that "Discipline is the soul of any army"; for "it makes small numbers formidable; procures success to the weak, and esteem to all."[31]

Though Washington was severely handicapped by recruitment problems because the House of Burgesses was much slower than the New England assemblies to offer enlistment bounties, and though he had to rely in part on men drafted from outside the militia, he nevertheless contended that his was an excellent regiment that deserved a place on the regular establishment. Twice Washington pressed his case to the uppermost British military authorities in America—when he traveled to Boston in 1756 to implore General William Shirley and when he journeyed to Philadelphia the following year to confront Lord Loudoun. The Virginia colonel carried with him in the latter endeavor a memorial from his regimental officers that shows how professional they had become in their own eyes.

It was important to the provincial officers to inform Loudoun that they were not militia—for which they, like Washington, had great contempt—at the same time that they argued for regular status. While militia were part-time or seasonal soldiers, poorly trained and ill disciplined, the "Virginia Regiment was the first in arms of any Troops" in America during the Seven Years' War. Their "three years hard & bloody Service"—without "agreeable recess in Winter Quarters"—for which they had "been regulary Regimented and trained" meant that only "Commissions from His Majesty" were required to make them "as regular a Corps as any upon the Continent."[32]

Did Washington and his officers, who failed in their quest for royal preferment, exaggerate their abilities and accomplishments? The Virginia colonel was hardly modest at this stage; he described himself as "much longer in the Service than any provincial officer in America" and possessed of abilities far above "the *common run* of provincial officers." But any number of British civilian and military officials had spoken warmly of his performance in arms. During the 1758 campaign against Fort Duquesne at the forks of the Ohio, General John Forbes complimented Washington by giving him command of a lead division and instructions to diagram a suitable order of march for the army. His regiment also elicited strong praise from Forbes for its "good behavior"; and later in the war General Robert Monckton informed General Jeffery Amherst that the Virginians had performed their "Duty as well as any old Regiment" on the royal establishment. If Washington and his soldiers were better than most provincial units, if they therefore were hardly typical of the evolving semiprofessional military tradition in colonial America, they nevertheless represented that tradition at its best, and their record suggested what it might become for colonial Americans generally in subsequent wars.[33]

Was there any immediate future for colonial semiprofessional forces in the king's service after 1763? Certainly imperial authorities, for the first time ever, decided to keep a substantial military contingent in North America following a war with the Bourbon powers. But this decision did not embrace provincial units but rather fifteen regiments of regulars totaling about six thousand troops, stretched over a thousand-mile rim from Florida to the Mississippi River to Canada and here and there in the older settlements. Both directly and indirectly, the army's presence in peacetime, coupled with Parliamentary taxation of America for its upkeep, created or exacerbated tensions and difficulties that contributed to the growing rift within the empire and to the eventual movement for independence.[34]

One wonders (to pose a counterfactual question) what the subsequent course of eighteenth-century Anglo-American relations might have been had Britain chosen semiprofessional colonial soldiers to protect the frontier, to police the newly acquired lands, and to guard against possible Franco-Spanish territorial aggrandizement—an idea favored by Benjamin Franklin.[35] Such a military structure could have drawn upon countless semiprofessional officers who had gained invaluable experience in the Seven Years' War, officers who in many cases had sought royal rank and now might receive it—or something close to it, however such an American army might be established; officers who, whether they fully understood it, had a psychological need to be recognized as military men the equal of British-born officers (and was this psychological need a possible explanation why former provincial officers enjoyed being addressed by their previous service rank?). It is tempting to speculate that a lack of fulfillment as a soldier lay behind Washington's ordering for Mount Vernon portrait busts of six great captains—both ancients and moderns, from Alexander to Frederick II—and his decision to have his first known portrait painted while wearing his blue Virginia regimentals.

No doubt this kind of postwar military opportunity would also have been attractive to thousands of former enlisted men from the various provincial forces. Although there is some reason to think that the rank and file generally had found military service less attractive than their officers—especially if they came under the control of British officers and their military code of justice—they had earlier been enticed by bounties and monthly pay in a society where currency was always in short supply.[36] Doubtless, too, there would have been competition for enlisted slots from the more than ten thousand colonials who had joined the British army during the 1750s and early 1760s. The very fact that hordes of provincials donned redcoats may itself imply that we have made too much of friction between colonial soldiers and their British counterparts.

What if London officialdom had created an American establishment? One wonders whether such an army would have been more effective and less controversial in the colonies after 1763 than the British regiments were. Certainly an American army would have been cheaper to maintain than an imported one, and a precedent existed from the last war for such expenditures (after 1757 Prime Minister William Pitt heavily subsidized the provincial armies). But Britain never formally considered its military options in the early 1760s.

This lack of an analytical examination of the problem of imperial defense and control of the interior contrasts sharply with the attitude of Spain toward its military requirements in the viceroyalty of New Spain or Mexico at the conclusion of the Seven Years' War. John Shy explains that there were two contrasting views. One favored "the creation of an indigenous professional army, with creole sons given at least junior commissions and trained and inspired by . . . European professionals." The second supported "the organization of an effective colonial militia which would be cheaper and larger and would fit more readily into colonial society than a professional army." Though both approaches were tried, achieving only modest results as the court at Madrid oscillated between the two, one can still say that methods of defending New Spain were at least debated and alternatives were seriously examined.[37]

If the use of American semiprofessionals was not considered in London, we can surely add that neither Britain nor her colonies themselves addressed the second Spanish option: the revival and reordering of the militia. While in Britain, during the Pitt administration, the militia had been reformed for the first time in a century—compulsory active service was confined to three-year terms under systematic training by regular army officers—the colonial militias continued their decline, which had begun more than half a century earlier.[38] But that indifference to the militia ended abruptly in 1774, following the Boston Tea Party and the dispatching of 3,500 British troops to Massachusetts in retaliation. The occasional tracts extolling the militia which had appeared over the decades (for example, those of Ebenezer Gay and Thomas Nairne) were now followed by a torrent of writings in favor of invigorating this venerable institution of the citizen soldier. Never had so much been written so eloquently and so quickly on the militia as appeared in 1774 and 1775.[39]

Why did militia apologists glorify an institution that, in its actual operation, was more myth than reality, that had never really stood up to professional armies in major combat, and that could scarcely do so in 1775? Perhaps the answer in part is that the colonists were prisoners of language. They had never developed a positive nomenclature for their own semiprofessional armies of the past, much less a European-style professional army. To use terminology currently fashionable among early American historians, it has been argued that militia reflected the "country" (or classical republican) ideology that was appealing to the revolutionists; that standing armies mirrored the "court" (or Walpolian consolidated-mercantilist) ideology; and, one should add, that semiprofessional provincial forces had no place in the American lexicon.

Even so, men who are captives of language may, in the midst of revolution, break the bonds of their captivity in order to prevail. Yet it has long puzzled more than a corporal's guard of scholars as to how Americans could turn from a glorification of the militia in 1774 to the adoption of a standing army—the Continental army—the following year. To be sure, it seems at first glance to have been a dramatic step, but it was even more a pragmatic and evolutionary step, an indication that historians (of military affairs at least) may well have exaggerated the rigidity or ideological dimensions of early American thought. Let me additionally suggest that although Americans waxed eloquently over the theoretical attributes of militia, they did so primarily to contrast their own values with those of the mother country and thus to find a common rallying cry to foster colonial unity—and not to make the militia a vehicle for bearing the brunt of a war against Britain.

Moreover, if we remain mindful of the provincial semiprofessional military pattern discussed in this essay, then the adoption of a professional army after Lexington and Concord is properly seen as a logical and predictable development—a third stage in the history of early American military institutions—from seventeenth-century militia to eighteenth-century semiprofessional forces to professional army in 1775. Even so, Washington's army was hardly as professional at the siege of Boston as it became later, which is to say that Americans continued to have the opportunity to ease into an army on the European model. In some respects the Continental army during its first year in the field appeared to be an extension of a semiprofessional colonial force of the Seven Years' War. Most of its general officers had held provincial commissions in the last imperial conflict; its articles of war were moderate compared to those of the British army; and its soldiers were enlisted for a year or less. Furthermore, the army itself had not been raised by Congress but rather was a New England provincial army (not unlike earlier New England armies) that had been assembled to bottle up General Thomas Gage in Boston.[40]

It may not be amiss to maintain that a fourth and final stage in the evolution of an American professional army began in 1776 and continued through the War of Independence. It included such developments as long-term enlistments, a sterner military code, the removal of marginal officers, the establishment of more uniform tactical procedures, and the importation of Prussian and French military ideas and practices (particularly owing to the influence of Friedrich Wilhelm von Steuben as inspector general and of such technical experts as Louis Duportail, who headed the corps of engineers).[41]

What, in the final analysis, was the significance of the colonial semiprofessional military experience? As for the colonial period itself, three observations may be made. First, it provided British-Americans with a reasonably effective way of waging offensive warfare and guarding peripheral outposts, a far better one than the militia could offer. Second, it afforded the provincials a great deal of valuable knowledge about eighteenth-century European military behavior. It is true, of course, that provincials performing with redcoats did not customarily receive frontline battlefield assignments and were more likely relegated to support duties—to pick-and-shovel brigades. Nevertheless, colonials often obtained rigorous training and not infrequently participated in combat. Third, the growing colonial preoccupation with British military ideas and practices lends support to the thesis of John Murrin that similar imitations were simultaneously taking place in such vital spheres as the court system, the practice of law, and the character of politics. The result was the "anglicization" of provincial life. Ironically, the American Revolution occurred when the colonies were more like the mother country than ever before.[42]

Finally, what can we say about the usefulness of the colonial semi-professional experience for Americans who won their independence between 1775 and 1783? Two points seem to stand out. First, Americans' sense of military accomplishment in the imperial wars may have given them a good deal of self-confidence for risking a violent break with Britain. For some Revolutionary military leaders, particularly Washington, that previous experience proved invaluable; that in itself makes the connection worth stressing. But the connection was doubtless far broader than that. It is well to remember that Revolutionary Americans fought two major wars in a single generation (1754–83). These two conflicts resulted in the fourth and third greatest efforts at manpower mobilization in American history.[43] Just as the Mexican War has been called a "rehearsal for conflict"—for the Civil War—so we may also argue that the Seven Years' War bore a similar relationship to the War of Independence. Second, the colonial semiprofessional experience enabled Americans to move by evolutionary stages to the creation of a Revolutionary army that became sufficiently professional by European measurements to acquit itself remarkably well against Britain—and to do so without arousing against it the deep-seated fears of standing armies that had been a part of their Whiggish heritage. For Americans to have accomplished all that during the War of Independence may seem amazing, but an examination of the semiprofessional military tradition helps to make their achievements explainable.

NOTES

1. Ebenezer Gay, *Well-Accomplished Soldiers*... (Boston, 1738), 28.
2. Julian P. Boyd et al., eds., *The Papers of Thomas Jefferson* (Princeton, 1950–),

2:195; *The Lee Papers*, New York Historical Society, *Collections*, vols. 4–7 (New York, 1871–74), 1:162.

3. Richard Hellie, *Enserfment and Military Change in Muscovy* (Chicago, 1971).

4. John A. Lynn, *The Bayonets of the Republic: Motivation and Tactics in the Army of Revolutionary France* (Urbana, Ill., 1984), esp. chap. 8, quotations on pp. 185, 192.

5. For an illuminating discussion of the subject, see Melissa Meriam Bullard, "The Magnificent Lorenzo de Medici: Between Myth and History," in *Political Culture in Early Modern Europe: Essays in Honor of H. G. Koenigsberger*, eds. Phyllis Mack and Margaret C. Jacob (Cambridge, 1987), 25–58.

6. *Bayonets of the Republic*, 192.

7. "A Letter From A Swiss Gentlemen to his Friend in Bern," *North Carolina University Magazine* 4 (Sept., 1855): 297.

8. Lyman H. Butterfield, ed., *Diary and Autobiography of John Adams* (Cambridge, Mass., 1961), 3:195.

9. Nathaniel B. Shurtleff and David Pulsifer, eds., *Records of the Colony of New Plymouth in New England* (Boston, 1855–61), 1:22.

10. "Military Leadership in an American Colonial Society: Connecticut, 1635–1785," Ph.D. diss., Yale University, 1984, xiv.

11. Jack S. Rodabaugh, "The Militia of Colonial Massachusetts," in *Military Analysis of the Revolutionary War: An Anthology by the Editors of Military Affairs* (Millwood, N.Y., 1977), 27.

12. For the English militia, see Michael Powicke, *Military Obligation in Medieval England: A Study in Liberty and Duty* (Oxford, 1962); Lindsay Boynton, *The Elizabethan Militia, 1558–1638* (London, 1967).

13. Quoted in Hellie, *Enserfment and Military Change*, 220.

14. "Changing Military Technology Among the Indians of Southern New England, 1600–1677," *American Quarterly* 25 (March 1973): 49–63, quotation on p. 52. Generalizations about seventeenth-century Indians' methods of warfare must be guarded at this juncture since much work is going on in this field, and there are sharp scholarly differences on the subject. See E. Wayne Carp, "Early American Military History: A Review of Recent Work," *Virginia Magazine of History and Biography* 94 (July 1986): 266–68.

15. Quoted in Radabaugh, "Militia of Colonial Massachusetts," 19. For chronic shortages of firearms elsewhere, see William L. Shea, *The Virginia Militia in the Seventeenth Century* (Baton Rouge, La., 1983), 53, 75, 130.

16. John M. Murrin, "Anglicizing an American Colony: The Transformation of Provincial Massachusetts," Ph.D. diss., Yale University, 1966, 61–76, quotations on pp. 62, 75.

17. Ibid., 77–97; Archibald Hanna, Jr., "New England Military Institutions, 1693–1750," Ph.D. diss., Yale University, 1950, 54–115.

18. Murrin, "Anglicizing an American Colony," 95.

19. Hanna, "New England Military Institutions," 116–58; G. A. Rawlyk, *Yankees at Louisbourg* (Orono, Maine, 1967).

20. Fred Anderson, *A People's Army: Massachusetts Soldiers and Society in the Seven Years' War* (Chapel Hill, N.C., 1984), 3, 59–60.

21. Murrin, "Anglicizing an American Colony," 137; Anderson, *A People's Army*, 48–50.

22. "Military Leadership in an American Colonial Society," quotations on pp. 182, 217.

23. Because of their common concerns about the Spanish and the southeastern tribes, South Carolina and Georgia developed similiar military institutions, including what have been called provincial navies. They consisted of a number of "scout boats"—made from giant cypress logs—averaging thirty-five feet in length, with two small sails and swivel guns fore and aft and carrying crews of ten. Larry E. Ivers, "Scouting the Inland Passage, 1685–1737," *South Carolina History Magazine* 73 (July 1972): 117–29; Ivers, *British Drums on the Southern Frontier: The Military Colonization of Georgia* (Chapel Hill, N.C., 1974).

24. Theodore Harry Jabbs, "The South Carolina Colonial Militia, 1663–1733," Ph.D. diss., University of North Carolina, 1973, chaps. 1–8.

25. Ibid., chaps. 9–10, Epilogue, quotation on p. 454; Robert L. Meriwether, *The Expansion of South Carolina, 1729–1765* (Kingsport, Tenn., 1940), 213–40; Lawrence H. Gipson, *The British Empire before the American Revolution* (Caldwell, Idaho, and New York, 1936–70), 9:55–86. For comparative purposes, see James Michael Johnson, " 'Not a Single Soldier in the Province': The Military Establishment of Georgia and the Coming of the American Revolution," Ph.D. diss., Duke University, 1980.

26. William L. Shea, *The Virginia Militia in the Seventeenth Century* (Baton Rouge, La., 1983).

27. R. A. Brock, ed., *The Official Letters of Alexander Spotswood . . . 1710–1712* (Richmond, Va., 1882–85), 2:212; Brock, ed., *The Official Records of Robert Dinwiddie . . . 1751–1758* (Richmond, Va., 1883–84), 1:344.

28. Richard L. Morton, *Colonial Virginia* (Chapel Hill, N.C., 1960), 2:534–35. Although in the seventeenth century Virginia had occasional experience with special ranger companies and other extended-service units, they failed to serve as a precedent for provincial military structures during the imperial wars. Shea, *Virginia Militia*, 65, 126–27.

29. The following discussion of Washington borrows liberally from my *George Washington and the American Military Tradition* (Athens, Ga., 1985), chap. 1.

30. "Orders," 8 Jan. 1756, W. W. Abbot et al., eds., *Papers of Washington: Colonial Series* (Charlottesville, Va., 1983–), 2:257.

31. Ibid., 2:23, 76, 124, 135, 257; 4:343, 344. See generally J. A. Houlding, *Fit for Service: The Training of the British Army, 1715–1795* (Oxford, Eng., 1981).

32. Washington to Dinwiddie, 10 March 1757, Memorial to Loudoun, 23 March 1757 *Papers of Washington*, 4:112–14, 120–21.

33. John C. Fitzpatrick, ed., *Writings of George Washington from the Original Manuscript Sources, 1745–1799* (Washington, D.C., 1931–44), 2:173, 177, 290–91; Monckton to Amherst, 9 July 1760, quoted in James W. Titus, "Soldiers When They Chose to Be So: Virginians at War, 1754–1763," Ph.D. diss., Rutgers University, 1983, 243, 264 n. 69.

34. John Shy, *Toward Lexington: The Role of the British Army in the Coming of the American Revolution* (Princeton, 1965); Peter D. G. Thomas, "New Light on the Commons Debate of 1763 on the American Army," *William and Mary*

Quarterly, 3d ser., 38 (Jan. 1981): 110–12; John L. Bullion, " 'The Ten Thousand in America': More Light on the Decision on the American Army, 1762–1763," ibid., 43 (Oct. 1986): 646–57.

35. Although they did not share the same reasoning, Franklin, Colonial Agent Richard Jackson, and Indian Superintendent William Johnson all had reservations about the decision to station thousands of redcoats along the North American periphery. Bernhard Knollenberg, *Origin of the American Revolution, 1759–1766* (New York, 1960), 89–90.

36. The best published account of motives for serving and of cultural conflict between provincials and redcoats is Anderson, *A People's Army*, esp. chaps. 2, 4, 6.

37. John Shy, "Armed Force in Colonial North America," in *Against All Enemies: Interpretations of American Military History from Colonial Times to the Present*, eds. Kenneth J. Hagan and William R. Roberts (Westport, Conn., 1986), 11–13, quotation on p. 12. See also Lyle N. McAlister, "The Reorganization of the Army of New Spain, 1763–1766," *Hispanic American Historical Review* 33 (Jan. 1953): 1–32.

38. J. R. Western, *The English Militia in the Eighteenth Century* (London, 1965).

39. John Todd White, "Standing Armies in Time of War: Republican Theory and Military Practice during the American Revolution," Ph.D. diss., George Washington University, 1978, chaps. 1–3; Lawrence Delbert Cress, *Citizens in Arms: The Army and the Militia in American Society to the War of 1812* (Chapel Hill, N.C., 1982), 46–50; Cress, "Radical Whiggery on the Role of the Militia: Ideological Roots of the American Revolutionary Militia," *Journal of the History of Ideas* 40 (1979): 43–60; Don Higginbotham, "The American Militia: A Traditional Institution with Revolutionary Responsibilities," *Reconsiderations on the Revolutionary War: Selected Essays*, ed. Higginbotham (Westport, Conn., 1978), 92–93, 95–97.

40. White, "Standing Armies in Time of War," 114–26; Higginbotham, *George Washington*, chap. 2; Robert K. Wright, Jr., *The Continental Army* (Washington, D.C., 1983), chaps. 1–4; Allen French, *The First Year of the American Revolution* (Boston, 1934); Charles Martyn, *The Life of Artemas Ward: The First Commander in Chief of the Amerian Revolution* (New York, 1921).

41. Higginbotham, *George Washington*, chaps. 3–4; Higginbotham, "The Early American Way of War: Reconnaissance and Appraisal," *William and Mary Quarterly*, 3d ser., 44 (April 1987): 230–73; Wright, *The Continental Army*, chaps. 5–7. See also Charles Royster, *A Revolutionary People at War: The Continental Army and American Character, 1775–1783* (Chapel Hill, N.C., 1979); E. Wayne Carp, *To Starve the Army at Pleasure: Continental Army Administration and American Political Culture, 1775–1783* (Chapel Hill, N.C., 1984).

42. Murrin, "Anglicizing an American Colony"; idem, "The Legal Transformation: The Bench and Bar of Eighteenth-Century Massachusetts," in *Colonial America: Essays in Politics and Social Development*, eds. Stanley M. Katz and John M. Murrin, 3d ed. (New York, 1983), 540–72. A somewhat different view of anglicization appears in Carp, "Early American Military History," 259–84, esp. 259–62, 275–76, 279–84.

43. Thomas L. Purvis, "Colonial American Participation in the Seven Years' War, 1755–1763," paper presented at the General Brown Conference at the University of Alabama, Tuscaloosa, 1983. This important essay is part of a large study in progress on the impact of the Seven Years' War on the North American colonies.

En avant!
The Origins of the
Revolutionary Attack

JOHN A. LYNN

WRITING IN THE SPRING of 1794, Jean-Baptiste Bouchotte, Republican Minister of War, directed the newly appointed commander of the Armée de la Mozelle: "Without cease act offensively; it is necessary to haggle with our enemies no longer, but to march intrepidly at them and charge them with the bayonet."[1] His dispatch reflected Bouchotte's conviction that the regenerated French people had created a new and powerful style of warfare, in which the sophisticated maneuvers of disciplined mercenaries had fallen before the energetic assaults of inspired levies. For him, battlefield tactics were the product of political revolution.

Bouchotte realized that he was witnessing a fundamental transformation in warfare. This watershed period of military history has recently been reexamined by European and American scholars. Published over the last decade, their findings challenge accepted notions, provide new interpretations, and supply needed details.[2] Such a many-faceted body of literature is all the more noteworthy since the field of military history generally suffers from a lack of historiographic depth—that diversity of perspective and argument that enriches other areas of historical inquiry. *Bayonets of the Republic,* by this author, is part of the new scholarship. *Bayonets* redefines troop motivation and tactical practice during the critical years 1791-94.[3] However, it does not trace the origins of the tactical system it describes. Certainly, a new definition of Republican warfare demands a new account of its evolution. That is the task of this article.

Here infantry receives pride of place; time will not allow a detailed

154

consideration of artillery and cavalry. Besides, infantry played the predominant role in the Revolutionary armies. Cavalry remained a negligible factor during 1793 and 1794, and while artillery was immensely valuable, it did not win battles for the French, with the notable exception of Valmy.[4] Victory required the bayonets of Republican battalions.

Within the tactical repertoire of French infantry, the "Revolutionary attack" deserves primary emphasis. This style of column assault supported by skirmishers captured the French imagination to endure as the most vivid image of warfare under the First Republic. The Revolutionary attack became part of the national mythology — a mythology that encouraged proponents of the tactical offensive and the bayonet for a century after Waterloo.

Conventional Wisdom versus the Reality of the Armée du Nord

Conventional wisdom concerning French combat style as it was supposed to have been practiced during the years that immediately followed the outbreak of war in 1792 holds that the traditional line formation disappeared from the tactical system of French infantry. Instead, the whole of tactics degenerated to little more than a series of mass assaults. While swarms of skirmishers harassed the enemy, the bulk of the infantry waited in crude battalion columns, ready to charge at the critical moment. Finally, supported by artillery, the spirited but undisciplined masses rushed forward crying "En avant!" and "Vive la République" to overwhelm their foes by sheer weight of numbers. Both the use of large quantities of skirmishers and the reliance upon attack columns are credited as major breaks with the past, but neither is portrayed as the result of intelligent innovation.

Instead, this form of brute assault is described as a *faute de mieux* reaction to necessity. The press of events determined that new levies swelling the ranks received no more than minimal training; moreover, emigration had robbed France of her seasoned officers, leaving her with only novices. As a consequence, Revolutionary battalions found "tactical subtleties wholly beyond the capacities of their training and experience."[5] After Revolutionary battalions suffered a series of setbacks, "French military pundits gradually came to recognize the limitations of their military material and advised the adoption of what may be termed 'horde tactics.' "[6] Unable to deploy and maneuver in line, French battalions had little choice but to disperse as skirmishers or clump together in compact masses. Fortunately, the tactics of skirmish line and column suited the revolutionary élan of the sans-culottes, who made up in enthusiasm what they lacked in skill.

That, in a nutshell, is the most-repeated analysis of the character and evolution of revolutionary tactics.[7] And while the works of Jean Colin certainly challenged this textbook account, they did not replace it.[8] Although the above account has been simplified in the interest of brevity, it has not been overly distorted. Lest it be dismissed as a straw man, poorly constructed for easy demolition, the quotations above come from no less than David Chandler's excellent *The Campaigns of Napoleon*.

In contrast, consider the examination of motivation and tactics in the Armée du Nord presented in *Bayonets of the Republic*. As the largest of the armies that defended France at the height of revolutionary turmoil the case of the Nord deserves to be weighted heavily.

By 1794, the Nord relied more upon a flexible and adaptable combination of tactical elements than upon the brute force of massed bayonets. To be certain, at all times the battalions in the Nord varied considerably from one to another in training and experience, so diversity must qualify any generalization. In the main, the infantry of the Nord did not abandon the traditional line, but rather took advantage of the line's superior firepower and employed it on defense and as a waiting formation. Skirmishers proved their worth, and at times entire battalions were deployed to fight in this style. Owing to its superior mobility, the column was the best formation for maneuver on the battlefield and for assault, if it came to that. The French could adopt a greater range of tactics than commonly believed because they were better trained and better led than normally recognized.

But if the French tactical system consisted of more than a clumsy formula imposed by necessity, then a different argument must be put forward to explain the creation of the system as a whole, and in particular its more novel elements—skirmishers and attack columns. In fact, a complex and varied list of factors combined to produce the revolutionary tactical system. These will be considered in turn.

The Stable Technology of Weaponry

Since the theme of this volume is the relationship between ideas and instruments of warfare, it is only appropriate to begin with a look at

French military technology. What immediately strikes an observer is its relatively static state during the eighteenth century.

Only artillery enjoyed any major technological advance. First adopted in 1765, the Gribeauval reforms in the matériel and organization of artillery remained the standard until 1827.[9] Improvements in casting and boring cannon allowed Gribeauval to shorten barrels, reduce windage, and decrease chamber thickness. With smaller powder charges, his pieces delivered the same force and range as earlier designs. Most importantly, the much lighter pieces of the Gribeauval system, mounted on redesigned carriages, were far more mobile than their predecessors. To be sure, his reforms constituted more an important refinement than a radical transformation of artillery technology, which would not be truly revolutionized until the introduction of rifled and breach-loading pieces in the mid-nineteenth century. Nonetheless, before the Industrial Revolution relatively small degrees of technical innovation could produce great effect.

With such superior matériel, it might be expected that French artillery would have dominated the battlefield from the onset of the Revolutionary wars. Yet it did not.[10] And what is crucial, while the greater mobility of Gribeauval artillery aided the more aggressive tactics of Revolutionary infantry, it neither suggested nor imposed the column attack.

Artillery may have fallen short of its potential during 1792–94 because, as a "system," Gribeauval's work received some hard knocks during the early years of the Revolution. For one thing, the practice of distributing two cannon to each infantry battalion ran exactly counter to Gribeauval's principles. On the whole, the French did not concentrate even their battery artillery well. For another, the influx of new officers may not have been able to employ his new system to advantage until they had gained sufficient expertise.[11] One must especially wonder, given the urgency of production and the improvisation characteristic of Revolutionary arms foundries, whether pieces manufactured to Gribeauval's standards of precision were produced.[12] They probably were not.

In contrast to artillery, the weapons employed by French cavalry changed not at all during the late eighteenth century. In fact, the cavalry rode to war with edged weapons that were no more than variations on tools of war that had been available since the dawn of the iron age.

As for infantry weapons, the main concern here, the union of fusil and bayonet was ninety years old by the time the Revolutionary Wars began. The fusil, a muzzle-loading, smoothbore flintlock, became the standard French infantry firearm in 1699, when it officially replaced the earlier matchlock musket.[13] During the seventeenth century, pikemen had stood together with musketeers to defend against charging cavalry and to provide battalions with an offensive shock potential; the bayonet was intended to transform the fusil into a short pike. Louis XIV was slow to appreciate the merits of the bayonet, but in 1703 he ordered his troops to carry it, and the pike disappeared.[14]

It is worth noting that although German and British specialist units employed rifled flintlocks during the late eighteenth century, the French never adopted such weapons, even for light infantry, until well after the Revolution. They regarded the expensive muzzle-loading rifle as fragile and prone to fouling compared to its more reliable smoothbore cousin. To the French, the smoothbore's more rapid rate of fire made up for its inaccuracy.[15] Only in 1839 would the French infantry replace their flintlocks with smoothbore, percussion-cap firearms, giving the flintlock a reign of 140 years.[16] Not until the 1850s did rifles become standard infantry issue; breach loaders came later still.

Few would deny that the era of the French Revolution witnessed a major transformation in the art of war, yet this occurred at a time when basic weapons improved in far less dramatic fashion. This fact demonstrates the fundamental truth that military technologies do not in themselves determine a single style of warfare but instead present armies with a menu of tactical possibilities. Selection of items from this menu can depend upon factors which may not be military in nature. Therefore, a shift in the style of warfare may reflect intellectual, social, institutional, or political change.

Perhaps only with the Revolution did Europeans learn the proper way to employ the muzzle-loading, smoothbore, flintlock musket and the bayonet in battle. If this observation holds true, it presents us with the paradox that not until the age of the smoothbore drew to a close did tactics evolve that properly maximized its strengths and minimized its weaknesses. But this should not surprise us. It can be argued that only with Trafalgar did the British master decisive tactics in the age of sail, and Trafalgar was the last battle that matched great fleets of ships of the line on the open sea.

The Pattern of Linear Warfare

After the War of the Spanish Succession, European armies based their tactics upon the thin line of infantry armed with fusil and bayonet. According to the *Règlement du 1er août 1791,* French regulars formed line in three ranks; therefore, a battalion of seven hundred men would stand 2 yards deep and about 160 yards long.

Several factors drove commanders to array their troops in linear order. It was a reasonable response to the limitations of the fusil. A smoothbore flintlock took considerable time to load. In the best of circumstances a skilled infantryman could discharge his musket two or three times every minute, but in the midst of battle's confusion and fear the rate of fire probably fell to something like one round per minute. Since the fusil was inaccurate at anything beyond close range, the line made the best of this weapon by packing the maximum number of infantrymen together across a given front so that every man could bring his fusil to bear against the enemy. The massed troops poured out a withering fire, while the law of averages ensured that it scored a good number of hits. On the defensive, this concentrated firepower could decimate an attacking battalion or squadron.

A linear order also allowed for a high level of troop control. Officers and NCOs could easily observe their men since they stood on open ground in only three ranks. At the same time, a thin line presented a less lucrative artillery target than a more densely packed column would have. Round shot smashing through a battalion arrayed in the standard French column could render twelve men *hors de combat* at a single blow.

There was also simply something neat and orderly about the line, making it in keeping with eighteenth-century opinion. This quality would have recommended it to officers steeped in the set of assumptions and propensities that we call the Enlightenment.

Since the line had dominated tactics for ninety years, any tactical system developed by the French in the last decade of the century could be expected to bear its stamp. Linear formations were fundamental to the conception of warfare held by French officers, and they shaped the drill regulations that guided the Revolutionary battalions. So French armies would modify, but could hardly be expected to abandon, this traditional formation.

The Military Enlightenment of
the Eighteenth Century

The second half of the eighteenth century was an era of criticism and innovation. Reformers interpreted French mid-century defeats as proof of flawed military institutions and practices. In response, they proposed major changes in everything from officer selection to tactics. Coming on the heels of this ancien régime reform movement, the Revolution promised a regeneration of all French institutions. It was a brave time in which experiments abounded.

An offspring of the Enlightenment, the Military Enlightenment bore a family resemblance, but it concentrated upon a broad range of professional and technical issues of interest to soldiers. At one extreme of the agenda, soldier-philosophes argued for a new aristocratic professionalism in the officer corps. Impassioned authors praised honor, duty, and competence, while condemning the practice of promoting wealthy men whose only qualification was the gold that allowed them to purchase expensive commissions. These critics ascribed professional commitment to the old nobility of modest means that regularly sent its sons to serve the king. Thus, the Ségur Law of 1781, which required new officers to demonstrate four generations of nobility, represented a triumph for reform. On a technological extreme of the Military Enlightenment's agenda, artillery officers feuded over the types of cannon to be employed in the field. "Reds" favored the traditional heavy pieces of the Vallière system, while "Blues" advocated the new lighter pieces proposed by Gribeauval.[17]

No debate produced more heat than the controversy over the proper tactics for French infantry, whose lackluster performance argued for a major change.[18] Two schools of opinion advanced strikingly different solutions. Proponents of the *ordre mince* praised the virtues of the line. They believed themselves justified by Prussian victories. The more extreme among them wanted to model French practices closely on those of Frederick the Great. In opposition, advocates of the *ordre profond* insisted that the column possessed the great advantages of mobility and shock. As early as 1724 the Chevalier de Folard had proposed huge unwieldy columns. In the 1750s Mesnil-Durand took up the brief for column warfare, which he dubbed the *ordre française*. His columns were less awkward than Folard's, but they were still massive.

Advocates of the column argued that the French had a natural propensity for shock combat—a style of warfare unsuited to the brittle immobility of the line. Even Voltaire contributed his opinion that "French artillery is very good, but the fire of French infantry is rarely superior and usually inferior to that of other nations. It can be said with as much truth that the French nation attacks with the greatest impetuosity and that it is very difficult to resist its shock."[19] Great commanders such as Maurice de Saxe shared this conviction as well. The most important military philosophe and a lion of the salons, the comte de Guibert spoke of his countrymen as "redoubtable in all attacks with cold steel.[20] While a believer in the value of columns, he opposed the radical departure from the linear tradition advocated by Mesnil-Durand. Guibert proposed new deployments for infantry and spoke of combining line and column in the order of battle—the *ordre mixte*.

In the midst of the paper debate, the matter was subjected to practical experiment. Troops encamped at Vaussieux on the Normandy coast carried out a large-scale test of Mesnil-Durand's system in 1778. Both Mesnil-Durand and Guibert served on the staff. Marshal Broglie, who commanded at the exercise, thought the test inconclusive, but most believed that it demonstrated the weakness of Mesnil-Durand's radical solution.

After a succession of drill books that appealed first to one school and then the other, the *Règlement du 1er août 1791* served the French throughout the Revolutionary and Napoleonic eras. The *conseil de guerre* that drafted it began to meet in 1787; Guibert served as the original secretary to the *conseil*. Therefore, the *Règlement* was not so much a creation of the Revolution as it was a product of the Military Enlightenment. Despite what some commentators have said, this *Règlement* itself did not represent a victory for the proponents of the *ordre profond* or the *ordre mixte*. Just counting pages, there is more detail on the line than on anything else. Certainly, the *Règlement* provided a variety of columns, including one called an attack column. On the whole, however, there was no particular emphasis on columns in the *Règlement*. As an advocate of the revolutionary attack commented in 1795, "movements by mass . . . are, so to speak, merely indicated in the *Règlement* of 1791."[21] Rather than close the tactical debate, the *Règlement* provided the means with which different alternatives might be put to the test of battle. It was an intelligent menu of possibilities, not a formula.

The fate of the attack column à la Guibert provides a useful commentary on the influence of the Military Enlightenment. He proposed that units advance toward the enemy in a fairly open column and deploy into line at short range to use fusil and bayonet to ultimate advantage.[22] Dumouriez tried this kind of assault as prescribed in the *Règlement* at the Battle of Jemappes. It resulted in a near disaster. As the advancing columns neared the Austrians, they halted to deploy into line; however, the fire from the Austrian defenders shook and disorganized the hard-put French troops. Even for the most experienced and best drilled of troops such a deployment under fire would have been extremely difficult, but for Dumouriez's battalions it approached the impossible.

The column made famous by the French was a different formation, a closed column by divisions, that the *Règlement* presented only for maneuver, not for attack. With this column, much broader than it was deep, troops marched straight at the enemy, never attempting to deploy into line before colliding with it. The column advocates of the Military Enlightenment clearly prepared the French to experiment with columns, but their final form was not the one prescribed by the soldier-philosophes. Rather it was one that evolved under the pressure of circumstance. The Military Enlightenment was a necessary but not sufficient cause of the new tactical system.

The Revolutionary Climate of Opinion after 1789

It would be difficult to imagine an intellectual environment more favorable to change than that of the exciting early years of the French Revolution. So many givens of French society were thrown open to question, from monarchy to marriage, how could the military escape such exuberance for innovation?

Indeed, the army was one of the institutions most profoundly affected by the Revolution. New standards of officer selection and promotion accompanied the elimination of privilege. Owing to emigration, the officer corps underwent a radical change in personnel. Of the officers serving in 1789, a mere 13 percent still wore the uniform of the Republic in 1794.[23] As the ranks swelled with volunteers and conscripts, the soldiers changed in character and motivation. Standards of military discipline and justice altered to suit the new troops. It would be going too far to claim that the Revolutionary commanders wrote on an absolutely clean slate, but they did work in an environment that favored innovation and suspected dedication to past methods.

The Commitment of the Nation to Mobilize for War

The unprecedented commitment of the French people to the defense of their ancient territory and their new society allowed the First Republic to mobilize the manpower produced by conscription and the devotion unleashed by nationalism. There is little mystery to this commitment. A great majority of the French gained from the destruction of aristocratic privilege. Peasants rejoiced in the de jure elimination of personal serfdom and the de facto end of feudal payments. Urban sansculottes seized a new-found leverage that promised political rights and economic security. The middle classes valued the advantages they gained through the recognition of legal equality and the elimination of aristocratic dominance over crucial institutions. Still, any catalog of Revolutionary gains based only on self-interest falls short because the French also experienced a spiritual identity with the nation and the state that no coldly rational list can express.

When they believed their Revolution threatened by an alliance of conservative powers, the French people saw the war effort as a defense of their own interests and convictions. As such, they encouraged, or at least allowed, their government to tap the full resources of society in terms of wealth, manpower, and emotional energy. While this mobilization met pockets of resistance, notably in the Vendée, its success was still overwhelming.

The French staked their lives and fortunes on the defense of the Republic. Now the government could summon the entire population to contribute to the war effort. At first, the assemblies relied only upon volunteers to swell the ranks. Certainly the choice to enroll for service bore witness to a high level of devotion among those individuals who did so. However, calling for volunteers was the path of least resistance for elected representatives since it aroused minimal public controversy and required minimal administrative effort. After voluntary enlistments provided the first waves of recruits, the government turned to conscription to guarantee an overwhelming flow of manpower. Conscription required the difficult decision to limit the hard-won freedoms of the French people by compelling young men to shoulder a musket. The National Convention did not make this choice lightly, so the fact that the representatives of the people voted for large-scale conscription testified to the dedication of the nation as a whole.

Those volunteers and conscripts who fought under the Tricolor differed from their enemies in more than numbers. It has become commonplace to speak of the enthusiasm of Republican troops. While contemporary rhetorical praise may overstate the case, there is no question that the troops who fought during the first few years of the war had a special élan that added to the force of their column attacks. At the same time, men who believed that the outcome of the war would have a profound effect on their own interests could be counted upon to show initiative in the field. Constant supervision was not thought necessary, so French commanders were more willing to throw out screens of skirmishers to fight as isolated marksmen or in small groups. This either made the tactics of the *tirailleur* possible or, more likely, thinkable, thus breaking the patterns of military conception in the eighteenth century. To this degree the usual arguments about the ties between political sentiment and tactics hold up.

The Influx of Recruits into the Army

Without doubt, there was little polish to Revolutionary troops, and the arrival of large numbers of unskilled levies put a tremendous strain on units and commanders. But is it fair to assert that rapid growth of the rank and file necessarily brought chaos and incompetence?

Timing alone challenges the influx argument. The Revolutionary attack, with its skirmishers, artillery, and columns, was well along the way to becoming a basic element of the tactical system in the fall of 1792, when the main combat force was composed of line regiments and battalions of the Volunteers of 1791. It would be hard to call the Volunteers of 1791 a flood of raw recruits; they were not a flood, since they numbered only about 100,000, and they were not raw, since they were supposed to be National Guard members. On the contrary, by the fall of 1792 the 1791 levy in the Nord comprised a body of reasonably skilled and experienced troops. The Volunteers of 1792, probably numbering in excess of 200,000, might qualify as a mass of unskilled men; however, they did not make their appearance before the late summer or autumn, and even then they were rarely engaged in action until 1793.[24] Still later came the roughly 150,000 recruits raised by the ill-titled "Levy of 300,000" decreed in February 1793 and the approximately 300,000 conscripts produced by the August 1793 *levée en masse*.[25] But the record establishes that before they arrived the tactical choices had been made.

Another way to challenge the influx argument is to examine certain givens in the train of logic behind it. The traditional position is based on several assumptions: that fighting as a skirmisher required few military skills, and these could be quickly taught to anyone; that the column placed less demands on soldiers than the line did, so it too could be quickly mastered; and that new men were put into combat without adequate time for training.

The notion that skirmishing was a "natural" method of combat requiring little formal training, and that, therefore, it suited the unskilled but devoted Revolutionary soldier must be questioned. Granted, French military pundits believed that you could not teach the skills of the *tirailleur* from a drill book, which explains why so little reference was made to open-order tactics in the *Règlement*. However, most commanders argued that skirmishing was best left to veterans, not to ill-trained novices.[26] While entire line battalions might disperse as skirmishers, should circumstance demand it, as at Hondschoote, if given the choice, commanders preferred to restrict open-order combat to specialists — either men from light infantry battalions or picked men from line companies. Why? On the one hand, commanders saw open-order tactics as a threat to the cohesion of their units. On the other hand, they recognized that *tirailleurs* required great skill — a skill learned in the field, not on the parade ground. In addition, skirmishers had to rely more on the kind of cohesion that only grows with time and experience. They, not troops in line or column, had to deal with what S. L. A. Marshall called the "isolation of the battlefield."[27] So *tirailleurs* were regarded as an elite, not as a lowest common denominator.

If the tactics of the skirmisher were not suited to the raw recruit, were those of the column? Not necessarily. It is reasonable to argue that it would have been easier for a novice battalion to stand in line than to maneuver in column. Given a body of only partially trained recruits, the simplest thing to do with them would have been to put them in that most basic of prepackaged battlefield formations, the line. In a line they could be easily supervised, and as long as they could load their fusils, they would have some military value. The compact column was clearly a more nimble formation, but to march in column still demanded more skill than to stand motionless in line. Remember, the column was a formation, not a mob. To be sure, the ranks within the column might break down in rapid maneuver, but they ought not to be lost altogether. Units were expected to deploy out of the attack column, so they ought to maintain order in it.

The Emphasis upon Training

The most damaging criticism of the influx argument is the fact that raw recruits were rarely put into battle before they had acquired the rudiments of training. From late 1791 through early 1793 recruits arrived as integral battalions. These battalions usually occupied garrisons or camps behind the lines and armed and drilled before moving up to face the enemy in a field army. Take for example the 1st Haute-Marne. Formed in August 1792, it did not leave its native department until April 1793 and did not enter combat until August—a full year after muster. One recruit in this battalion described the spring of 1793 as a time of intense instruction.[28]

Recruits who came to the front as part of the February 1793 Levy of 300,000 or the August 1793 *levée en masse* were distributed to existing battalions, where veterans could leaven the new men. How long did it take to create a trained infantryman in such circumstances? The military savant, General Félix de Wimpffen gave this estimate: "Everybody knows . . . infantry recruits with six weeks service are in a condition to serve usefully, when they are incorporated with veterans."[29] Later, no less an authority than Napoleon stated, "Infantrymen, after three months of service, ought to be first class in maneuver and able to undergo fire as well as the others."[30] These statements need not be taken as gospel; they are presented only as an antidote to the notion that the French could not possibly have fielded competent battalions because of the limitations of time and the demands of numbers.

Revolutionary commanders put a high premium on training; Rochambeau, Dumouriez, Custine, and Jourdan deserve special notice as being insistent on time spent in drill. Documents at the Archives de la Guerre establish that commanders did everything in their power to ensure that troops drilled regularly (usually twice a day, if war and weather permitted). During his tenure as commander of the Nord, Custine formed a special training camp at Cambrai under the direction of General Meunier. It was designed to create over a thousand new trainers for the army and to regularize such details as march-step and column deployment.[31] Jourdan, who literally put his head on the line by insisting that his troops devote the winter of 1793–94 to training, even ordered troops to train in barns if rain or cold made it impossible to drill out of doors.[32] These Revolutionary generals also recognized that units needed to gain some field experience under controlled conditions, so they encouraged small-scale actions to acclimatize troops to combat.

It is reasonable to expect that company grade officers shared their generals' concern with training. Consider that the majority of the company grade officers had experience in the old army, as rankers or NCOs. For example, 60 percent of the infantry captains of 1794 had served in the army before the Revolution, and half had at least nine years service before 1789; 55 percent of the captains had served as corporals in the old army, while only 4.6 percent had been officers.[33] The surprisingly high percentage of experienced soldiers in company grade slots may suggest a functional level of competency in company and battalion drill since, in a sense, the army of Revolutionary France was an army commanded by drill sergeants.

At this point it is important to recognize that the commitment of the rank and file expressed itself in the energy they devoted to training. Observers at the time noted how intensely the new recruits applied themselves to military training and how quickly they improved in drill-book matters. Representatives on mission, Celliez and Varin reported to Bouchotte, "The soldiers devote themselves to drill with an indefatigable zeal." The result of such efforts was that "the veteran soldiers are astonished when they see the precision with which our volunteers maneuver."[34] To the degree that troops believed that it was necessary to master the manual of arms and basic maneuvers before they could be of use to the Republic, the same commitment that made them spirited in the charge and the same initiative that made them responsible and resourceful as skirmishers could cause them to apply themselves to learning traditional military arts. By all accounts they did.

There is no question that the influx of recruits exerted pressures on the tactical system. First, they made it necessary to keep things simpler than otherwise might have been the case. But this did not mean that the French were condemned to clumsy "horde tactics." Second, periodic arrivals of new units or new men caused the level of tactical ability to fluctuate over time and from unit to unit. Third, Republican battalions did not master the details of drill to the level practiced both by ancien régime units and of the later Grande Armée. However, the soldiers of the First Republic did not have to perfect every deployment in the *Règlement du 1er août 1791* in order to conduct themselves on the battlefield in a rational and orderly fashion. Prudent commanders selected a small and practical list of formations and deployments from the vast repertoire of the *Règlement,* and within that list the troops could be expected to perform in workmanlike manner. This gets us back to the matter of selection.

The Cadre of Military Leaders
Who Advocated Innovation

The Revolutionary attack was not simply determined by the pressure of circumstance, although that pressure's influence was significant. Questions of necessity, such as technological determinacy or the influx of recruits, ought to be depreciated, and the value of choice in the development of tactical patterns ought to be emphasized. Therefore, it is important to consider those who made the choices. In short, we need to look at the officer corps, both the major commanders and the entire corps as a professional body.

It is useful to trace the ties that bound many major Revolutionary commanders to the Military Enlightenment, with its debates over new tactical forms. Officers who held high rank in the Nord were unquestionably aware of the column/line debate. Consider the central figure of Dumouriez, for example. He was an intimate of Guibert. Commenting on that military intellectual's taste for the salons, Dumouriez wrote to his friend, "We are like the mice of the fable, you are the city mouse and I am the country mouse."[35] While he served as Minister of War, before he ever joined the Nord, Dumouriez advised Luckner to put his volunteers in column.[36] Later, as commander of the Nord at Jemappes, Dumouriez followed Guibert's system, which prescribed that attack columns deploy into line before closing with the enemy. As already explained, this turned out to be a mistake, and it would not be the attack column à la Guibert that triumphed.

Frankly, it would be hard for a professional of the late eighteenth century to avoid the controversy over tactical forms, since it expressed itself not only in a body of critical literature but in drill books and field tests as well. Both Luckner and Rochambeau, for example, served as generals at the camp at Vaussieux.[37]

Revolution brought even more profound change to the officer corps than it did to the rank and file. In 1789 roughly 90 percent of officers were from aristocratic families; by mid-1794 this figure had fallen to 2 or 3 percent.[38] As already stated, nearly 90 percent of officers serving in 1789 had left the service by 1794.

It is reasonable to assume that those experienced officers who remained, and who often held high rank, were open to experimentation and change. Certainly, political conservatives, those with an inflexible devotion to the ancien régime, could be expected to leave the army after June 1791. It may be reasonable to expect a degree of professional conservatism to have left with them. Conversely, perhaps professional liberalism went hand in hand with political liberalism among those who opted to throw in their lot with the new state. This was certainly the case with Dumouriez and Jourdan. Of course, this is speculation, but it would be unreasonable to dismiss it in a cavalier manner.

Looking at the new officer corps as a whole, the percentage of officers serving in 1794 who had been officers in 1789 varied by rank. While 43 percent of generals had been officers in 1789, among colonels this figure fell to 40 percent; for captains the figure was a scant 5 percent. With such turnover within the cadre, particularly among company grade officers, it is not unfair to speak of a kind of tabula rasa within the officer corps. There is no reason to believe that revolutionary officers had any particular stake in maintaining the tactical practices of the ancien régime. They owed their commands to the Revolution, rather than to their position in the ancien régime.

Add to this tabula rasa effect the revolutionary climate of opinion already mentioned, and innovation appears more inevitable than surprising. Those commanders who inherited experimental concepts of maneuver and attack from the Military Enlightenment, and who confronted a rapid influx of new levies composed of troops of a kind Europe had not seen before, were free from the social and intellectual bounds of the military modus operandi of the ancien régime—free to forge a new tactical system that carried the Republic to victory.

The Political Influences Favoring the Revolutionary Attack

An analysis of the influence exerted by the last factor to be considered here—the climate of political opinion—must by nature be highly speculative, and it will be labeled as such. Yet, clearly, political opinion had an impact on tactical development, though one that, by the nature of things, is hard to trace.

The cult of the bayonet was full of political overtones. Of course, the very atmosphere seemed to be politically charged during the Revolutionary years. With so much being read as political, it would have been a small wonder if something as vital as military doctrine escaped this reading. It is reasonable to suggest that representatives of the government exerted subtle and not so subtle influences upon those who were to make the tactical choices for the armies in the field.

The National Assembly, Legislative Assembly, and National Convention and their committees thought it apropos to speak of military matters beyond declarations of war or questions of finance. They devoted time to military discipline, manpower procurement, and to the proper choice of weapons and tactics. They heard members even praise the pike as a weapon particularly suited to French lads and voted to buy this weapon in large quantities.[39] The influential publication of the Convention, the *Bulletin,* repeatedly described Republican victories as if there were a formula for victory. General Maximilien Foy complained, "The people . . . reading in the *Bulletin of the Convention* only stories of battalions in mass, lines broken through, and redoubts assaulted at the charge innocently believed that fusils and cannon had lost their value, and that all was taken with the bayonet."[40]

The Committee of Public Safety went on record in 1794 proclaiming that "the success of our arms is due primarily to the use of the bayonet."[41] This declaration reveals the hand of the committee's most influential military figure, Lazare Carnot. When he drafted a plan of operations for the spring of 1794, he directed that commanders "on every occasion engage in combat with the bayonet."[42] As we have already seen, Bouchotte, the Hébertist minister of war, echoed such sentiments. Representatives on mission and *commissaires* of the Ministry of War encouraged the Revolutionary attack. A Jacobin representative, Delbrel, wrote at the front, "Every time we have attacked we have won, and . . . every time we have been attacked we have almost always been defeated."[43]

There is no question that the government expressed a tactical policy. Was it a time when an officer could afford to take such a policy lightly? Hardly. Military commanders were under constant scrutiny, particularly after Dumouriez turned on the Parisian government. After two commanders of the Nord fled their posts for political reasons—Lafayette and Dumouriez—one former commander, Luckner, and two active commanders of the Nord, Custine and Houchard, went to the guillotine. Immediately after the treason of Dumouriez, the government ordered that the families of all officers serving with the Nord be put under a kind of detention as hostages to the officers' conduct.

It would have required extreme thick-headedness to be oblivious to the risks involved in giving off the wrong political signs. An officer's conduct was put under a microscope: small matters such as the continued use of uniform buttons stamped with the fleur-de-lis instead of a republican symbol could cause the dreaded *commissaires* to accuse an officer of incivism.[44] At a time when officers could be put to death for wearing the wrong buttons, is it too much to suppose that the government's promotion of a particular tactical doctrine of the offensive encouraged the use of the attack column?

In addition, the adamant praise of the bayonet found in military correspondence may have been put there precisely because officers were aware that correspondence might be read by the *commissaires*. Praise of the offensive and the bayonet may well have been a way of demonstrating that one possessed acceptable sentiments. So we see a very technical tactical report by the highly professional Meunier preceded by a banner headline in unusually large script "Bayonet and Republic."[45]

The rhetoric of the cult of the bayonet overstated the reality. However, to deny that such rhetoric was an accurate description of tactical reality does not exclude the possibility that it influenced the form of that reality.

Conclusion

Examination of the tactical system that won the great victories of 1794 is more important than mere antiquarian concern with past military techniques, for the mythology surrounding that system played a major role in determining tactical choices for the next century.

In particular, to explore the nature and evolution of the headlong assault is to probe the factual basis for an influential French conception of warfare. Developed as a tactical expedient that met the practical demands of the battlefield within the context of weapons technology, military theory, and political ideology, the revolutionary attack was immediately enshrined in patriotic legend. Indeed, from the start, the popular image of the column assault mixed fact with myth. This is what makes it such a fascinating, and at times frustrating, subject of study.

The perception, or misperception of a Republican formula for victory became an important statement of faith in the cult of the bayonet. To be sure, tactical doctrine oscillated during the 1800s. At times it emphasized the effects of firepower and maneuver in the "defensive-offensive."[46] However, in or out of favor, the cult of the bayonet was never without its devotees. Official doctrine just prior to the Franco-Prussian war directed, "No fire, but a determined advance to close on the enemy with bayonet and at the charge."[47] A more cautious and fire-oriented doctrine replaced this immediately following the war, but the shock attack regained its primacy by the mid-1880s. Briefly set back by French reaction to the Boer War, it would triumph again in the decade before World War I.

In the early twentieth century, the history of the armies of the First Republic became part of the military and political debates over defense policy and tactical doctrine. Jean Colin's important works on eighteenth-century infantry tactics can be seen as attempts by one professional soldier and historian to discredit the cult of the bayonet.[48] He called upon the past as an ally to resist present partisans of mass assaults in an age when machine guns and rapid firing artillery had rendered such tactics suicidal. However, his efforts met with little success. Instead, the popular notion of Revolutionary victory was used to buttress a French self-image of their armies as inspired and irresistible.

Over the decade preceding World War I, proponents of the tactical offensive came to dominate the army. Ferdinand Foch, the future Marshal of France, was a pivotal figure among them, but the ultimate high priest of the offensive à outrance was Colonel de Grandmaison. Today when the subject of European military institutions on the eve of World War I is enjoying renewed attention, it is appropriate to recognize that French conceptions of warfare in the Third Republic bore the stamp of a mythology born in the First. The continuity is startling. Consider this passage from the 1913 Regulation Concerning the Command of Large Units, written under the influence of Grandmaison. It reads like the directive by Bouchotte that began this essay: "The French army, returning to its traditions, no longer knows any other law than the offensive.... All attacks are to be pushed to the extreme ... to charge the enemy with the bayonet in order to destroy him."[49]

NOTES

1. Archives de la Guerre (AG), MR 6081, Jourdan, "Mémoires militaires."
2. The most important volumes in this new scholarly literature are Samuel F. Scott, *The Response of the Royal Army to the French Revolution: The Role and Development of the Line Army 1787–93* (Oxford, 1978); Jean-Paul Bertaud, *La*

Révolution armée: Les soldat-citoyens et la Révolution française (Paris, 1979); and Isser Woloch, *The French Veteran from the Revolution to the Restoration* (Chapel Hill, N.C., 1979). Consider as well the fine Jean-Paul Bertaud, *La vie quotidienne des soldat de la Révolution, 1789–1799* (Paris, 1985), a more popular approach to the subject.

3. John A. Lynn, *The Bayonets of the Republic: Motivation and Tactics in the Army of Revolutionary France, 1791–1794* (Champaign, Ill., 1984). Unless otherwise noted, all descriptions of motivation, training, and tactics are taken from this volume.

4. Some argue that artillery was crucial. For an example of such arguments see Richard A. Preston and Sydney F. Wise, *Men in Arms*, 4th ed. (New York, 1979), 181–82.

5. David G. Chandler, *The Campaigns of Napoleon* (New York, 1966), 67.

6. Ibid.

7. It is only fair to point out that since 1970 three works have appeared that presented more balanced, and more accurate, views of the Revolutionary tactics. Two of these, Jean-Paul Bertaud, *La Révolution armée*, and Steven Ross, *From Flintlock to Rifle* (London, 1979) derived their treatments from my dissertation. The third, Gunther Rothenberg, *The Art of War in the Age of Napoleon* (Bloomington, Ind., 1970) seems to have reached the proper conclusions by the very sensible method of splitting the difference between extreme opinions.

8. In his *La tactique et la discipline dans les armées de la Révolution: Correspondance du général Schauenbourg du 4 avril au 2 août 1793* (Paris, 1902), Jean Colin insisted that the French relied upon the line to the exclusion of the column. He wrote, "attack columns and mass formations were abandoned for some time; at least we no longer find any trace of them in 1793 and 1794." Colin, lxiv. Here this excellent soldier-historian was flat wrong, since the Armée du Nord regularly employed columns on the offensive. Perhaps the Armée de la Mozelle, upon which Colin based his generalizations, pursued a different tactical course than the Nord did.

9. The most detailed discussion of Gribeauval's work is Howard Rosen, "The System Gribeauval: A Study of Technological Development and Institutional Change in Eighteenth-Century France," Ph.D. diss., University of Chicago, 1981. He stresses the system as a whole, rather than just the technical ameliorations of artillery. Brief descriptions of the Gribeauval reforms are contained in Robert S. Quimby, *The Background of Napoleonic Warfare* (New York, 1957), and Matti Lauerma, *L'artillerie de campagne française pendant les guerres de la Révolution* (Helsinki, 1956).

10. Certainly, the historian of revolutionary artillery, Matti Lauerma, denies that French artillery dominated the battlefield early in the war, with the obvious exception of Valmy.

11. Although it is often stated that the artillery did not suffer much from officer turnover during the Revolution, this is not true. By April 1794, 81 percent of the artillery officers of July 1789 were no longer in uniform; even though the comparable figure for infantry was higher, 95 percent, the artillery still witnessed an exodus of its old officers. Given the high level of education and training required by the artillery, this exodus was probably particularly damaging. G. Bodinier, "Les

officiers de l'armée royale et la Révolution," in *Le métier militaire en France aux époques des grandes transformations sociales,* ed. André Corvisier (Vincennes, 1980), 68.

12. On the manufacture of cannon during the Revolution see Camille Richard, *Le Comité de Salut public et les fabrications de guerre sous la terreur* (Paris, 1922), especially chapter VI, "Les fonderies en bronze," 228–76. Before the Revolution the French had only two foundries for field guns, at Douai and Strasbourg. By September 1794 Paris alone boasted six new foundries, and there were thirteen more in the Departments. Did this multiplication of manufacture maintain the high standards necessary for the Gribeauval system? Research is still required to establish whether it did or not; however, Richard supplies several examples of complaints about the quality of guns produced in the new foundries.

13. Gabriel Hanoteau, ed., *Histoire de la nation française,* tome 7, *Histoire militaire et navale,* 2 vols. (Paris, 1925), 1:435–36. Bernard Brodie and Fawn Brodie, *From Crossbow to H-Bomb* (New York, 1962), 181, say the switch came in the 1680s, and Richard A. Preston and Sydney F. Wise, *Men in Arms,* 4th ed. (New York, 1979), 244, date it at 1690.

14. Hanoteau, 1:436.

15. The tactical experts Generals Hugues Meunier and Philibert Duhesme both favored the smoothbore carbine as the best light infantry weapon. AG, MR 2041, Meunier, "Changements," and Duhesme in Peter Paret, *Yorck and the Era of Prussian Reform* (Princeton, 1966), 272. See report by Scharnhorst on field test of smoothbore and rifled weapons in Paret 271–73.

16. Hanoteau, 2:266.

17. Several works deal at length with the Military Enlightenment in France. On questions of professionalism, the status of the army, and officer selection see Emile G. Léonard, *L'Armée et ses problèmes au XVIIIe siècle* (Paris, 1958), and relevant chapters of Jean Chagniot, *Paris et l'armée au XVIIIe siècle* (Paris, 1985). On the Ségur Law see David D. Bien, "La réaction aristocratique avant 1789: l'exemple de l'armée," *Annales, économies, sociétés, civilisations* 29 (1974): 23–48, 505–34. On organizational reform see Albert Latreille, *L'oeuvre militaire de la Révolution: L'armée et la nation à la fin de l'ancien régime* (Paris, 1914). For a brief overview of reform measures in English, see John A. Lynn, "A Pattern of French Military Reform, 1750–1790: Speculations Concerning the Officer Corps," *Proceedings of the Consortium on Revolutionary Europe* (Gainesville, Fla., 1979), 113–28.

18. On tactical debates concerning infantry see the excellent Jean Colin, *L'infanterie au XVIIIe siècle: La tactique* (Paris, 1907), and Robert S. Quimby, *The Background of Napoleonic Warfare* (New York, 1957).

19. Voltaire in Léonard, 235.

20. Jacques Antoine Hippolyte de Guibert, *Essai général de tactique,* vol. 1 (London, 1773), 7.

21. Hugues Meunier, *Rapport fait au ministre de la guerre par son ordre sur l'instruction du général Schauenburg, concernant les exercices et manoeuvres de l'infanterie* (Paris, an VII), 17.

22. For those who desire a technical description of the Guibertian attack column of the *Règlement,* it was formed by the companies on either flank forming a

column behind the two center companies. It was defined as a "double column." The interval between the companies stacked one behind the other equalled half the front of the company, that is, a fairly big interval. The interval was necessary to allow for deployment at close range. The column which served the Revolutionary armies as their attack column in reality was formed in a different manner, with an interval of only two yards, or the depth of a company.

23. Bodinier, 67–68.

24. Concerning the size of the contingent raised by the Volunteers of 1792, see Lynn, *Bayonets of the Republic*, 52.

25. On the Levy of 300,000 and the *levée en masse*, see Bertaud, *La Révolution armée*, 101–3, 137.

26. See the discussion in Lynn, *Bayonets of the Republic*, 265–68. It is interesting to compare French preferences with those of the Army of Flanders two hundred years before. Geoffrey Parker states how Alva believed that while any troops could fight in a pitched battle, only skilled veterans could be counted on for "actions," the term for small-scale engagements and skirmishing. Geoffrey Parker, *The Army of Flanders and the Spanish Road* (Cambridge, 1972), 13.

27. See the discussion of the isolation of the battlefield in S. L. A. Marshall, *Men Against Fire* (Gloucester, Mass., 1978).

28. For information concerning the position and strength of the 1st Haute-Marne, see situation reports in AG, B¹*250 and B¹*251. Jacques Fricasse provides a personal view of this battalion in his *Journal de Marche du sergent Fricasse* (Paris, 1882).

29. Address to the National Convention, 15 December 1789, in *Archives parlementaires,* première serie, ed. J. Mandival and E. Lauent, 10:587.

30. In Jean Morvan, *Le soldat impériale,* vol. 1 (Paris, 1904), 282.

31. Hugues Meunier's "Changements en errata au *Règlement de 1791*," AG, MR 2041, is based on his tenure in command of this training camp.

32. AG, B¹*223, 20 December 1793.

33. Bertaud, *La Révolution armée*, 183.

34. AG, B¹13, 5 June 1793.

35. Arthur Chuquet, *Dumouriez* (Paris, 1914).

36. Eugène Carrias, *La Pensée militaire française* (Paris, 1960), 205.

37. Quimby, 233.

38. Figures for the composition of the officer corps have been taken from Jean-Paul Bertaud, *La Révolution armée*, Bodinier, and Scott.

39. See John A. Lynn, "French Opinion and the Military Resurrection of the Pike, 1792–1794," *Military Affairs* 41 (February 1977): 1–7.

40. Maximilien Foy, *Histoire des querres de la Péninsule* (Paris, 1827), 1:101.

41. Committee of Public Safety decree of 4 March 1794 in H. Coutanceau and H. Lepus, *La campagne de 1794 à l'armée du Nord*, part 1, vol. 1 (Paris, 1903), 404.

42. Carnot in H. Coutanceau and Clément de Jonquière, *La campagne de 1794 à l'armée du Nord,* part 2, vol. 1 (Paris, 1908), 5.

43. AG, B¹19, 23 September 1793.

44. For an example of orders concerning buttons, see AG, B¹*121, 11 August 1793.

45. AG, MR 2041, Meunier, "Changements."

46. See B. H. Liddell Hart, "French Military Ideas before the First World War," in *A Century of Conflict,* ed. Martin Gilbert (New York, 1967), 135–48; Douglas Porch, "The French Army and the Spirit of the Offensive," *War and Society,* eds. Brian Bond and Ian Roy (New York, 1975), 117–43; Jonathan House, "The Defensive-Offensive: A New Look at French Infantry Tactics on the Eve of World War I," *Military Affairs* 30, no. 4 (December 1976): 164–68; and Joseph Arnold, "French Tactical Doctrine 1870–1914," *Military Affairs* 42, no. 2 (April 1978): 61–67.

47. Quoted in Liddell Hart, 141.

48. These works include both his *L'infanterie au XVIIIe siècle: La tactique,* already cited, and his *La tactique et la discipline dans les armées de la Révolution* (Paris, 1902).

49. Quoted in Liddell Hart, 140.

Weapons and Ideas in the Prussian Army from Frederick the Great to Moltke the Elder

DENNIS SHOWALTER

THE TIME FRAME of this volume encourages interrelated revisions of Prussian/German military history. Scholars continue to describe the army as the single most powerful embodiment of preindustrial mentalités and behaviors in modern Germany. Soldiers are presented as extending Junker traditions far beyond their time, into the nineteenth and twentieth centuries. According to conventional wisdom, a Prussian army that at mid-eighteenth century stood as a model for Europe decayed because of stubborn reliance on increasingly outmoded forms of war. Swept away in the cataclysm of 1806, it rose like a phoenix during the Wars of Liberation, thanks to the efforts of the reform movement. From 1815 to 1860, however, the Prussian army was reshaped by a generation that sacrificed the humanistic visions of the Era of Reform to caste concerns imperfectly masked by an increasingly rigid, increasingly narrow professionalism. The operational efficiency demonstrated in the Wars of Unification was correspondingly misleading — a superficial manifestation camouflaging the system's fundamental unfitness to meet the tests of total war and people's war applied from 1914 to 1918.[1]

A survey of Prussian military history from Frederick the Great to Moltke the Elder suggests an alternative interpretation. Prussia's policies between 1740 and 1860 were determined in principle and in detail by a common set of factors growing out of her dual status as a German *Kleinstaat* and a European power. The year 1806 was not a turning point the army simply missed. Instead, the military reforms both confirmed tendencies and concerns a half-century old and carried them forward as a kingdom became an empire.

I

Among possible areas illustrating this thesis, technology stands out. Its exact relationship to military performance remains problematic. In the aftermath of World War I, the soldiers of nineteenth-century Europe have been commonly derided as romantics in an industrial age, blind alike to the constraints and the opportunities offered by modern technology.[2] On the other hand, a recent wave of criticism has washed over military establishments, alleging that they are obsessed by machinery, that they sacrifice war's intellectual and moral elements to soulless bean-counting and allow techniques to replace the human factor.[3] David Mets has presciently suggested that this backlash reflects undue preoccupation with the Korean and Vietnam experiences. There have been times, he argues, when technology was in fact among war's decisive factors. There have been other times when it might have been decisive, but decision makers were unready to accept it.[4]

The first key in evaluating military technology's importance to Prussia's evolution involves reexamining the military career of Frederick the Great—a career whose parameters were, until recently, set by the nineteenth-century *Federkrieg* between Hans Delbrück and the uniformed historians of the German General Staff. Delbrück's insistence on the French Revolution as a watershed between limited and total war was paralleled by the General Staff's presentation of Frederick as a seeker of decisive victories in the Napoleonic model.[5]

The debate over Frederick as a proponent of *Niederwerfungsstrategie* or *Ermattungsstrategie* significantly obscured the matrix of the Prussian way of war. The growth of particularist absolutism in Germany in the century following the Treaties of Westphalia was accompanied by a flourishing of paternalism. In part this paternalism was a legacy of the Lutheran and Calvinist Reformations, with their respective emphases on a ruler's obligations before God to his subjects. In part it reflected the survival of estates that were able, even if they no longer formally assembled, to exercise significant restraints on the exercise of central power. Stronger in central Europe than across either the Rhine or the Vistula, paternalism implied both control of and concern for the welfare of a ruler's—and, eventually, an administration's—subjects. But it was most consistently manifested in issues of state security.[6]

The increasing focus of German historians on questions of domestic politics has combined with the growing popularity of presenting history as the long duration of trivia to push diplomatic and military problems off their traditional place at stage center. Yet for the governments and the peoples of eighteenth-century Germany, defense was at once a sine qua non and a ne plus ultra. Folk and institutional memories of the Thirty Years' War had lost nothing through recording and repetition. They were reinforced by more immediate experiences at the hands of the armies of Louis XIV. The limited wars of the eighteenth century were limited only by comparison to their predecessors. Armies still fed themselves largely from the countryside. If they did so by contributions and requisitions rather than simple pillage, the results could be no less devastating. The new style of damage involved not destruction, but exhaustion. Demands for food and cash, for labor, housing, and not least, for wagons and animals, impoverished any region unfortunate enough to be fought over or camped in for any length of time.[7]

While it is an exaggeration to apply abstract, social-contract theories to the German states of the eighteenth century, it is nevertheless appropriate to speak of a mutual understanding between rulers and subjects that the crucial function of government—the principal legitimator of its expanding authority, overriding even the claims of domestic reform—was to provide security against external foes.[8] The problem was exacerbated by the fact that the small size of the post-Westphalian states made literal self-defense impossible. German rulers of the Age of Absolutism would have applauded the lines written by Oscar Hammerstein and delivered so unforgettably by Yul Brynner:

> Shall I join with other nations in alliance?
> If allies are weak, am I not best alone?
> If allies are strong with power to protect me,
> Might they not "protect" me out of all I own?

The challenge lay in building a state too powerful to be ignored or abandoned without significant risk. The process involved a broad spectrum of activities. In the absence of central authority and central institutions, economic recovery and economic development in eighteenth-century Germany devolved to the individual states. Their role was further enhanced by the religious settlements of 1648, which diverted significant political and intellectual energies into sustaining details of the theological status quo, while encouraging service-minded men to seek opportunities in the secular world.

This represented a new and vital growth. The "well-ordered police state" of the eighteenth century was sufficiently confident and coherent to transform the Enlightenment into a public manifestation. Enlightened principles penetrated Germany in the context of a developing government apparatus. The territorial princes demanded academic training for their officials in order to improve the utilization of their limited human and material resources. They found support among reformers who saw influencing administrations as a major way to effect quick and enduring changes. The states of absolutist Germany did not usurp private initiatives. Rather they preempted them, as the new cameral sciences fell more and more under the regulatory power of the government.[9]

The effects and legacies of this pattern were most remarkable in Prussia. In the century from Frederick the Great to Moltke the Elder, Prussia's geographic and diplomatic position made it either the hammer or the anvil of central Europe—particularly after the decline of Sweden left that dual role vacant in the minds of statesmen and princes.[10] This uncomfortable position was both a cause and a consequence of Prussia's military structure. The buildup begun by Frederick William I took Prussia well beyond the parameters of a military middle power. Hesse-Kassel is only the most familiar of those German states whose armed forces were large enough and efficient enough to encourage the cultivation of those states as more or less permanent clients by a great power, yet which remained too small to exert an independent influence in any major war.[11] The Prussian army, however, increasingly became a dangerous adversary in its own right. She posed a particular objective challenge to both France and Austria, as being too powerful to be a trustworthy second on the diplomatic dueling ground.

Frederick William I adopted, from principle as well as out of pragmatism, a foreign policy of conciliation—of not merely standing well with his more powerful neighbors but of reassuring them of his essential goodwill at every opportunity, while pursuing only modest territorial goals.[12] Such volitional affirmations, however, were heavily discounted in an age dominated by *l'esprit géométrique* and its emphasis on objective calculations. Nor did eighteenth-century diplomacy foster harmony of interests. Europe's foreign offices contemplated with equanimity the dismantling of such great powers as Spain or Austria. Sweden and the Ottoman Empire suffered major territorial losses. Poland disappeared from the map altogether. It was scarcely unreasonable for Prussia to act on the aphorism later attributed to Bismarck, that the pike in Europe's fish pond prevented her from becoming a carp.[13]

Perception of the situation was only the first step. Whatever its claims to European power after 1740, the Kingdom of Prussia remained an underdeveloped nation—underdeveloped even by German standards. The fine-tuning of Frederick William I and Frederick II only increased Prussia's vulnerability to the disruptions of a long war. State identity and state loyalty in the widely extended kingdom remained strongly instrumental, reflecting the provision of security from foreign invasion and domestic disorder as much as any common positive commitment. Military strength and diplomatic influence coexisted with an economy that lagged significantly behind that of other great powers. Mirabeau's famous aphorism that Prussia was an army in possession of its own state reflected a fact as familiar to Prussia's potential foes as it was to Prussia's government: the immense strain Prussia's peacetime military establishment placed on its resources. Furloughing conscripts for most of the year, encouraging or requiring soldiers to take jobs in the civil economy during off-duty hours, freeing an increasingly broad spectrum of the population from any civic obligations beyond paying taxes for the army's upkeep—these policies only highlighted Prussia's status as the major power least capable of sustaining a war of attrition of the kind Europe had known as its norm since the Renaissance.[14]

In this context, it is important to remember that Prussia was on the far end of a spectrum rather than in a category by itself. The persistence, indeed the prevalence, of attritional war in the eighteenth century was a product of necessity rather than an affirmation of choice. No preindustrial system possessed enough mobilizable resources to deliberately waste them in such a cavalier fashion. For this reason, war was increasingly perceived as involving the direct control of territory for the purpose of mobilizing its human and economic resources. Sieges were giving way to field operations, particularly in central Europe. There the growing size and limited budgets of the new monarchies combined to make impossible the dense network of fortresses covering such traditional, and wealthy, centers of conflict as Flanders and northern Italy. As field armies increased in size, professionalism, and reliability, they offered an alternative, and far more flexible, benchmark for evaluating a state's power. Regular pay and systematic management, comprehensive logistics and bureaucratized discipline—these provided the kinds of certainties once only given by permanent fortifications.[15]

They also provided a matrix for decisive operational action. The military logic of the Age of Reason combined with commonsense evaluation of Prussia's strategic and economic position to suggest that the state's optimal force structure should be front-loaded: geared for maximum immediate efficiency to produce maximum immediate results. But the catalytic agent for institutionalizing this concept was Frederick II himself. Before 1740 he was essentially a book soldier whose knowledge of the craft of war had been developed by studying basic contemporary and classical sources on the subject. These works were less likely to describe war as the province of confusion than to assert the necessity for control, for fighting at one's own choice on one's own ground, for keeping troops and subordinate commanders alike carefully in hand, for developing and executing plans of battle and campaign. As much to the point, these treatises insisted such control was possible—at least for a great captain.[16]

Frederick's emphasis on control reflected his belief that wars were best fought in a context of clear, positive goals susceptible of becoming subjects for negotiation. The First Silesian War is a prime example. It involved direct territorial acquisition: the redrawing of lines on a map. The Second Silesian War was influenced, if not determined, by Frederick's concern for Prussia's position in a European power structure whose equilibrium seemed to be at significant risk. The Seven Years' War was, even more than its predecessor, a preventive war against a coalition that at the least debated plans to wipe Prussia from the map of Europe.[17] But even in the later conflicts, Frederick continually asserted the necessity for pursuing concrete, practical ends:

> I believe that no intelligent man, when he considers matters calmly, will begin a war in which he knows that he will be forced onto the defensive from the start. Putting all lofty sentiments aside, I maintain that any war which fails to lead to conquests is a war which weakens even the victor in the conflict, and which undermines the strength of the state. Therefore you should never embark on hostilities unless you have an excellent prospect of making conquests. This will determine the way you go to war, and give that war an offensive character.[18]

For Frederick, the optimal way to achieve these ends was neither to exhaust one's adversaries nor to destroy them, but rather to establish by an initial victory, or series of victories, the wisdom of negotiations as an alternative to further struggle. Thus, when urged to launch a pursuit of the Austrians after winning the field at Chotusitz, he answered, "You are quite right, but I don't want to defeat them too badly."[19]

Nor was this attitude simply a manifestation of an age of limited wars. Many of Napoleon's decisive campaigns—Italy in 1796–97, Friedland, even Austerlitz—arguably achieved their primary results by reinforcing the arguments of peace advocates among France's enemies, as opposed to breaking actual capacities to resist.

Frederick's initial and naïve expectations of battle as the payoff were rudely shattered at Mollwitz and Chotusitz. The Second Silesian War further developed his sense of the differences between strategy and "a walking tour that happened to end in a few bloody acres. . . ."[20] These experiences, however, enhanced rather than modified his commitment to order and control, particularly on the battlefield. Prussia's relative geostrategic weaknesses, particularly against the Franco-Russian-Austrian constellation emerging in the 1750s, made quick tactical and operational successes not merely important, but vital. And this in turn required an army capable of achieving decisions against its exact counterparts: forces armed and trained in the same way, with the same strengths and weaknesses.[21]

Frederick was throughout his career more traditionalist than innovator, a seeker of the attainable rather than the ideal. He did not create new military forms. Instead he developed those he inherited to their logical limits. This was more than reflex conservatism. For example, the social matrix of the Prussian army was by no means inflexible. Soldiers of the eighteenth century owed much of their negative image to the generalized perception among enlightened classes and individuals that military life and military systems epitomized disorder and irrationality.[22] Caste prejudice was also a factor. Integrating the common man, particularly the countryman, into Europe's public life depended heavily on the growth of both romanticism and industrialism.[23] Soldiers came far down the queue. The best they could hope for till the Franco-Prussian War was the image of romantic outcasts.

Images, however, do not necessarily incorporate reality. Well before the French Revolution, Europe's military theorists perceived the utility of improving the quality of the rank and file, of giving soldiers a stake greater than board and lodging in the system for which they fought. The familiar litanies of obscurantism and oppression obscure the fact that eighteenth-century armies were not entirely composed of otherwise useless outcasts. The cantonists of Prussia, the conscripts of Hesse-Kassel, the volunteers of Great Britain, fit remarkably similar profiles. They were men with essentially respectable backgrounds, often with definable trades or expectations, products of deferential societies, who adjusted reasonably well to the demands of military discipline, particularly as they perceived its value as a survival mechanism.[24]

As for the mercenaries, the foreigners who made up a large proportion of Prussia's infantry were far from regarding themselves as the dregs of humanity. Instead they saw themselves as men who followed the honorable profession of arms by their own choice, cosmopolitans with interesting pasts, if not necessarily promising futures. Native Prussians were considered by comparison crude and unsophisticated boors.[25]

This was not a mix to delight the modern nationalist. But neither was it an amalgam brought to battle only by brute force. Its more extreme manifestations of antisocial behavior were likely either to be confined to relatively small groups or to be the product of specific operational circumstances perceived as breaches of contract.[26]

A second argument against challenging the internal structure of eighteenth-century armies was the effectiveness of the existing system. The colonial wars of the eighteenth century proved the value, and the worldwide adaptability, of forces organized on European models. The sepoy armies of India were perceived as products of organization and discipline. Racial identity played almost no role. The notion that "native" troops required European stiffening would have seemed absurd to Crown and East India Company officers who saw the states of south and central India fall like ninepins to expeditions containing only limited European elements.[27] In the North American wars, local forces on both sides proved useful the more closely they acculturated to European models or worked in symbiosis with them. To cite only the most familiar example, Rogers' Rangers were not in themselves a battle-winning force. Their techniques of woods fighting were transmitted not to provincial regiments, but to the royal army, by officers such as Thomas Gage and Lord George Howe, who incorporated ranger methods into line battalions and raised such units as the Royal Americans and the 80th Foot, Gage's Light Infantry.[28]

Failure to cultivate methods of open-order fighting in Europe's armies reflected less a general absence of vision than a belief that these techniques could easily be relearned as necessary—grafted onto a basic structure that had proven its flexibility and adaptability from the Carnatic to the Ukraine.[29] A reasonable parallel might be drawn with the ambiguous fate of counterinsurgency in the post-Vietnam U.S. army. Critics deploring its eclipse are met with the reasonable response that no armed force can prepare for every possible contingency, that it makes best sense to focus on those major threats against which improvisation is most difficult.

II

For Frederick II, then, the key to optimizing the military system lay in improving its internal efficiency. Initially this appeared to have little or nothing to do with technology. But technology does not involve an exclusive concentration on machines. The essential tools of eighteenth-century war were the soldiers themselves, and they could be as difficult to replace as modern battle tanks or jet fighters. Eighteenth-century battle drill, with its blend of flexibility and complexity, raised the human and professional demands made on the man in the ranks to heights unknown since the Roman Empire. Various forms of militia systems survived throughout this period. They were, however, increasingly uncompetitive. The often-cited risks of domestic destabilization should the rabble be armed were less significant than the growing gap between the demands of the modern battlefield and the routines of civil society—a gap widening with every decade of stability and order provided by the absolute state.

From the French Revolution to the Second World War and beyond, soldiers and scholars alike have overwhelmingly asserted the superiority of the citizen in arms. Like Cromwell's plain russet-coated captain, the citizen, fighing for a cause he knows or at least accepts, compensates for any lack of specific skills with his enthusiasm and intelligence. Ultimately he is a better bet than the professional, the man who substitutes technique for commitment. The shortcomings of this line of argument, indicated as early as World War I, have become plain as the stresses of the modern battlefield combine with the demands of an increasingly technical weaponry to expand demands on soldiers at war's cutting edge. In this context it is useful to suggest parallels between the contemporary tanker, gunner, or rifleman, and his eighteenth-century ancestor. Both must master a broad spectrum of arcane skills as a matter of life and death. Goodwill was by itself insufficient to make a musketeer fit for the firing line, any more than it qualifies a modern recruit for a place in an infantry fighting vehicle or an assault helicopter. Even in the French Revolution, the survival of the old regular army attests to the importance in battle of a level of technical expertise that ultimately depended heavily on training.

How could this training best be applied? At the beginning of his career the Prussian king agreed with such contemporaries as Maurice de Saxe that fire action had ossified the battlefield. Victory under such circumstances would go to the general best able to disrupt his enemy's position by rapid movement. The concept of the oblique order, the concentrating of superior force against one point followed by a rapid advance, had its operational roots in the Silesian Wars.[30] But its execution depended on training, discipline, and motivation.

Trained soldiers were scarce enough and valuable enough to be worth preserving. Positive reinforcements existed for the men in Prussia's ranks. Under Frederick II, enlistment bounties were increased, standards of treatment were improved, and the rights of furlough and civil employment were steadily extended. One of the enduring myths of Prussian military history is that the army suffered an average loss of 20 percent from death or desertion. Willerd Fann has shown the desertion rate from 1713 to 1740 was a modest 1.9 percent; the death rate was even lower, at 1.4 percent.[31] Wartime rates, of course, were significantly higher, particularly after the incorporation of the Saxon army in the Seven Years' War. Nevertheless, much of the Prussian army's concern with desertion was preventive maintenance.

Frederick was too much the rationalist to accept entirely any myths and cold steel. If he believed that a determined advance with fixed bayonets was by itself likely to convince an enemy of urgent business elsewhere, he also favored using a volley or two to change the minds of any that held their ground. After 1740 Prussia's infantry formations were thinned and extended, with the goal of bringing as many muskets as possible against the enemy. During the Second Silesian War, Prussian infantrymen proved able to breach enemy positions without firing a shot, opening the way for the heavy cavalry to complete the victory by riding down a scattered enemy. But the limits of this tactic became painfully clear from the start of the Seven Years' War. Prussia's first contacts with the revitalized army of Maria Theresa showed the results of improved Austrian fire discipline combined with an artillery that concentrated on Frederick's infantry instead of his guns. In front of Prague fourteen Prussian battalions, muskets at the shoulder, were stopped in their tracks before the main Austrian position, then routed by a counterattack. A few weeks later, at Kolin, nine battalions halted and disrupted by Austrian fire were ridden down by a cavalry charge.

Over 14,000 of Frederick's best men fell at Prague; 13,000 more died at Kolin. If both battles might be counted as victories, Frederick was enough of a classical scholar to be haunted by images of Pyrrhus. But the king's genius lay in his adaptability. In victory or defeat, Frederick never again neglected fire action. Where once he spoke of a volley or two, his assault formations were increasingly expected to deliver as many as a half-dozen in succession before pushing forward over the bodies of their opponents. At least in theory, a Prussian infantry battalion was expected to maneuver as swiftly and efficiently as the oblique order demanded, while being able to deliver two thousand rounds a minute on command. Leuthen, generally considered the greatest of Frederick's victories, was as much a triumph of firepower as a demonstration of the oblique order. At Leuthen, Prussia's musketeers took their ammunition wagons into battle for the first time; some men fired three times the regulation allowance of sixty rounds during the day.[32]

Frequent negative references to the Prussian soldier as a machine or an automaton have obscured the fact that by 1765 he was seen as part of an integrated weapons system. The complex geometric evolutions perfected after the Seven Years' War were less absurd than their critics suggested. All of them were ultimately designed to facilitate the individual soldier's quick deployment into battle formation and his disciplined execution of small arms drill under the worst, most confusing circumstances. Similarly the musket he carried, although dismissed by one critic as "neither firearm, pike, nor club,"[33] was in its definitive form a weapon refined and developed along the lines of the modern submachine gun or assault rifle. Prussia's gun designers and its practical soldiers alike favored ease of usage and enhanced rates of fire over ballistic qualities. The *Infanteriegewehr M1782,* the culmination of a century's effort, featured an iron ramrod that was durable and unlikely to swell and stick in a barrel heated by rapid fire. The musket's great windage facilitated loading. Its imbalance, particularly the muzzle-heaviness caused by the iron ramrod plus a heavy bayonet, enhanced its value as a quick-firing weapon by limiting the normal tendency of excited men in combat to shoot too high. Foreign observers of peacetime maneuvers laughed as battalions fired volleys into the ground. Men who faced Prussian musketry in the field were less amused.[34]

The Seven Years' War, however, also demonstrated the essential shortcoming of the infantryman as weapons system: its production took too long and depended on too many variable factors. Medieval commanders had frequently complained that the usefulness of English longbowmen was limited by their collective fragility. Cold, hunger, or sickness took the power from an archer's arm and robbed his eye of its accuracy. Heavy wartime casualties combined with the physical and moral stresses of constant campaigning had a similar effect on Prussia's infantry. As the quality of his foot troops declined, Frederick turned increasingly to the army's newest branch of service.

The basic weapon of the Prussian heavy artillery in 1756 was a twelve-pounder, designed to sacrifice firepower for maneuverability and deficient in both respects. Most of these unfortunate weapons were lost in early defeats, replaced by older, heavier twelve-pounders stripped from fortresses and mounted on improvised field carriages. This expedient solution also responded to a certain gigantism among Prussia's gunners, who simply felt more comfortable with the heavier pieces. Their *Brummer* performed spectacularly at Leuthen, tearing open Austrian positions and providing significant psychological support to an infantry that began the battle with pardonable misgivings at being once more used as cannon fodder. For the rest of the war it was an article of faith among Prussian officers that their men fought better when heavy guns were available.

Heavy artillery was only part of Frederick's increased emphasis on battlefield firepower. Like all European armies, the Prussian infantry included "battalion guns," designed to supplement musketry directly by canister and case shot. Initially, Frederick favored light pieces for this service—a logical consequence of his belief in the intimidating power of rapid movement. In 1742 each infantry regiment received new three-pounder guns, whose significant lack of range and hitting power were so marked that in the Second Silesian War the infantry often advanced without them. Frederick responded by ordering the design of a heavier gun with improved ballistics.

These new six-pounders began entering service in 1755. From the beginning of the Seven Years' War they became targets for the longer-range, more accurate Austrian artillery. Initial support for abolishing them faded, however, as the infantry's quality declined. Frederick and most of his generals increasingly agreed on the role of battalion guns for direct fire support, and as rallying points in action. As the war dragged on, the Prussian army also made increasing use of short-barreled, high-trajectory howitzers, whose explosive shells and large charges of small shot proved invaluable at close quarters. New three- and six-pounders, longer-ranged than their predecessors, took the field as regimental guns alongside the infantry.[35] A half-century later, Napoleon was to draw similar conclusions. Regimental artillery, considered unnecessary in the Grande Armée of 1805, reappeared unobtrusively in 1809.[36]

Frederick favored in principle the use of artillery en masse, first to silence enemy batteries, then to play on the area of his intended breakthrough.[37] This doctrine proved increasingly difficult to implement as the declining strength and morale of the infantry made them correspondingly dependent on artillery firepower. By war's end, most of the Prussian army's heavy guns were assigned to infantry brigades on a permanent basis. The king's major attempt at compensating for this development came with the creation in 1759 of horse artillery, which he regarded as a mobile reserve of guns to be used at the commanding general's discretion. Frederick's belief in the arm's potential was not, however, entirely justified by its performance in battle. In particular, the light six-pounders with which the batteries were equipped lacked the fire effect to be useful in a major battle.[38]

The steady increase in the proportion of artillery in Prussia's field armies, to as many as six guns per thousand muskets in the war's last years, represented for Frederick an excess rather than a triumph. The heavy guns in particular required a larger number of draft horses and heavy-duty wagons than were commonly available anywhere in Germany in order to maintain their supply of ammunition—ammunition that could neither be requisitioned nor improvised. The effect of large artillery trains on unpaved roads, even in the dry season, further restricted the army's movements. These disadvantages did not mean Frederick changed his mind about the importance of artillery fire, though. In preparing for the Potato War of 1778 he conceded that Austria would have more guns, but declared, "by concentrating our howitzers and cannon at a single point we will gain the local superiority, and perhaps be able to beat them."[39]

Frederick's acceptance of Austrian numerical superiority implied another major brake on the development of artillery in Prussia: its cost. The false starts with the too-light three-, six-, and twelve-pounders and the limited improvement represented by wartime designs meant that cannon were constantly being recalled for the expensive process of recasting. Frederick particularly feared the consequences of being drawn into an arms race with Russia and Austria—a race he insisted Prussia had no chance of winning when a single campaign consumed three times as much gunpowder as the state could produce in a year.[40]

The King's caution persisted in the context of Prussia's economic recovery after 1763. Frederick's mercantilist commitment to expanding commerce and industry required increasing state intervention in the context of domestic investors short of capital and reluctant to take risks. The exasperation of the business community at what it regarded as unwarranted interference, the often-cited inefficiency of Frederick's *dirigisme* in everyday terms, should not obscure the increase in production, the growth of a skilled labor force, and the rapid increase in public revenue—three times larger at Frederick's death than at his accession.[41]

A large proportion of this income was earmarked for military purposes. But less and less of the army's budget went for material. The postwar introduction of a new family of artillery pieces and the adoption in 1782 of a new infantry musket remained isolated improvements. Shoddy uniforms, underfed horses, and worn-out weapons alike testified to a comprehensive pattern of cheeseparing. Like the U.S. military of the 1980s, Prussia faced a problem of prioritizing. What was more important: numbers or serviceability? At what point could—or should—spare parts and practice ammunition be sacrificed to maintain numbers? Was state security best served by maintaining a relatively large number of formations that had to be supplemented before taking the field or by smaller forces ready in every particular for war?

For Frederick there was only one answer. Or perhaps it is more accurate to say that he denied any need for making trade-offs. Technology could not support a *Qualitätsarmee* of the kind possible in later centuries. Also, the Prussian army's manpower could not be allowed to shrink, particularly in view of the continuous improvements France, Russia, and Austria were making in their armed forces. Frederick had come to perceive operational efficiency as the product of a symbiosis between human and material factors. Prefiguring arguments current in the last quarter of the twentieth century, the aging king insisted on the importance of intangibles. His often-stated emphasis on externals, on the precise execution of drill movements and maneuver instructions, was only the tip of a structural iceberg devoted to maintaining the largest possible army at the lowest possible relative cost. From Frederick's perspective, drills cost nothing and enhanced qualities easier lost and more difficult to regain than simple material efficiency.

But the king's growing misanthropy led to the equation of skills with discipline. The stick virtually replaced the carrot. Rigid emphasis on aristocratic origins arguably did less to diminish the efficiency of Prussia's officer corps than the absence of a retirement system. Particularly in a society where few families possessed truly independent means, this not only encouraged staying on as long as possible but also generated a reluctance among even martially inclined noblemen to make a profession of arms. Among the rank and file, the exponential increase in exemptions from the cantonal draft and the use of military service as a form of criminal punishment did much to diminish the enthusiasm of native Prussians. Foreign recruits also found conditions of service in Prussia increasingly unattractive, particularly in the context of Great Britain's extensive hirings of German auxiliary troops in the 1770s and 1780s.[42]

III

The German Enlightenment was shaped by two related principles: the importance of free inquiry and the possibility of institutional reform.[43] No system was perfect; none was entirely new: the problem was finding the best ways to improve a given order. For Frederick II the answer had involved working within existing parameters. An increasing number of Prussian officers regarded this as an inappropriate response. Apart from the problems occasioned by Frederick's advancing age, his most prominent subordinates were practical soldiers. Concern for the changing craft of war correspondingly tended to be taken outside the Prussian army's mainstream, discussed and debated in organizations like the Military Society of Berlin, founded in 1802, or by soldiers like Gerhard von Scharnhorst, who transferred from Hanoverian service in 1801. The dominant concerns of these military *Vorreformer* focussed on moral factors. Their focus on the individual soldier reflected the humane aspects of the German *Aufklärung*. Frederick William II, who succeeded his uncle in 1786, had at best a casual interest in military affairs, but he manifested it by ameliorating the worst aspects of Frederician discipline and by improving provisions for soldiers' families and former soldiers. Given the increasingly brutalized condition of the rank and file, these reforms had less than the hoped-for effect. In any case, they were perceived as merely an entering wedge.

The Frederician legacy had geared the Prussian army to fight decisive battles. The Potato War of 1778 and the 1787 incursion into Holland demonstrated the army's shortcomings when confronted with limited war. In particular, the light troops were regarded as auxiliaries, expected at most to establish conditions for a major encounter. When there was no will to fight such a battle, as in Bavaria, or when there was no real opponent, as was the case in Holland, the Prussian army had difficulty responding. The experiences of the Russian and Austrian armies in their wars against the Ottoman Empire sparked further Prussian interest in light troops as something more in their own right than scouts, marauders, and cannon fodder. In 1787 Prussia introduced sharpshooters to the infantry battalions and created a force of fusilier battalions, intended as permanent light infantry.

The success of these innovations was limited. The sharpshooters tended to become merely a source of noncommissioned officers. The fusiliers, like the dragoons of an earlier era, tended to assimilate to the forms of the line. But fusiliers and sharpshooters did at least provide a matrix for responding to the upsurge of military vitalism accompanying the French Revolution. An increasing number of military theoreticians across the Rhine saw the Republic's armies as introducing a new and unique form of warfare. In particular, the French use of skirmishers and their encouragement of initiative at the lowest levels seemed to combine Enlightenment concepts of *Bildung*, or self-development, with the metamorphosis of soldiers into citizens. The Frederician concept of the rank and file as human components of a weapons system, as military cyborgs, gave way to the image of the soldier as warrior, with the personal, individual element all-important at all levels. Just as the future infantryman would have to act on his own responsibility, so commanders and staffs would have to respond to challenges instead of merely pushing buttons.[44]

Evaluating the military reform movement in Prussia is complicated by its virtually automatic appeal to scholars and soldiers alike—particularly by comparison to its opponents. Nineteenth-century nationalists and twentieth-century Marxists can agree that the reformers had their hearts in most of the right places and sought to move in most of the right directions. Their critics emerge as mean-spirited reactionaries, clinging to outmoded forms and attitudes no matter what the cost to the society they purported to serve.[45] Yet the Prussian reformers' understanding of the French way of war reflected preconceptions and wishful thinking as well as realities. The armies of the French Republic did recognize and adjust to the enthusiasm of their rank and file. But from the beginning that enthusiasm was tempered and shaped by training and discipline.[46] Nor does it represent a concession to Borussian patrioteers to suggest that in 1806, an army between eras faced an adversary at the peak of its efficiency, commanded by one of history's greatest captains at the height of his powers. Defeat at such hands may pitilessly expose weakness, but it is by no means prima facie evidence of irreversible dry rot.

Nevertheless the Prussian recovery after Jena evoked rewriting of the Frederician contract, reharmonizing the needs of the state and its people. Both the reformers and their critics, both the Scharnhorsts and the Marwitzes, moved away from the technical aspects of professionalism in evaluating the Prussian army's requirements. Both factions saw will as important; each stressed the human aspects of war. For conservatives, the soldier had to become a self-consciously dutiful subject. For the reformers, an initial concept of the soldier as citizen evolved into the image of military service as preparation for citizenship itself. The soldier no longer needed to belong to a special class. In the words of Baron vom Stein, one's years in uniform were to become the most honorable period of one's life.[47] Whether this citizen would know how to fight was of secondary importance.

Changing attitudes were reflected in questions of armament and doctrine. The Prussian army's increased interest in open warfare had in 1801 resulted in the adoption of a new musket. The *Nothard-Gewehr*'s angled butt, rear sight, and reduced windage improved its accuracy enough to make it a far more suitable skirmishers' weapon than its predecessor. By 1806, however, only seven battalions had been rearmed, and the losses sustained as the French overran Prussia highlighted the Nothard's one outstanding flaw. It was too small-bored to use foreign ammunition—a decisive drawback for an army that expected to fight long before it would be able to supply its own needs. The result was a compromise, the New Prussian Musket of 1809. Its bore was large enough to take any ball used in Europe, but its overall design was along the lines of the Nothard: a musket suitable for the aimed fire of skirmishers.

Like Frederick II, Scharnhorst recognized the significance of firepower, but he saw it in terms of accuracy as opposed to volume. The revised drill regulations of the Prussian infantry designated half the men in each regiment for training as skirmishers. Target practice with live ammunition became a regular event, with cash prizes for the best shots. The light troops were given their own inspectorate, under Hans

David Yorck, former commander of the army's rifle regiment. His emphasis was on fire tactics, which he defined as "hitting the enemy with the bullet."[48]

All of these reforms were as much psychological ploys as tactical innovations. Even Scharnhorst proposed practice allowances of no more than 27 rounds a year for recruits and 18 for trained soldiers, and these steadily reduced as the army sought to save gunpowder.[49] Real marksmanship correspondingly remained the function of specialized formations of riflemen. The ultimate intention of the process was to strengthen the individual soldier's self-confidence, rather than any specific technical skills. The Prussian soldier of the Wars of Liberation was ideally part of a disciplined military community. He fought according to a tactical doctrine based on the close coordination of skirmishers with small flexible columns. In principle, the enemy was to be worn down by lengthy firefights, then tested for weak spots by local attacks against targets of opportunity.

The reformers' emphasis on operational mobility meant that heavy guns were discounted in favor of light six-pounders, particularly in early operations. Instead of being massed in Napoleonic—or Frederician—style, artillery was distributed by batteries among the brigades, and later the corps, of the reorganized Prussian army, on the principle that a dozen guns at hand at the right time were preferable to fifty on the spot a half-hour later. Cavalry was similarly dispersed in squadrons and regiments instead of being massed in the style of Seydlitz.

These amalgamations were a product of Scharnhorst's belief in combined arms. They reflected the losses suffered by the cavalry and artillery in 1806–7. But underlying this process was the fact that infantry best fit the reformers' image of the citizen-soldier able to substitute enthusiasm for training. Each in its own way, cavalry and artillery were technical arms, demanding kinds and levels of skill impossible to acquire overnight and unsusceptible to even the purest patriotic zeal.

The Prussian army of the War of Liberation was much more the force of a *Kleinstaat* than its Frederician predecessor had been. Not intended to strike decisive, independent blows, it was governed by a doctrine stressing the use of combination punches to develop and discover weak spots, followed by breakthroughs in a small-scale version of Liddell Hart's expanding torrent. Success depended less on adherence to a battle plan than on individual responses to circumstances on all levels.[50] Strategically, as well as operationally, the Prussian army was limited, seen as operating within a coalition held together by a common denominator no less firm for being low: the defeat of Napoleon. Until the Emperor's first abdication, it was Prussian statesmen and Prussian generals who stressed the importance of keeping the alliance intact by fighting the French wherever and whenever possible, leaving the aftermath of victory to take care of itself.[51]

On the whole, the reformers' concepts tested well enough against the realities of the Wars of Liberation. Yet even in those years the Prussians faced continuous difficulty in generating combat power. Clausewitz's descriptive "The Nature of Battle Today" sets the scene:

> What usually happens in a major battle today? The troops move calmly into position in great masses deployed in line and depth. Only a relatively small proportion is involved, and is left to conduct a firefight for several hours, interrupted now and then by minor blows — charges, bayonet assaults and cavalry attacks — which cause the fighting to sway to some extent to and fro. Gradually, the units engaged are burned out, and when nothing is left but cinders, they are withdrawn and others take their place. So the battle slowly smolders away, like damp gunpowder.[52]

Tactically the army was at its best in the early stages, before its dilution by men untrained in, and officers unskilled in, the new methods. The relative tendency toward mass characteristic of the Prussian army in the Waterloo campaign was only partly a reflection of the problems of digesting new levies from newly annexed territories. It was also a response to the problem of achieving a decision in the context of the new tactics with any but the highest-quality troops and officers.

IV

The problem of quality became even more acute after 1815. The Prussian/German army is consistently attacked for its caste-bound reluctance to implement true universal service, for favoring instead the development of soldiers as a Praetorian Guard for the status quo. Without denying the evidence marshaled in support of this approach, it nevertheless offers an incomplete picture. Prussia was no more able to sustain great-power status with a professional army after 1815 than before 1806. In sharp contrast to its predecessor, however, the new Prussian military system, as seen by the reformers, depended heavily on popular enthusiasm, to the point of expecting voluntary participation in drills and exercises—particularly as the natural increase in the Prussian population after 1815 made it impossible to finance a full term of active service for every able-bodied man except at the expense of other material requirements, whose neglect had contributed so much to the decline of Frederick II's army. The result was analogous to that of the selective service system as implemented in the U.S. between the Korean and Vietnam Wars: an expectation of universal service in law and principle, heavily modified in reality.

The reformers were swimming against powerful political tides. Prussia's unwritten constitution, dating back to the Great Elector, implied very little about the duty of assuming burdensome personal obligations, particularly to a state that, in the peaceful years of Metternich's Europe, seemed to deliver few obvious benefits in return. This lack of popular enthusiasm was particularly apparent in the decline of the reform movement's favorite child, the Landwehr. Scharnhorst and his colleagues originally expected public zeal and energy to sustain this national reserve force even in the face of financial strictures. Within three years after Waterloo, however, the Landwehr had lost its novelty. Its commissions were no longer sought by martially ambitious young men. Its drills were no longer attended by a public eager to watch the show, and to stand its brave defenders to drinks afterwards.[53]

Whether sustained enthusiasm for Landwehr service would have improved the Prussian army's operational efficiency is at best questionable. The argument for reducing time in the active army's ranks, for creating what amounted to a national militia system, had strong advocates in and out of Prussia. But here again a reasonable parallel may be drawn, this time between men like Karl von Rotteck and certain contemporary advocates of the integration of women into the U.S. armed forces. In both cases broader sociopolitical agendas, public and hidden, can be said to override limited questions of operational efficiency. For Rotteck, a militia would fight well because it must fight well. Arguments to the contrary were merely the excuses of reactionaries, to be dismissed rather than refuted.[54]

Those military reformers who continued in service after 1815, men like War Minister Hermann von Boyen, men like Grolman and Clausewitz, did not see the situation quite so simply. Postwar experience with the Prussian Landwehr showed that a mass of several hundred men, if worked to exhaustion, could be taught the rudiments of company drill in a few weeks. They could be given some sense of group identity, and of the meaning of military order. Of skirmishing, fieldcraft, marks-manship, and all the other skills demanded by the Regulations of 1812, they remained essentially ignorant.[55]

Beyond the drill grounds, the Prussian army of the Age of Metternich faced a second set of problems. The essence of the Revolutionary/Napoleonic approach to war was improvisation. The military institutions of the Republic and the Empire alike functioned in a state of constant flux. How could a state with a past and a future, a state like Prussia, best institutionalize this complex legacy? Charismatic leaders and systems depend heavily for their sustenance upon constant rein-fusions of emotional fervor—"second revolutions" followed by thirds and fourths, or at least their appearances.[56] A common result of this process is the intimidation of one's neighbors. Yet far more than its Frederician and Reform-Era predecessor, Biedermeier Prussia was con-cerned with maintaining its existing place in a stable international system. Its foreign policy focused on what a later generation would describe as crisis management—maintaining stability by a mixture of negotiation and compromise backed by a credible possibility of using force. But a mass army organized along Napoleonic lines, whether a militia in the style advocated by Rotteck or the more flexible and deadly instrument of the reformers, was credible only as an ultimate weapon. Its possessor would be correspondingly vulnerable to pressure and manipulation on issues less than existence-threatening. Were Prussia to risk depending heavily on popular enthusiasm as an element of its military efficiency, might it not also risk inheriting France's position as an objective threat to Europe's order?[57]

Prussia's soldiers were in a double bind. The institutional legacy of the reform movement implied an ethic best applicable to total wars for indefinite aims. The state's geographic and diplomatic circum-stances, however, continued to highlight the utility of a front-loaded military system, able to conduct prompt, decisive operations for specific objectives. This meant retaming Bellona: applying principles of limi-tation and control to both the structure of the armed forces and the conduct of operations.

One possible solution involved evaluating technology as a combat multiplier for a numerically reduced army. Yet for twenty years, Prussian factories delivered smoothbore flintlocks. Prussian artillery pieces were so inaccurate that sentries had to be posted to warn passers-by during target practice, and so heavy that their own users often condemned them as unfit for field operations.[58]

This lack of technical progress in part reflected the existence every-where in Europe of large stocks of proven war matériel more or less adequate to its purpose. At a time when mass armies made increasing demands on budgets, no state was eager to embark on an arms race whose costs would have to be borne by cuts elsewhere in the military establishment. Caution was also a function of the presence of too many talented officers bored by routine, with too little to do. This led to a fiddling preoccupation with details of weapons design, and a corre-sponding commitment to delaying innovation until perfection should be reached on the drawing board. More generally, Prussia's soldiers were frequently appalled by the impact of industrialization, suspicious of the social, political, and environmental consequences of the factory system, and dubious as to the proper level of state involvement in the process of economic development. But positive involvement with the industrial revolution was above all restricted by the vitalist heritage of the military reform movement.[59]

The concept that men were the decisive element in war was rein-forced by the continued association of firepower in the Frederician style with Frederician rigidity: levels of mass inappropriate to Prussian tactical doctrine and levels of control impossible to achieve on a modern battlefield. A major goal in Prussian weapons design was to avoid this kind of inflexibility. The percussion musket adopted in 1839 to replace the Napoleonic flintlock had a recoil so heavy only the strongest men could hold it on target. Its merits were nevertheless debated in terms of skirmishing tactics: the theoretical accuracy of individual shots.[60] The artillery system adopted in 1842 was tested not for hitting power, but for mobility: the capacity to keep up with cavalry and infantry under the most trying circumstances.[61] Critics of the breech-loading needle gun introduced to service in 1841 stressed its Frederician short-comings: lack of range and accuracy compared with the muzzle-loading rifles coming into service elsewhere. Others argued breech-loaders wasted ammunition by encouraging rapid firing at nothing in particular—a distinctive "Frederician" characteristic.[62]

The needle gun, indeed, was so controversial that much expert opin-ion favored issuing the weapon to picked men or selected units. The debate was resolved only in 1848, when revolution led to a general issuing of the available needle guns. They proved so popular that talk of withdrawing them was soon stopped as harmful to morale. In the course of the next decade, breech-loaders were integrated into a tactical doctrine continuing to emphasize skirmish lines and small columns. The revised infantry drill regulations of 1847 put more emphasis on close formations than the preceding ones issued in 1812. But the men in those formations were still regarded as consciously committed individuals, going forward not from fear or compulsion, but as a result of enthusiasm tempered by training in the best ways of reaching an enemy position alive.[63] The third year of active service, which was such a major element in the Prussian constitutional conflict of the 1860s, was intended to do more than transform the conscript into a dutiful subject. It was also regarded by its advocates as time necessary to internalize the skills of marksmanship, fire discipline, and prompt response to changing conditions that were the essence of the modern foot soldier.[64]

Innovations in artillery material similarly reflected the growing decentralization of fighting power. Specifically, skirmish lines armed with modern rifles seemed increasingly invulnerable to the traditional designs of guns and howitzers. Was the challenge best met by rifled guns, whose long range and flat trajectory made them precision weapons, but whose explosive rounds had limited blast effects? Or was the field piece of the future a large-caliber smoothbore gun able to check skirmishers by firing shell and shrapnel rounds at close and medium ranges?[65]

These kinds of debates served to revitalize the Prussian army as well as polarize it. From the 1840s, soldiers began applying themselves to technical problems, developing working acquaintances with civilian designers and industrialists like Alfred Krupp, evaluating the impact of firepower on the modern battlefield. But the prospective combat multipliers offered by a developing military technology seemed to lead in wrong directions—or directions that at least challenged Prussia's objective strategic requirements. The prospects for controlling the progress of a modern battle diminished as the size of armies grew, as the killing zones of rifles and cannon increased to four or five times Napoleonic norms. Field commanders had not abandoned hope of mastering the modern battlefield. Professional literature of the 1850s was replete with proposed innovations in tactics, training, and command that were expected to generate decisive battles.[66] But the nature of mid-century armies and mid-century weaponry alike discouraged excessive reliance on these predictions. Victory, if achievable, seemed to be the more likely result of a bitter dogfight followed by an ex post facto tallying of results.

Prussian planners correspondingly tended to shift their emphasis to the higher levels of operations and strategy. The War Ministry even during the 1820s and 1830s moved ever further away from the days of heroic improvisation. Boyen's shock at what he considered the ossification of that office on his recall in 1840 was in good part his revulsion at anything but the most limited systemization.[67] The General Staff, as well, developed as an organization whose main purpose was providing for the most efficient use of Prussia's limited resources in the greatest number of contingencies.

This process received added impetus as soldiers began adapting to the introduction of railroads. In the 1840s and 1850s, their direct military utility was questionable. Roadbeds, rolling stock, and track networks were limited in their ability to transport combined armed forces of any strength. Since most lines were built by private enterprise, their strategic worth was at best a secondary issue. These facts combined to make rational calculation the key factor in the successful utilization of railroads for military purposes. Appeals to patriotism and threats of punishment were useless in the face of broken axles, hotboxes, or tracks leading to no particularly desirable destination from an operational point of view. Railroads also complicated logistics. No matter how many men they might bring to a given spot, no more than 30,000 or so could be supplied by a single major road as long as horse transport connected supply dumps with caissons, haversacks, and nosebags. An army of 100,000 or 150,000 did not really march, but rather inched its way cross-country, using every possible dirt track and cowpath for the supplies on which its efficiency depended. Apart from the expected quantum jump in ammunition consumption by rapid-firing weapons, the conscript citizen-soldiers of an *Ordnungsstaat* like Prussia were not the best material for self-reliant foragers in the Napoleonic tradition.[68]

The need for control at higher levels that the railroads helped to generate blended nicely with Prussia's geostrategic requirements. Otto von Bismarck is frequently and legitimately described as Europe's last Cabinet warrior. However willing he might have been to use the solvents of liberalism and nationalism, however extreme might have been his rhetoric, Prussia's Minister-President recognized that wars end by negotiation. He insisted on keeping that option always open.[69] Less familiar, and less generally accepted, was Moltke's adherence to similar principles. Moltke's insistence that the conduct of war itself must be determined by military considerations, and his bitter criticism of Bismarck's attempts to influence operations during the Wars of Unification, must be understood in the context of his perception of the course of these operations. Prussia was relatively no better able geographically, socially, or economically to sustain protracted operations in 1860 than it was in 1740. Like Frederick II, Moltke accepted the desirability of decisive victories at the start of a war. Like Frederick, he believed that decisive battles were possible if the Prussian army took advantage of technical multipliers. And once these victories were achieved, by Moltke's own logic the soldier must withdraw in favor of the statesman.[70]

Though Moltke and Bismarck differed sharply over what constituted a decisive victory, both men accepted its importance for Prussian grand strategy. Even before Moltke's appointment as its chief, the Prussian General Staff had begun evaluating the possibilities of so coordinating and supplying the movement of large forces on separate lines of advance that they could support each other while concentrating against an enemy from several directions at once. Here technology offered both a promise and a threat. The electric telegraph, introduced on the railway system in the 1840s, was adapted for military purposes in the 1850s.[71] On the surface, the new development offered prospects for making the task of the high command easier than at any time since the advent of mass armies. Rapid communication over long distances and indirect routes made possible improved control of logistics arrangements. With schedules and movements controlled by telegraph, railway networks could be harnessed to concentrate and supply masses of troops with a minimum of confusion. Commanders in the field could remain in constant touch with their capitals. The movement of individual parts of an army could conceivably be coordinated by a single headquarters.

The latter possibilities inspired fear as well as enthusiasm — fear of depriving commanders of necessary initiative by binding them too closely to higher authority. Encouraging subordinates to make and execute independent decisions, within the framework of a given operational plan, involved risks. Stubbornness, eccentricity, even genius could bring about disastrous confusion. Nevertheless, Moltke was convinced that the advantages obtained by overcontrolling subordinates were illusory.

No commander in the field could be more unfortunate, Moltke declared, than to have in his headquarters someone who could call him to account every day and every hour, subjecting his plans and decisions to criticism, offering advice without responsibility. But if a delegate from supreme headquarters was bad enough, a "telegraph wire in the back" was worse.[72]

More than principle was involved here. The clumsiness of telegraph apparatus and the vulnerability of the wires on which it depended meant that it could hardly be counted on to maintain touch with units in the field. And the haphazard nature of tactical communications along with the slowness of runners and dispatch riders meant that specific information was likely to be both sporadic and outdated. Depending on communications from headquarters as a guide to action was to trust an illusion.

Solving the problem involved further developing the General Staff. This body had not been originally conceived as an instrument of operational control. It emerged from the improvisations of the War of Liberation with the related responsibilities of evaluating Prussia's potential enemies, preparing contingency plans for mobilization and deployment, and digesting the experiences of previous campaigns. But for chiefs like Karl von Grolman and Baron Karl von Müffling, the kinds of officers assigned to the staff were just as important as their mission. After 1806 the Prussian army had established a comprehensive and increasingly efficient educational system for its officers. But the very existence of these schools increased the risk of making the General Staff a kind of postgraduate institution dominated by glorified clerks who could pass examinations. Grolman and Müffling insisted on regular rotation of staff officers to field assignments. Müffling developed a system of annual rides designed to bring his subordinates out of their offices and into contact with the terrain over which troops would actually operate. The General Staff also began institutionalizing the concept of mission performance. Two of the major perils of staff work in all European armies in the years after 1815 were tendencies to wait for orders and evade responsibility. Instead Grolman and his successors encouraged officers assigned to the General Staff to act independently within their spheres of action.

The small size of the corps—45 officers in 1824, 64 in 1859—and the fact that its members were experienced officers who had passed through the same schools encouraged at least professional harmony. Neither Moltke nor his predecessors had any desire to create a parallel hierarchy to the official chain of command. They were motivated instead by a far more modest desire: to provide division, corps, and army headquarters with at least a few officers trained in the same pattern, formed in a common mold, and able to evaluate situations from a common framework.

If the Frederician musketeer was one kind of military cyborg, the Moltkean general staff officer was another. He was part of a nervous system enabling a coherent response to changing circumstances while keeping headquarters aware of the general progress of events. No battle plan might survive contact with an enemy, but the institution of the General Staff in combination with the electric telegraph offered the possibility of adapting to that confusion Clausewitz described as the essence of war. At the very least, Prussia would be one degree less confused than her enemies. In the Wars of Unification, that limited edge proved enough.[73]

Moltke, in short, recognized the parameters of technology as applied to strategy and operations in the same way Frederick had recognized the parameters of tactical technology. The key to the successful application of either involved concentrating on what machines could do, and applying that to Prussia's geostrategic requirements. Strategic/operational control did not mean for Moltke foreseeing and regulating every move, any more than Frederick proposed to dominate a battle like a chess master. But precisely because war is the province of uncertainty, these great practitioners shared a determination to maintain war as the servant of state policy, rather than allowing it to become an end in itself. Under virtually all conditions, societies retained some military capacity. The goal of warfare was to convince governments to use that capacity no longer. To Moltke as to Frederick, a "battle of annihilation" had a limited context: one not of crushing an enemy root and branch but of convincing him to stop fighting and talk. The increasing difficulty of controlling war at its cutting edge only enhanced the need for control where it could be exercised: by using technology as a force multiplier in order ultimately to limit war's consequences.

NOTES

1. Cf., inter alia, Martin Kitchen, *A Military History of Germany* (Bloomington, Ind., 1975); Bernd F. Schulte, *Die deutsche Armee 1900–1914: Zwischen beharren und verändern* (Düsseldorf, 1977); and Manfred Messerschmidt, "Preussens Militär in seinem gesellschaftlichen Umfeld," in *Preussen im Rückblick,* ed. Hans-Jürgen Puhle, Hans-Ulrich Wehler [*Geschichte und Gesellschaft, Sondernummer* 6 (1980)], 43–88.

2. As in Alfred Vagts, *A History of Militarism*, rev. ed. (New York, 1959), 155ff., or T. E. H. Travers, "Technology, Tactics and Morale: Jean de Bloch, the Boer War, and British Military Theory, 1900–1914," *Journal of Modern History* 51 (1979): 264–86.

3. The standards for this form of criticism were set in Richard A. Gabriel and Paul Savage, *Crisis in Command: Mismanagement in the Army* (New York, 1978). Cf., more recently, Gabriel, *Military Incompetence: Why the American Military Doesn't Win* (New York, 1986), and, from differing perspectives, Edward N. Luttwak, *The Pentagon and the Art of War* (New York, 1985), and Martin van Creveld, *Technology and War* (New York, 1989).

4. David R. Mets, "What If It Works? Air Armament Technology for Deep Attack," *Military Review* 66 (December, 1986): 13–15.

5. Cf. Gordon A. Craig, "Delbrück: The Military Historian," in *Makers of Modern Strategy from Machiavelli to the Nuclear Age*, rev. ed., ed. Peter Paret, Gordon Craig, Felix Gilbert (Princeton, 1980), 342 ff., and Arden Bucholz, *Hans Delbrück and the German Military Establishment* (Iowa City, 1985), 30ff.

6. Cf. Marc Raeff, *The Well-Ordered Police State: Social and Institutional Change through Law in the Germanies and Russia, 1600–1800* (New Haven, 1983); F. L. Carsten, *Princes and Parliaments in Germany from the Fifteenth to the Eighteenth Century* (Oxford, 1959); and James Allen Vann's case study, *The Making of a State: Württemberg 1593–1793* (Ithaca, 1984).

7. Martin van Creveld, *Supplying War: Logistics from Wallenstein to Patton* (Cambridge, 1977), 23ff.

8. Cf., inter alia, Fritz Hartung, *Enlightened Despotism* (London, 1957), and Leonard Krieger, *An Essay on the Theory of Enlightened Despotism* (Chicago, 1979). The security question also crops up in the contributions to Franklin Kopitsch, ed., *Aufklärung, Absolutismus und Bürgertum in Deutschland* (Munich, 1976). Charles Ingrao, "The Problem of 'Enlightened Absolutism' in the German States," *Journal of Modern History* 58 [Supplement] (1986): S161–S180, perceptively surveys the literature.

9. Useful case studies include Helen Liebel, *Enlightened Bureaucracy versus Enlightened Despotism in Baden, 1750–1792* (Philadelphia, 1965); Eberhard Weis, "Der Aufgeklärte Absolutismus in den mittleren und kleineren deutschen Staaten," *Zeitschrift für bayerische Landesgeschichte* 42 (1979): 31–46; and Charles Ingrao, *The Hessian Mercenary State: Ideas, Institutions and Reform under Frederick II, 1760–1785* (Cambridge, 1987).

10. Gregor Schöllgen, "Sicherheit durch Expansion? Die Aussenpolitischen Lageanalysen der Hohenzollern im 17. und 18. Jahrhundert im Lichte des Kontinuitätsproblems in der Preussischen und Deutschen Geschichte," *Historisches Jahrbuch* 104 (1984): 22–45. Cf. Michael Roberts, *The Swedish Imperial Experience, 1560–1718* (Cambridge, 1929).

11. Rodney Atwood, *The Hessian Mercenaries from Hessen-Kassel in the American Revolution* (Cambridge, 1980), 7ff., is a good introduction to this issue. Cf. also Ingrao, *Hessian Mercenary State*.

12. A. W. Koch, *A History of Prussia* (London, 1978), 95ff., is a sympathetic summary. Useful for background is Richard L. Gawthrop, "For the Good of Thy

Neighbor: Pietism and the Making of Eighteenth-Century Prussia," Ph.D. diss., Indiana University, 1984.

13. This point is highlighted in Paul Schroeder, *Austria, Great Britain and the Crimean War* (Cornell, 1971), 402–3. Heinz Duchhardt, "Friedenswahrung in 18. Jahrhundert," *Historische Zeitschrift* 240 (1985): 265–82, establishes the limits of peace in an age of limited war.

14. Cf., inter alia, Otto Büsch, *Militärsystem und Sozialleben im alten Preussen*, rev. ed. (Frankfurt, 1981), and Bernhard R. Kroener, "Armee und Staat," in *Panorama der Friedericianischen Zeit*, ed. J. Ziechmann (Bremen, 1985), 393–404. The limits of Prussian national identity are established in Henri Brunschwig, *Enlightenment and Romanticism in Eighteenth-Century Prussia*, trans. F. Jellinek (Chicago, 1974), and Hans Kohn, *Prelude to Nation-States: The French and German Experience, 1789–1815* (New York, 1967), 119ff.

15. Cf. William H. McNeill, *The Pursuit of Power: Technology, Armed Force and Society since A.D. 1000* (Chicago, 1982), 117ff., and Christopher Duffy, *The Fortress in the Age of Vauban and Frederick the Great, 1660–1789* (London, 1985).

16. Jay Luvaas, "Frederick the Great: Education of a General," in *The John Biggs Cincinnati Lectures in Military Leadership and Command, 1986*, ed. H. Bausum (Lexington, Va., 1986), 23–37.

17. Particularly useful for evaluating Frederick's approach to war is the recent work of Theodor Schieder, particularly "Friedrich der Grosse und Machiavelli— Das Dilemma von Machtpolitik und Aufklärung," *Historische Zeitschrift* 234 (1982): 265–94, and *Friedrich der Grosse: Ein Königtum der Widersprüche* (Frankfurt, 1983). On the outbreak of the Seven Years' War, see Winfried Baumgart, "Der Ausbruch des siebenjährigen Krieges. Zum gegenwärtigen Forschungsstand," *Militärgeschichtliche Mitteilungen* 11 (1972): 157–65, still a useful survey of the literature. Cf. also L. Jay Oliva, *Misalliance: French Policy in Russia during the Seven Years' War* (New York, 1964), and C. W. Ingrao, "Habsburg Strategy and Geopolitics during the Eighteenth Century," in *East Central European Society and War in Pre-Revolutionary Europe*, ed. G. Rothenberg, et al. (New York, 1982), 49–66.

18. Frederick II, "Pensées et règles générales pour la guerre" [1755], *Oeuvres*, 30 vols. (Berlin, 1843–57), 28:124–25.

19. Cited in Christopher Duffy, *Frederick the Great: A Military Life* (London, 1985), 44. Cf. Frederick II, "Das politische Testament von 1752," *Die Werke Friedrichs des Grossen*, 10 vols. (Berlin, 1913), 7:164ff.

20. Luvaas, "Education of a General," 35.

21. On the essential similarity of European armies during this period, see particularly André Corvisier, *Armies and Societies in Europe, 1494–1789*, trans. A. Siddall (Bloomington, Ind., 1979).

22. Hans Speier, "Militarism in the Eighteenth Century," *Social Order and the Risks of War* (Cambridge, Mass., 1969), 230–52.

23. John Gagliardo, *From Pariah to Patriot: The Changing Image of the German Peasant, 1770–1840* (Lexington, Ky., 1969); Eugen Weber, *Peasants into Frenchmen* (Stanford, 1976).

24. Charles Ingrao, " 'Barbarous Strangers': Hessian State and Society during

the American Revolution," *American Historical Review* 87 (1982): 954–76, esp. 961–62, Sylvia R. Frey, *The British Soldier in America: A Social History of Military Life in the Revolutionary Period* (Austin, Texas, 1981), 4ff.

25. F. C. Laukhard, *Magister F. Ch. Laukhards Leben und Schicksale von ihm selbst beschrieben,* 13th ed., 2 vols. (Stuttgart, 1930), 1:248–49.

26. Franz Uhle-Wettler, *Höhe- und Wendepunkte deutscher Militärgeschichte* (Mainz, 1984), 33ff., and Hans Bleckwenn, *Unter dem Preussen-Adler* (Munich, 1978), 72, appropriately point out that a relatively small number of hard cases received a disproportionate number of the most draconic punishments, and that such men gave soldiers in general a bad name. Moreover, the vivid accounts of the system's horrors were likely to be composed by critics: officers who favored a discipline based on honor and mutual respect, or soldiers already distinguished from the common run by their literacy, who perceived themselves as having been enlisted by guile or force. That they hated the Prussian army is understandable, but deserters and malcontents are seldom a reliable guide to the internal dynamics of any armed force. Such works as Ulrich Bräker's *Der arme Mann im Tockenburg* (Zürich, 1789; reprint, Munich, 1965), often cited for the army's routine on the eve of the Seven Years' War, are best taken at a certain critical distance. Willerd Fann, "On the Infantryman's Age in Eighteenth Century Prussia," *Military Affairs* 41 (1977): 165–70, stresses the rootedness foreigners and old soldiers generally had in their regiments.

27. Cf. John Pemble, "Resources and Techniques in the Second Maratha War," *The Historical Journal* 19 (1976): 375–404, and Lorenzo Crowell, "The Madras Army in the Northern Circars, 1532–1833: Pacification and Professionalism," Ph.D. diss., University of North Carolina, 1982.

28. Peter E. Russell, "Redcoats in the Wilderness: British Officers and Irregular Warfare in Europe and America, 1740 to 1760," *The William and Mary Quarterly* 35 (1978): 629–52.

29. Peter Paret, "Colonial Experience and European Military Reform at the End of the Eighteenth Century," *Bulletin of the Institute of Historical Research* 37 (1964): 49–56, and "The Relationship between the Revolutionary War and European Military Thought and Practice in the Second Half of the Eighteenth Century," in *Reconsiderations on the Revolutionary War: Selected Essays,* ed. D. Higginbotham (Westport, Conn., 1978), 144–57. Cf. also David Gates, *The British Light Infantry Arm c. 1790–1815: Its Creation, Training, and Operational Role* (London, 1987).

30. Duffy, *Frederick the Great,* 308ff., is the most recent survey of the oblique order's evolution.

31. Willerd Fann, "Peacetime Attrition in the Army of Frederick William I, 1713–1740," *Central European History* 9 (1978): 323–34.

32. Cf. Christopher Duffy, *The Army of Frederick the Great* (New York, 1974), 89ff.; Curt Jany, *Geschichte der Preussischen Armee von 15. Jahrhundert bis 1914,* rev. ed., 4 vols. (Osnabrück, 1967), vol. 2 passim; and Dennis E. Showalter, "Tactics and Recruitment in Eighteenth-Century Prussia," *Studies in History and Politics/ Etudes d'Histoire et de Politique* 3 (1984): 15–41.

33. Cited in F. Meinecke, ed., "Aus den Akten der Militärreorganisationskom-

mission von 1808," *Forschungen zur brandenburgischen und preussischen Geschichte* 5 (1892): 139.

34. W. Eckardt and O. Morawietz, *Die Handwaffen des brandenburgisch-preussisch-deutschen Heeres, 1640-1945* (Hamburg, 1957), 43ff., is technically accurate, but typically critical in evaluating the M1782.

35. Duffy, *The Army of Frederick the Great*, 110ff. See also the older, detailed accounts of C. von Decker, *Die Schlachten und Hauptgefechten des Siebenjährigen Krieges . . . mit vorherrschender Bezugnahme aus den Gebrauch der Artillerie* (Berlin, 1837); L. von Malinowski and K. von Bonin, *Geschichte der brandenburgisch-preussischen Artillerie*, 3 vols. (Berlin, 1840-42).

36. David Chandler, *The Campaigns of Napoleon* (New York, 1966), 360, 670.

37. Frederick, "Instruction für meine Artillerie," [1782] *Die Werke Friedrichs des Grossen*, 6:337ff.

38. Cf. R. von Bonin, "Über die Errichtung, Formation and Ausrüstung der Preussischen reitenden Artillerie," *Archiv für die Offiziere der Königlich Preussische Artillerie-und Ingenieur-Korps* 9 (1839): 202-37, (hereafter cited as *Archiv*); von Strotha, *Die Königlich Preussische reitende Artillerie vom Jahre 1759 bis 1816* (Berlin, 1868).

39. Frederick to Prince Henry, 11 June 1778, in *Politische Korrespondenz Friedrichs des Grossen*, 46 vols. (Berlin, 1879-1939), No. 26458.

40. Frederick, "Das militärische Testament von 1768," *Die Werke Friedrichs des Grossen*, 6:225ff.

41. On Prussia's postwar recovery, see most recently C. A. B. Behrens, *Society, Government, and the Enlightenment: The Experiences of Eighteenth-Century France and Prussia* (New York, 1985), 125ff., and W. O. Henderson, "Die Wirtschafts und Handelspolitik Friedrichs des Grossen," in *Panorama der Friedericianischen Zeit*, ed. J. Ziechmann, 477-85.

42. The decline of the Prussian army can be traced in Duffy, *Army of Frederick the Great*, 199ff., and John E. Stine, "King Frederick William II and the Decline of the Prussian Army, 1786-1797," Ph.D. diss., University of South Carolina, 1980.

43. H. B. Nisbet, " 'Was ist Aufklärung?': The Concept of Enlightenment in Eighteenth-Century Germany," *Journal of European Studies* 12 (1982): 77-95.

44. Stine, "King Frederick William II," 91ff.; Charles E. White, "The Enlightened Soldier: Scharnhorst and the Militärische Gesellschaft in Berlin, 1801-1805," Ph.D. diss., Duke University, 1984; and G. Wollstein, "Scharnhorst und die Französische Revolution," *Historische Zeitschrift* 227 (1978): 325-53.

45. As in Gordon A. Craig, "The Failure of Reform: Stein and Marwitz," in *The End of Prussia* (Madison, Wis., 1984), 8-26.

46. John A. Lynn, *The Bayonets of the Republic: Motivation and Tactics in the Army of Revolutionary France, 1791-94* (Urbana, Ill., 1984).

47. In Max Lehmann, "Zur Geschichte der preussischen Heeresreform von 1808," *Historische Zeitschrift* 126 (1922): 442-43.

48. Cf. Eckardt and Morawietz, 45ff.; Dennis E. Showalter, "Manifestation of Reform: The Rearmament of the Prussian Infantry, 1806-13," *Journal of Modern History* 44 (1972): 364-80; and "Instruktion des Generals von York für den leichten Truppen zu den Übungen im Jahre 1810," in C. F. Gumtau, *Die Jäger und Schützen des preussischen Heeres*, vol. 3 (Berlin, 1838), 79ff. (appendix).

49. "Allgemeine Regeln zur Befolgung in den Übungen," in G. H. Klippel, *Das Leben des Generals von Scharnhorst,* vol. 3 (Leipzig, 1871), 541.

50. White, "Enlightened Soldier," 177ff., and Peter Paret, *Yorck and the Era of Prussian Reform, 1807–1815* (Princeton, 1966), 154ff., admirably summarize the scholarship on this subject while drawing conclusions differing significantly from those of the present author.

51. Gordon A. Craig, "Problems of Coalition Warfare: The Military Alliance against Napoleon, 1813–1814," in *War, Politics and Diplomacy: Selected Essays* (New York, 1966), 22–45.

52. Carl von Clausewitz, *On War,* ed. and trans. M. Howard, P. Paret (Princeton, 1976), 226.

53. Dennis E. Showalter, "The Prussian Landwehr and Its Critics, 1813–1819," *Central European History* 4 (1971): 3–33, is best balanced by Peter Paret, *Clausewitz and the State* (New York, 1976), 286ff., and Alf Lüdtke, " 'Wehrhafte Nation' und 'innere Wohlfahrt': Zur militärischen Mobilisierbarkeit der bürgerlichen Gesellschaft. Konflikt und Konsens zwischen Militär und ziviler Administration in Preussen, 1815–60," *Militärgeschichtliche Mitteilungen* 30 (1981): 7–56; more comprehensively by *"Gemeinwohl," Polizei und "Festungspraxis": Staatliche Gewaltsamkeit und innere Verwaltung in Preussen, 1815–1850* (Göttingen, 1982).

54. On this issue, Reinhard Höhn, *Verfassungskampf und Heereseid: Der Kampf des Bürgertums um das Heer (1815–1850),* (Leipzig, 1938), remains useful despite its *Völkisch* tones and sympathies. Cf. the case study by Reinhard Meilitz, "Das badische Militärwesen und die Frage der Volksbewaffnung von den Jahren des Rheinbundes bis zur 48 er Revolution." Ph.D. diss., University of Freiburg, 1956. The limits of even the best kind of popular levies when unsupported by organized forces had been indicated by the Tirol uprisings of 1809. Gunther Eyck, *Loyal Rebels: Andreas Hofer and the Tyrolean Uprising of 1809* (Lanham, Md., 1986).

55. Frederick Meinecke, *Das Leben des Generalfeldmarschalls Hermann von Boyen,* vol. 2 (Stuttgart, 1899), 225ff.

56. Ann Ruth Wilner, *The Spellbinders: Charismatic Political Leadership* (New Haven, 1984).

57. The impact of even the German Confederation on French military planning during the period is a major theme of Gary Cox, "Facing the Germans: The Beginning of French Strategic Planning, 1815–1848," Ph.D. diss., University of Virginia, 1987. Cf., more generally, Enno E. Kraehe, *Metternich's German Policy,* vol. 2, *The Congress of Vienna, 1814–1815* (Princeton, 1983); and Heinrich Lutz, *Zwischen Habsburg und Preussen: Deutschland 1815–1866* (Berlin, 1985).

58. Beitner, *Die königliche preussische Garde-Artillerie,* vol. 1 (Berlin, 1889), 281.

59. Dennis E. Showalter, "Weapons, Technology and the Military in Metternich's Germany: A Study in Stagnation?," *The Australian Journal of Politics and History* 25 (1978): 227–38, will best be read in the context of Eric Dorn Brose's forthcoming monograph on government and industrialization in Prussia during the early nineteenth century. I am indebted to Professor Brose for sharing early versions of his arguments and conclusions.

60. Eckard and Morowietz, 63ff.

61. "Übersicht der hauptsächlichsten Veränderungen in der Einrichtung bei der

Feldartillerie des Systems von Jahre 1842 im Vergleich zu dem von Jahre 1816," *Archiv* 20 (1846): 18–60.

62. For details of the debate see Dennis E. Showalter, *Railroads and Rifles: Soldiers, Technology, and the Unification of Germany* (Hamden, Conn., 1975), 81ff.

63. Jany, *Preussische Armee*, 4:200. Cf. the Cabinet Order of 6 June 1848, in *Militärische Schriften weiland Kaiser Wilhelms des Grossen*, ed. Pr. Kriegsministerium, 2 vols. (Berlin, 1897), 2:80–81.

64. Cf. the *Exercir-Reglement für die Infanterie der Königlich-Preussische Armee* (Berlin, 1847), with Prince William's extensive memoranda and correspondence in *Militärische Schriften Kaiser Wilhelms*, 1:304ff. It is worth noting that the new regulations satisfied not only Boyen (Meinecke, *Boyen*, 2:521–22), but Frederick Engels, who in 1855 described them as "without a doubt by far the best in the world." Engles, "Die Armeen Europas," in *Ausgewählte Militärische Schriften* (Berlin, 1958), 434.

65. Cf. such contemporary polemics as "Die gezogenen Geschütze: Kritische Untersuchungen über ihre Vortheile und Nachtheile, von einem deutschen Artillerie-Offizier" (Darmstadt, 1861); "Die Anwendbarkeit gezogenen Geschütze," *Archiv* 38 (1855): 39–46; and "Über Bewaffnung und Organisation der Feld-Artillerie," *Archiv* 56 (1864): 13–43.

66. Cf., inter alia, "Streifereien auf dem Gebiete der modernen Taktik," *Allgemeine Militärische Zeitung* (1957), Nos. 5–10, 29–32, 57–58, 79–80, 83–88, 93–104; Helmuth von Moltke, "Bemerkungen von 12. Juli 1858 über Veränderungen in der Taktik infolge des verbesserten Infanteriegewehre," in *Moltkes Militärische Werke*, ed. Gr. Generalstab, 13 vols. (Berlin, 1892–1912), sec. 2. Abteilung, *Thätigkeit des Generalstabs im Frieden*, 2:7ff. (hereafter cited as *MMW*); and [Prince Frederick Charles] *Eine militärische Denkschrift [Über die Kampfweise der Französen]* (Frankfurt, 1860).

67. Meinecke, *Boyen*, 2:541ff.

68. Showalter, *Railroads and Rifles*, 23ff.; van Creveld, *Supplying War*, 77ff.

69. Otto Pflanze, *Bismarck and the Development of Germany* (Princeton, 1963), 458ff.; Lothar Gall, *Bismarck: The White Revolutionary*, trans. J. A. Underwood, 2 vols. (London, 1986), 1:295ff.; Eberhard Kolb, "Der schwierige Weg zum Frieden: Das Problem der Kriegsbeendigung 1870/71," *Historische Zeitschrift* 241 (1985): 51–79.

70. Eberhard Kessel, *Moltke* (Stuttgart, 1957), and Rudolf Stadelmann, *Moltke und der Staat* (Krefeld, 1950), remain the best of the sympathetic studies. Gerhard Ritter, *Staatskunst und Kriegshandwerk*, vol. 1 (Munich, 1965), 247ff., stresses the limits of Moltke's approach.

71. Martin van Creveld, *Command in War* (Cambridge, Mass., 1985), 107ff.; Dennis E. Showalter, "Soldiers into Postmasters: The Electric Telegraph as an Instrument of Command in the Prussian Army," *Military Affairs* 37 (April, 1973): 48–52.

72. *MMW*, 3. Abteilung, *Kriegsgeschichtliche Arbeiten*, 3:11.

73. On the origins and functioning of the staff system, Dallas D. Irvine, "The Origin of Capital Staffs," *Journal of Modern History* 10 (1938): 161–79, and "The French and Prussian Staff Systems Before 1870," *Journal of the American Military*

History Foundation 2 (1938): 192, remain useful introductions. A satisfactory history of the institution itself remains to be written. Walter Goerlitz, *Der deutsche Generalstab, Geschichte und Gestalt,* 2d ed. (Frankfurt am Main, 1953), is more complete than its abridged English translation, *History of the German General Staff,* trans. Brian Battershaw (New York, 1961), but is still more anecdotal than analytical. T. N. Dupuy, *A Genius for War: The German Army and General Staff, 1807–1945* (Englewood, N.J., 1977), is disappointingly unoriginal.

The British Army and "Modern" War: The Experience of the Peninsula and of the Crimea

HEW STRACHAN

IT IS A TRUISM among military historians that, while the armies of Europe blazed a trail of technological and organizational modernization in the nineteenth century, Britain's army lagged behind. On Queen Victoria's death, the army did not have a general staff, a permanent divisional and corps organization, or enlistment by conscription.

The conventional explanation for this state of affairs is the remarkable persistence in the nineteenth century of colonial wars. Between 1815 and 1914 the British army only once fought an organized European army—in the Crimea—but it almost never ceased combat, in wars both lesser and greater, against a bewildering variety of extra-European opponents. Between 1837 and 1846, the Queen's regiments suppressed a rebellion in Canada, suffered defeat in Afghanistan and victory in China, overran the Sind, annexed Gwalior, fought the Maoris and crushed the Punjab. In an even shorter time span, between 1878 and 1881, they fought, albeit with mixed fortunes, the Afghans (again), the Zulus, and the Boers. Whereas the Prussian army could develop its institutions against a reasonably constant geographical and strategic background, the British army could not. As G. F. R. Henderson put it in 1900: "It is useless to anticipate in what quarter of the globe our troops may be next employed as to guess at the tactics, the armament and even the colour... of our next enemy. Each new expedition demands special equipment, special methods of supply and special tactical devices, and sometimes special armament."[1] Furthermore, as Henderson's remarks testify, it was not simply in its broad structures that the British army was shaped by colonial demands. The colonies provided

211

a continued and important role for cavalry when the devastation of modern firepower had diminished its significance in mainland Europe; the infantry still met onrushing Dervishes in square, when that same firepower would, in a European context, have forced not concentration but dispersion.[2]

It has, however, been argued elsewhere that to see colonial warfare as inhibiting change is to miss the point.[3] In practice the colonies were one of a triumvirate of pressures underpinning the army's institutional and tactical development. The second was British domestic reform, inaugurated with the 1832 reform bill, which in the next couple of decades embraced many state institutions.[4] The third, and most relevant in a military context, was technological innovation. The army of Britain, the first industrialized nation of the world, constantly confronted the issue of weapons modernization and its doctrinal implications from the late 1830s onwards. Most dramatic as steps on this path were the adoption of the Minié rifle in 1851 and its replacement by the Enfield in 1853; the entire infantry was now equipped with a weapon accurate to 800 yards — rather than a smoothbore musket inaccurate at even 150 yards.[5]

If the army considered war against a European opponent, it did so largely in the context of home defense against a French invasion. The Crimean War, with the dispatch of a British expeditionary force to fight a European adversary, was in this context an aberration. But although the practice of warfare for the British army in the nineteenth century was unequivocally colonial, in the propagation of theory it looked to Continental precepts, to the examples of Frederick the Great and of Napoleon. Rarely indeed did British military writers illuminate their analyses by reference to the sort of operations of which their readers had the greatest experience. C. E. Callwell's *Small Wars* is important not least because it stands in isolation. Callwell, by dint not only of his treatment of colonial warfare but also of his *Military Operations and Maritime Preponderance* (1905), deserves far greater recognition as the publicist of specifically *British* forms of strategy; the fact that he was not one of those selected for treatment in Jay Luvaas's *The Education of an Army* illustrates how the main currents in British military thought ran elsewhere.

But the point being made here is not simply that the British army failed to study its colonial experiences. That British soldiers should have regarded Continental, not colonial, warfare as the real thing is

not in itself odd; what is strange is that, despite its Continental preoccupations, it did not study those European wars in which Britain itself
had been directly engaged and even taken the major part. The Peninsular
War had been a vital component in a collaborative effort to defeat the
most brilliant commander Europe had ever seen. The post-1815 international system in Europe lay under the threat of the Cossack—
the Russian army in the East stretched a long and seemingly barbaric
shadow over the West. But in 1854–56 this army, the largest in Europe,
and the victor in 1812 and 1813, was defeated in the Crimea through
another joint effort in which Britain's army played a major part. The
achievements of the British army were therefore highly creditable by
any absolute standards. But professional commentators were drawn
instead to consideration of Napoleon's campaigns in Italy and his
defensive strokes in 1813–14, and to the wars of German unification
in 1866 and 1870. The strategy, which they and their European contemporaries embraced, was—in Delbrück's terminology[6]—a strategy
of annihilation. Short, sharp campaigns had by their speed of maneuver
brought rapid and decisive battlefield success. Waterloo—being a short
campaign concluded with a decisive battle—was not too different to
prevent its being assimilated into the general pattern if necessary.

In 1914, therefore, British generals, like those of France and Germany,
went to war seeking a speedy resolution on the battlefield. Maneuver
and mobility were the keynotes, and war was limited because it was
brief. In the event, none of this was true. It was Delbrück's "strategy
of attrition," not his "strategy of annihilation," that best described the
Great War. Tactically, defensive firepower dominated, and the armies
responded with gigantic schemes of field fortification, which evoked
techniques of earlier siege operations. Strategically, or, perhaps more
accurately, operationally, exhaustion—not a decisive battle—became
the means to victory.

What is striking in this for the student of the British army is the
comparison between the tactical conditions of the First World War
and those of the Crimea, and—at the operational level—between those
of the First World War and those of the Peninsular War. This may
seem a somewhat simplistic comparison (and it is not necessarily pre-
supposed that such connections are anything other than contrivances),
but given the military penchant for drawing "lessons" from history,
here is a case where lessons that might have been drawn were not. For
British military theorists before 1914 tended to neglect both the Cri-

mean and the Peninsular Wars; even if they overcame this neglect, they did not study the Crimea as an example of trench warfare or the Peninsula as an illustration of the strategy of attrition. If they had, the British army might have been better prepared intellectually for the conditions of 1914–18. The irony, therefore, is that Britain's Continental military experience could have been made to reveal "lessons" more relevant to "modern" war than were precepts derived from Napoleon or Moltke.[7]

That this occurred will not necessarily be very surprising. It would have required intellectual courage and a degree of foresight—both in large measure—to have gone against the prevailing trend. And if anyone had, he probably would have been consigned to oblivion and left without influence. But the historiographical fates of the Crimean and of the Peninsular Wars up until 1914 are nonetheless worthy of consideration. The remainder of this essay will therefore develop this last theme and ask why it was that the army did not learn all that it might have from either episode.

II

The Crimean War may have deflected attention from the more fundamental and ongoing challenges confronting the British army. But it was a European war fought after the onset of technological innovation and after the commencement of a period of reform in British military institutions. It is therefore the pivot in any argument about the British army and its response to "modern" European war. Although in outward form much of the Crimean War seemed to belong to the age of Marlborough rather than of Moltke, in its essentials it could be—and has been—described as the first "modern" war. Steamships supported the allied armies; the telegraph linked them to their capitals; railways were constructed between the base at Balaclava and the forward positions. Ultimately the efficiency of these communications allowed Britain and France to apply their superior economic strength to the theater of operations, and so exhaust the Russians into abandoning Sebastopol and conceding defeat. The Crimean War, although not a particularly long war, was a war of attrition. The great battles decided little, if anything. It was the continuation of the campaign that brought victory.

The Crimean War was also a war of attrition in tactical terms. Kinglake described the defense of Sebastopol as "that protracted conflict which we have almost been ready to call a continuous battle."[8] The battle — or siege — lasted eleven months. Field Marshal Sir Evelyn Wood looked back on the war forty years later, and concluded: "I must go fully into the question of our siege works, and batteries, for it was in them our soldiers died from starvation, want of clothing, and overwork; and it was in them we wore down the strength of the Russians till they withdrew across the harbour, Alma, Balaklava, and Inkerman being but incidents in the war, albeit of a glorious kind."[9] His contemporary, E. B. Hamley, produced a related observation from the more immediate vantage point of 1855; the allies had won the war by the continuous nature of the siege, since its length ensured the drain on Russian resources that its rapid conclusion would have prevented.[10]

Use of the description "siege" is itself unfortunate. It was a word redolent of Vauban and the self-important technicalities of science applied to wars in the Age of Reason. By calling the fighting at Sebastopol a "siege," Victorians pointed backward not forward. They could argue that Sebastopol's investment was never complete and that, since it could still be supplied from outside, its defense was prolonged. According to this argument, complete encirclement would have brought rapid capitulation. But, in the view of Sir John Burgoyne (Raglan's de facto strategic advisor and a distinguished engineer), this was totally to misunderstand the nature of the operations. As early as 18 October 1854 he acknowledged, "It is not a fortress we are attacking, but an army deeply entrenched in strong ground, and with an immense provision of heavy artillery."[11] Although Burgoyne criticized Kinglake, since he felt the latter persisted in seeing Sebastopol as a fort held by a garrison,[12] he was being somewhat unjust. Kinglake held that Todleben had created an entrenched position, requiring a whole army (not simply a garrison, as in a fortification) to defend it against the attack of another army.[13] E. B. Hamley came to a similar conclusion.[14]

Trench warfare was therefore the dominant military experience of the Crimea. The frontage of the allied lines was 7 miles, that of the Russians 5 miles.[15] There were 12 miles of British trenches; and to construct them 38,894 shovels, 13,322 pickaxes, 9,319 spades, and 529,587 sandbags were brought up to Balaclava between 10 February and 8 September 1855.[16] The French constructed 50 miles of trenches, using 14,000 tons of engineering materials, including 80,000 gabions, 60,000 fascines, and a million sandbags.[17] The trenches themselves were "two or three yards wide and two or three feet deep, with the earth thrown up to form a parapet towards the enemy."[18] The guns were separated by traverses, faced with gabions and sandbags, and zigzags (or "communication trenches" in the parlance of a later war) linked the first and second parallels. In the winter the trenches filled with snow and liquid mud.[19] The duties were exhausting and trying for the men; the attackers had insufficient numbers to mount reliefs as regularly as regarded desirable. British soldiers tended to be insufficiently active in raiding or sniping and to be reluctant to undertake the hard labor of digging.[20] By contrast, the Russian defense was conducted in a very lively manner, with sorties and night raids, countermining, and—above all—aggressive artillery fire. Under cover of darkness the Russians would mark out and dig fresh trench lines and prepare rows of rifle pits (effectively holes for individual snipers) that would later be developed into a connected trench line.[21]

As well as being a sappers' war, it was also a gunners' war. Todleben's plan of defense aimed to stop the attack by firepower; he concentrated, in his own words, "upon all the approaches of the town a powerful front and flank fire of artillery and musketry, endeavouring to sweep with as much fire as possible all the bendings of the broken ground by which the enemy might appear."[22] In the first bombardment in October 1854, the allies had to curtail their firing as they had only three to four days' supply of ammunition.[23]

Already, in January 1855, Burgoyne was amazed by the consequences: "The expenditure of ammunition by the Russians has been extraordinary: the whole surface of the ground from immediately in rear of our own batteries to about 2000 yards from the place, is thickly strewed with shot (of very heavy calibre), blind shells, and splinters, in a degree that astonishes you . . . while they are twice as thick along the straight lines of the deep ravines."[24] The number of heavy guns steadily mounted. A report of December 1855 computed that the Russians had a total of 1,254 guns available,[25] but of these less than half were both heavy and in a position to be brought to bear against the allies. In the fifth bombardment on the town, the Russians had 586 heavy guns mounted, and the allies 638. The bombardment was officially timed to last from 17 to 21 August 1855, but in practice fire was continued until the sixth and final bombardment, begun on 5 September. On this occasion, the allies had 775 heavy guns, all of heavier caliber than those used in the sieges of the Peninsular War, and including—for the British—seven 68-pounders and seven 10-inch guns. The Russians had 1,209, of which

586 were employed.[26] The allies were reckoned to have fired 1,350,000 rounds of artillery ammunition during the siege (and 50 million rounds of small arms ammunition);[27] the British siege guns alone fired 251,872 rounds.[28] Kinglake reports that in the closing stages of the siege, "even General Todleben was fain to break away in describing it from the colder language of science, and to treat the bombardment as an abnormal exertion of force—as violent, terrible, murderous."[29]

The point is clear: herein are the prefigurings of the First World War. The relevance of the Crimea was not lost on Pétain in 1916, as his forces struggled to recapture Fort Douaumont at Verdun. He wrote: "It was most encouraging as one looked from the Souville observation post, to see them gaining each day a few feet of ground, and at once organizing for the defence their rudiments of trenches. Often, as I gazed at them with admiration, I reflected that they were carrying on the tradition to which the siege of Sebastopol had given birth."[30]

But in Britain the lesson was lost. In part, this was the consequence of the context in which the siege was set. Before the Crimean War, the threat of French invasion had sparked an enthusiasm for the construction of fresh fortifications, especially around naval bases such as Portsmouth. The costs of forts built of mortar, and the rapidity with which they might become outdated by improved gunnery, led an architect, James Fergusson, to propose a system using earth as its primary building material.[31] The proponents of the Fergusson approach seized on Todleben's defense of Sebastopol as vindication of their views. Sir Harry Jones, the senior royal engineer at the conclusion of the siege, was disposed to agree; earth parapets could be restored overnight after heavy fire, when those of masonry would have been completely destroyed.[32] Burgoyne, Fergusson's principal prewar opponent, did not at first accept this argument. The Russians had used earthworks by necessity, not from choice; the strength of their position was primarily due to the number of their guns and their dispersion (not—as in Fergusson's system—their concentration).[33] The future first commandant of the Staff College, Patrick MacDougall, in *The Theory of War* (1856), poured scorn on earthworks and held that the siege of Sebastopol had done no more than confirm the principles of Vauban and his successors.[34]

In due course, principally thanks to the advent of rifled artillery and to the influence of the American Civil War, MacDougall revised his views.[35] Burgoyne also came round to earthworks during the 1860s.[36]

But the opportunity for the full tactical impact of such conclusions to be absorbed by the British army had been lost; cautious revisionism was swamped by the acclamation of the Prussian victories of 1866 and 1870. No link was made between Sebastopol and the lines of Torres Vedras, another entrenched position that was not a fortress with a garrison but a defensive screen for a field army. Field fortification remained an art of the engineer; it was an expedient for detached outposts, not a method of warfare for whole armies. Histories of the Crimean War failed to highlight the strategic consequences of their tactical employment.

The historiography of the Crimean War before 1914 is a disappointment. It was a field dominated by A. W. Kinglake's *The Invasion of the Crimea*. But Kinglake was a professional writer, not a professional soldier. Soldiers did not imagine that they were likely to receive much instruction from him; indeed their view was, if anything, the reverse — that Kinglake should be kept right by them. Furthermore, Kinglake did not take the war to its conclusion but to the death of Lord Raglan. Thus the central military operation of the war, the "siege" of Sebastopol, was not the core of Kinglake's book. Understandably, he was drawn to big battles, and so the Alma, Balaclava, and Inkerman each received a volume of its own. The causes of the war and the administration of the allied effort both demanded another volume each. His last two volumes inevitably had more to say about the siege, but the concluding volume did not appear until 1887, twenty-five years after the first, and by then other wars had intervened.

The trend was confirmed by the self-interest of Garnet Wolseley and his acolytes. The Crimean War became a benchmark by which to measure the subsequent improvement in the administration and efficiency of the army. It provided a vivid cautionary tale of what might happen in the event of financial and parliamentary neglect; it was the backcloth against which the victories of Roberts and of Wolseley himself could shine all the more brightly. Its serious study at an operational level was not compatible with its use for propaganda purposes. After 1871 the wars of German unification, and to a lesser extent the American Civil War, seemed to provide a much more revealing insight into the nature of modern war. Furthermore, the achievements of Moltke supported the "strategy of annihilation" argument — maneuver had brought decisive battle-field success in the space of single, short campaigns.

Jay Luvaas has called Frederick Maurice's *War* (a reprint of Maurice's contribution to the *Encyclopaedia Brittanica*) "one of the most famous works on the subject of war published in England during the nineteenth century."[37] It may therefore be appropriate to look at *War* in the light of its comments on the Crimea. Not that there is much to say, for Maurice is dismissive: "In England there yet survive officers who talk as though the experiences of the Crimea were the only "practical' experiences; as though the blood-stained fields of France and Turkey supplied us only with "theoretical' lessons. It is the old story."[38] In his appendix on military literature, he highlighted works on Napoleon, the Waterloo campaign, 1866, and 1870. "Neither [the Crimean campaign or the Franco-Austrian campaign of 1859] is, I think, for a military student, so valuable as any one of Napoleon's earlier campaigns, or, for strategical study, as those of Frederick the Great."[39]

The reasons for Maurice's dismissal of the Crimea are not hard to find. For him the great change in modern war, as exemplified by the Germans, was the perfection of army organization;[40] this had been the British army's gravest defect in 1854. Furthermore, his views on strategy itself would not allow much value to be placed on a campaign where siege operations had dominated. Modern artillery, he felt, would make all types of fortification more vulnerable, and great movements would be less impeded by forts than in the past.[41] Predictably the aims of these "great movements" would be "first, to break up the organic force of the opposing army by dealing in concentrated force with fractions of the enemy, and secondly, to threaten, and if possible to destroy, the enemy's connection with the sources fromwhere he draws his supplies."[42] There was little that was attritional—either tactically or strategically—in all this.

Maurice was not unique in his rating of the Crimean War's significance. Sir Edward Hamley, although he wrote two books on the war, and although he himself served in it, gave it almost no attention in *The Operations of War*. T. Miller Maguire, in his *Summary of Modern Military History* (1887) devoted four pages to the war, as opposed to twenty-eight on Waterloo. F. N. Maude did not mention the Crimean War once in *The Evolution of Modern Strategy* (1905) and the same went for J. W. E. Donaldson's *Military History Applied to Modern Warfare* (1907).

Potentially the Crimean War had much to say about "the tools of war," but in practice it was not much studied by the British army. For all its technological innovations, in tactical terms it was too often seen—and is still too often seen—as the last of an old style of warfare, not the first of the new.

III

The historical analysis of the Peninsular War suffered a fate almost diametrically opposed to that of the Crimea. In tactical terms, the Peninsula belonged firmly to an evolved eighteenth-century tradition; the British infantry was equipped with smoothbore muskets, Wellington employed limited quantities of field artillery in a conservative fashion, and sieges (properly understood, if frequently improperly undertaken) against conventional masonry fortifications were as common as battles. By 1854 the technology and tactics associated with the Peninsular War were under direct challenge. But before 1854 it was at this level, the tactical, that the Peninsular War was primarily studied.

However, there was a different approach to the understanding of the Peninsular War, albeit one not clearly articulated until after the First World War. It is an interpretation that, in British accounts of the war, first begins to find prominence in Liddell Hart's *Strategy: The Indirect Approach,* although Liddell Hart himself pointed out that Fortescue's *History of the British Army* was tending in the same general direction.[43] Neither work was available to soldiers in 1914; Fortescue's Peninsular War volumes were not completed until 1920 (although the first appeared in 1910), and Liddell Hart's book began life as *The Decisive Wars of History* in 1929. Indeed, it required the experience of the Great War to highlight the attritional aspect of the Peninsular War.

In Liddell Hart's view the means to victory in the Peninsula was not the sequence of battles and sieges fought by Wellington's army. It was the combination of the presence and threat of that army in the field with "an intangible web of guerrilla bands."[44] French strength in the Peninsula was not crushed in a decisive battle, but was eroded by numerous simultaneous and small threats forcing dispersion and, ultimately, exhaustion. "The foundation of the British success," Liddell Hart wrote, "lay in Wellington's shrewd calculation of the military economic factor"; "indeed, by treating the Peninsular war as a chronicle of Wellington's battles and sieges it becomes meaningless."[45] Liddell Hart presented this strategy as one of "indirect approach," not of "attrition" (which for him carried far more awful connotations). But the very title given by Napoleon himself to the war, and used by its most recent historian,[46] the "Spanish Ulcer," reinforces the attritional argument. On the level of grand strategy, Napoleon was defeated by the combination of his wars in Eastern Europe, and especially Russia, with the continued drain of Spain. Decisive battlefield success, when eventually it came, was the fruit of this long process of erosion and exhaustion, not of speedy maneuver. It all bears a strong resemblance to the interpretation of the Great War given by Douglas Haig (albeit with hindsight) in his final dispatch; the battles of 1916 and 1918 were not to be considered individually but as a long, wearing-out fight culminating in the victories of autumn 1918.[47]

In the nineteenth century, study of the Peninsular War was dominated by W. F. P. Napier's *History of the War in the Peninsula*. His contemporaries knew well enough Napier's intemperate nature, his hot-headed advocacy of particular lines of argument, and his fury when crossed. His quite naked support of his brother, Sir Charles Napier, in *The Conquest of Scinde* was a case in point. But, despite all the controversy his *War in the Peninsula* provoked, the account was soon installed as the definitive statement on the subject. It gave more sustained analysis to the problems of war than any book hitherto published in English, and in the couple of decades after its publication it was widely read, discussed, and quoted. This was a double-edged boon for British military thought. The advantages of having a major work of military history in English had to be set against any errors of interpretation.

By contrast with Liddell Hart's, Napier's account was a history of battles and sieges, the abridged edition being brought out under that very title.[48] Most of Napier's general observations were at a tactical or operational level; but at three points he tried to embrace a wider strategic view. First, he argued that Wellington's campaign furnished "lessons" for British commanders in future Continental wars, because the duke reconciled the conduct of the war with the obstruction of "politicians who depending upon private intrigue prefer parliamentary to national interests."[49] Second, the victory was that of Britain (or England, as Napier preferred): "English steel, English gold, English genius, English influence, fought and won the battle of Spanish independence."[50] Third—following from this second argument and constantly reiterated—the victory was not that of the Spanish guerrillas, who were characterized as "weak in fight and steeped in folly."[51] Guerrilla warfare for Napier was inherently inferior: "The Partida system in Spain, was the offspring of disorder, and disorder in war is weakness accompanied by ills the least of which is sufficient to produce ruin."[52] Napier never attempted a coherent summary of his doctrine on war. But his leading ideas are nonetheless clearly stated at random points in his books;[53] like Jomini and others, he saw the essence of Napoleonic warfare as the protection of one's own lines of communication and the ability to master one's opponents. For those initiated into military theory when Napier's influence was at its height, the Peninsular War could therefore readily become a sequence of maneuvers threatening French communcations, while preserving those of Britain, and forcing the French to withdraw or to fight.

Keys to understanding the difference in the two approaches are the Talavera campaign of 1809 and the retreat to the lines of Torres Vedras in 1810. For Liddell Hart the Talavera campaign was a failure of Wellington's generalship; by advancing to seek battle, Wellington enabled the French to concentrate against him and so sacrificed the advantages inherent in French dispersion.[54] For Napier the retreat after Talavera was attributable entirely to the lack of Spanish support.[55] The Torres Vedras campaign was, in Liddell Hart's view, the supreme embodiment of Wellington's Peninsular strategy. The British retreat forced the pursuing Masséna to lengthen his line of communications in a country denuded of supplies and swarming with partisans. The French armies had to disperse to feed, but then became vulnerable to the guerrillas; the proximity of Wellington forced them to concentrate, but then they starved. Whereas Liddell Hart saw Torres Vedras as the high point of the strategy that exhausted the French through extending their lines of communication over hostile terrain, Napier presented the lines of Torres Vedras as "one stupendous and impregnable citadel," designed for the defense of Portugal since the frontier line itself could not be held.[56] Napier made scant allowance for the operational difficulties encountered by Masséna in Portugal, and instead attributed French weakness to the absence of Napoleon and the inadequacies of his subordinates.[57] Rather than a triumph for British strategy, Torres Vedras was a French failure. The attritional nature of what Wellington was about eluded Napier entirely. Decisive battle remained the key; Masséna should have pressed the opportunity provided for him at Busaco,[58] and at the outset of the 1811 campaign Wellington planned—according to Napier—to concentrate the Spanish and British armies in the region of Madrid for a conclusive victory.[59]

It would be a mistake to see the "attritional" analysis of the Peninsular War simply as the superior wisdom of hindsight. It did not require the First World War to illustrate what Wellington was about, for Liddell Hart's approach to understanding what had happened was one shared by Sir George Murray, Wellington's quartermaster general in the Peninsula and (for some at any rate) his de facto chief of staff. Murray had himself harbored a project such as Napier's, and some, therefore, attributed his criticism of Napier's work—published anonymously in the *Quarterly Review*—to personal pique. But what is striking in the present context is how much closer Murray's understanding of the war is to that of Liddell Hart than of Napier. Next to Wellington himself, Murray was the person best qualified in Britain to comment on the strategy of the Peninsular War, and for Murray the attritional aspects of that strategy were fundamental.

Murray castigated Napier for his denigration of the Spanish. It was, after all, a war originated by the Spanish people on Spanish ground for the object of Spanish national independence.[60] The guerrilla war which the Spaniards mounted was an end in itself; it was not the prelude to a regular war, but was the most effective method open to the Spanish of striking the French.[61] Furthermore, the Spanish efforts were continued throughout the war, and the vital element in allied success was the fusing of their guerrilla operations with regular war so that "every movement, whether for the purpose of advance or of retreat, was a continued combat."[62] The British won most of the general actions in which they engaged from the outset of the war but achieved nothing decisive before 1813. Until then "the war in the Peninsula continued to be a warfare of 'surges and eddies,' "[63] a sustained process of constantly eroding French strength. In conclusion, Murray attacked Napier's tendency to "reduce the practical art of war into an abstract science of mathematical problems."[64] "There are," Murray confessed, "general principles [in war]... but there is an almost endless variety in the application of those principles to the like variety of forms in which war presents itself"; in some circumstances, therefore, "desultory and harrassing warfare" will bring greater success than pitched battles.[65]

But Murray's views did not prevail. Napier's "abstract science" was far more consonant with the Jominian orthodoxy of the day. C. H. Smith, in his article in the *Aide-Memoire to the Military Sciences*, first published in 1846, summarized Wellington's operations in the Peninsula thus:

Meantime the Duke of Wellington began in the Peninsula by creating
a military base; then, although he manoeuvred with inferior forces,
by carrying the mass alternately on the north and on the south of
the Tagus, he widened and strengthened his frontier. Next, after having
finally checked Massena in the position of Torres Vedras, he com-
menced operations on a single prolonged line, always in the direction
of the enemy's communications with France, and, therefore, so dangerous to them, that in order to compel his army to retreat towards
the Portuguese position, they were obliged to collect far superior
forces, and to abandon the whole south of Spain. Soon after, Madrid
itself, and then the north, were similarly lost by the operations and
movement of battles ever turning the communications of the French
and the Pyrenees themselves gave no lasting security; . . . No stronger
example of the superior advantage of a right use of lines of operations
in the direction of an enemy's flank and rear can be produced, than
the result of these operations in the north [of Spain].[66]

It is hard to imagine a picture of the Peninsula War more removed
from that of Liddell Hart or of Murray. But it was a picture that
became hallowed by repetition. E. B. Hamley's *The Operations of War*
discussed the Torres Vedras campaign as an example of operational
maneuver and of Masséna's choices in this regard; the lines themselves
were an exceptional expedient and, by implication, Wellington's own
strategy on this occasion revealed little.[67] Hamley, of course, like Napier, admired Napoleon and saw him through the eyes of Jomini.
Colonel Patrick MacDougall, Napier's son-in-law, hardly considered
the Peninsular War in *The Theory of War* (1856), and his concerns in
Modern Warfare as Influenced by Modern Artillery (1864) were more
narrowly tactical. He discussed Wellington's battles as examples of
actions fought on defensive positions, but he did not see these defensive
battles as part of a Wellingtonian grand attritional design.

Although in the 1860s and 1870s the Jominian legacy in Britain kept
alive Napier's ideas on strategy, the Peninsular War itself was eclipsed
by the aftermath of the Crimean War. The accusation that the British
army had rested on its laurels, that nothing had changed between 1815
and 1854, was too deeply felt — even if in many respects inaccurate —
for soldiers to show much enthusiasm for the study of Wellingtonian
precepts and precedents. For the rest of the century the campaigns in
the Peninsula received only passing attention. Lieutenant Colonel Charles
Chesney, professor of military history at the Staff College, writing in
the *Edinburgh Review* in 1866, blamed the disasters of the Crimea on

the influence of the Peninsula. He therefore neglected the latter in his historical survey of the art of war; as, in any case, his conclusion was that wars were getting shorter, the Peninsula was hardly relevant.[68]

C. W. Robinson, a former instructor at the Royal Military College Sandhurst, published his *Lectures upon the British Campaigns in the Peninsula, 1804–14; Introductory to the Study of Military History* in 1871. Not only is it remarkable that these lectures were given at all; it is also striking how well they summarize the Napierian view of the Peninsula. Napier was Robinson's principal source, and his central thesis was to show the vital importance of bases and lines of communication; it was the maintenance of these as ends in themselves, rather than the supply problem toward whose solution they were the means, that determined the unity of armies in the field. The logistical difficulties and the role of the guerrillas were mentioned but were not integrated into an overall strategic view. Masséna's campaign of 1811, which is particularly relevant in developing the case for the strategy of attrition, was described as a "campaign of battles and sieges, and of fighting in several quarters," but "not of a character well adapted to illustrate any of the broader movements of strategy."[69]

By the 1890s some writers had begun to question the neglect of the Peninsular War. In 1887, T. Miller Maguire, who used Napier in his "summary of modern military history," castigated the fashion among English officers to "ignore the military history of their nation, and to sneer at the value of the operations in the Peninsula."[70] He did not really follow his own advice, for he devoted six pages to the entire Peninsular War as against twenty-eight on the Waterloo campaign. But he did cite the campaign of 1810 as showing the best method of conducting defensive war. The French were refused battle and their communications lengthened and harried by partisans; thus "famine, exhaustion, isolation and despair compelled the offensive army to undertake a difficult retreat and to evacuate Portugal."[71]

Maguire had posed British soldiers in the last decade of the nineteenth century a difficult question. The prevailing wisdom was that wars were short, and getting shorter; that masses should be concentrated against fractions of the enemy; and that offensive maneuver, which threatened to master the enemy's lines of communications, would bring decisive battlefield success in the space of a single campaign.[72] Their interpretation of Napoleon's strategy, and of Moltke's in 1866 and 1870, provided the supporting evidence. But yet the British army's own successes, won by a great commander, did not seem to conform to the pattern. Wellington's tactics, and even strategy, were defensive — so said Maguire, and Charles Chesney had hinted at a similar conclusion before him.[73]

Although the consequences of confronting the dilemma threatened to bring about a strategic reinterpretation of the war, it never happened. In part this was because the prime focus of thinkers like G. F. R. Henderson, Frederick Maurice, and even Lord Roberts was on the tactical defensive — the key to Wellington's success in battle — not the strategic.[74] In part it was rendered possible by a concentration on Waterloo, where a single tactical success had decisively concluded a campaign. And one solution to the whole conundrum — that adopted by Henderson — was to say that appearances were deceptive, that at bottom Wellington was an offensive-minded general who fought offensively more often than not, and whose defensive battles were no more than temporary expedients.[75] Thus, when in 1899 Lord Roberts highlighted the significance of the lines of Torres Vedras, he flattered to deceive; he stressed that the lines' function was to give Wellington a secure base (rather than to complete the exhaustion of Masséna's army), and so he subsumed them within Jominian orthodoxy.[76] Frederick Maurice, writing in the same volume as Roberts, emphasized that supply was the key to French problems in the Peninsula but drowned this observation in a conventional blow-by-blow account of Wellington's battles.[77]

None of this is to say that the Peninsular War was being brought down from the shelves of professional libraries and dusted off. It was, however, the prelude to a mini-boom in Peninsular War studies before the First World War.

The two most convincing explanations for this revival of interest are, in chronological order, first, the impact of naval thought and the challenge presented to the army by the primacy of seapower in the event of war against a European opponent, and second, the successful resistance through guerrilla operations by a weaker power (the Boers) against a stronger one (the British). T. Miller Maguire, writing about Wellington's campaigns in 1906, recognized what had happened: "The study of British campaigns was then [1898] quite unfashionable, and, indeed was supposed to be unworthy of scientific soldiery, and I was ridiculed for my eulogies of Wellington and his matchless infantry. But since then, the value of sea-power, the resisting force of patriotic though small nations when well led, the necessity of supplementing even absolute command of the sea by military expeditions against Continental States, have been clearly demonstrated."[78]

The maritime part of this argument will be considered in the final part of this essay; of the importance of guerrillas (which chimed so well with Britain's colonial experience), there is little to say. For even in the first decade of the twentieth century, British views on the Peninsula became bogged in the Napierian interpretation.

In 1905 and 1906 the Peninsular War was, mirabile dictu, prescribed for students preparing for the Staff College entrance examination; for militia, yeomanry, university, and colonial army candidates for regular commissions; and for those taking promotion examinations. The first group was to study the war's course from 19 May 1812 to 31 August 1813, the second from March 1811 to 31 October 1813 (with reference to the period 19 May 1812 to 12 August 1812), and the third from March 1811 to 31 October 1813 (with special reference to the period May 1813 to 30 June 1813). No detailed questions were to be set on the actions of the Spanish and Portuguese armies, and no questions of any kind when the actions of these armies had no bearing on those of the British troops.[79] These limitations, both chronological and geographical, assured that no broad idea of the war's strategy was likely to emerge from its study. Guerrilla operations were once again consigned to the wastebasket. By beginning in March 1811, the Torres Vedras campaign—so fundamental to an attritional interpretation of Wellington's strategy—was excluded. The focus of the syllabus was on battles, through descriptions borrowed from Napier, and on operational maneuver in the Jomini/Hamley mold. One of the best of the crammer's texts produced to meet the new market was that of T. Miller Maguire. "He is a good strategist," he wrote, "who so arranges his plans as to compel his foe to abandon important positions or fight. Whatever description or definition be adopted, Wellington's strategy was excellent; indeed, it was Napoleonic, and what can be greater praise?"[80]

Occasionally, less orthodox views, like that of Captain J. W. E. Donaldson, who acknowledged the importance of the guerrillas and their role in sapping the strength of the French army, emerged.[81] But the norm in the crammers' prescribed readings was far less controversial. The best of the authors did at least discuss the whole war and not restrict themselves to the period 1811–13. But one of them, Captain

Lewis Butler, had little to say about guerrillas, and in his account of the Torres Vedras campaign, he dwelled on the battle of Busaco rather than the campaign's strategic significance.[82] The other, and probably the most widely used of all the texts, was Major General C. W. Robinson's expansion of his 1871 lectures. For Robinson, Spanish movements were "comparatively unimportant,"[83] and the lines of Torres Vedras were to defend Portugal (not to exhaust the French).[84] A note of self-doubt does creep in: "Too much implicit confidence is not to be placed in entrenchments and earthworks, though their value in strengthening a position should never be overlooked; and it may be added that this remark must not be pushed too far, or taken to apply to a series of formidable defensive lines, compact, well-garrisoned, and with the flanks secure, such as were the 'Lines of Torres Vedras.'"[85] But the sense of caution was fleeting. Robinson saw Wellington in the same light as Henderson had done—an offensive general who controlled his natural instincts if circumstances so demanded.[86] The principles of modern war that Robinson drew from his study of Wellington included all the ingredients of maneuver strategy—turning movements, mass on the decisive points, attacks against the flanks, and so on.[87]

Sir John Fortescue's and Sir Charles Oman's works were to oust the Napierian view of the Peninsula. Oman in particular was to give full weight to the Spanish contribution. But by 1914 he had only reached the fifth volume of his seven and only taken his account to 31 August 1812. Therefore, when European war again broke out in 1914, neither he nor Fortescue had yet provided the material for a fresh synthesis of the Peninsular War—whether for instructional purposes or for the development of strategic doctrine. Thanks to the recovery of interest in Wellington and the Peninsula in the couple of decades before 1914, British commanders were not as ignorant of those events as they might have been in the 1860s, 1870s, or 1880s. But they did have a restricted and partial view of the Peninsular War. For most it was no more than an episode of the Napoleonic Wars, albeit one in which British troops had played a major part, and therefore confirmed the principles of Jomini and his British equivalent, Hamley.

The tendency in the historiography of both the Crimean and the Peninsular Wars before 1914 was to use the wars as mirrors on the institutions of the British army, not on the army's employment in the field. Napier's history established a notion of British military superiority; the heroes of his account are the English (as he would call them) infantry of the line—dogged, stoical, and tough. The Peninsular War became a potent force in the growing self-regard of the British army and of its individual regiments. The Crimean War, of course, gave rise to a reverse process; it became a cautionary tale of bureaucratic infighting and administrative complacency. But there were strategic and tactical precepts to be drawn from both wars. A strategy of attrition had prevailed in the Peninsula, and not only the strategy but also the tactics of attrition had done the same in the Crimea. Both were to dominate in the First World War. None of this commentary, in itself, is meant to suggest that there are "correct lessons" to be derived from military history, nor does it presuppose that there are such things as principles of war or that military history had a didactic purpose. It is simply a reflection that, in an age when much of the purpose of military history was instructional, the lessons that might have been valuable were not drawn from either war. If the British army had paid greater attention to its own military history rather than to that of France and Germany, it might have learned more.

IV

This, however, is not the whole story. As already mentioned, part of the pre-1914 revival of interest in the Peninsular War was attributable to the maritime context in which the British army continued to find itself. Furthermore, this approach was one in which the Crimean War also could be embraced.

The relevance of the Peninsular War in showing how Britain could threaten land operations all along a Continental coastline, how, once landed, the army could rely on seapower for secure supply, and how only by such operations could seapower be translated into practical effect on land, had been recognized by Napier himself. The point was made by Lord Roberts in 1899, when he took the opportunity to stress the need for "a thoroughly efficient army in readiness to take advantage of our naval superiority."[88] And Frederick Maurice, like Napier and many others before him, bewitched by the romantic figure of Sir John Moore, concluded that Wellington's war was exceptional, but Moore's campaign at Corunna was not. In any future Continental war, major land operations were "scarcely conceivable," and the latter—a rapid foray, with the possibility of quick withdrawal—was therefore the likely pattern for the employment of the army.[89] Corunna showed, he wrote to A. T. Mahan, "that sea-power does not consist merely in the acquiring by the navy of the domain of the sea, and the pressure thereby exerted on the land, but that, for its full effect, it requires the trained co-operation of the navy, transport, and army, in order that the blow may be driven home on land."[90]

Because he saw Wellington's campaigns in the Peninsula as a full-dress Continental war, Maurice had not extended his view of the appropriate military operations for a maritime power to include it. But C. E. Callwell did. In 1897, he had commented on his contemporaries' lack of interest in the Peninsular War.

> Napier is regarded as out of date in the British army. His fascinating volumes are not to be studied in the hope of gleaning from their pages lessons on the military art. They are read as a tribute to their literary merit, to their purity of style and force of description, to their vivid picturing of episodes which famous regiments cherish as traditions. And yet strategical principles are taught by them which are as fresh and opportune at the present time as they were in the pre-Crimean days, when every officer versed in his profession was familiar with the incidents in the Peninsula—principles more applicable to the conditions of the British Empire than any which can be deduced from Königgratz or Gravelotte. For the operations in Spain and Portugal hinged upon sea-power.[91]

For Callwell, Corunna was no more than a hit-and-run raid;[92] by contrast, Torres Vedras, "a maritime fortress,"[93] allowed Wellington to stay on the Continent and, thus, to apply Britain's maritime supremacy in protracted land operations. In 1905 he had developed his thinking to the point where his view of the lines of Torres Vedras and of their position in the history of the Peninsular War had come very close to that of Liddell Hart and also to that of a strategy of attrition. He wrote in *Military Operations and Maritime Preponderance*:

> While Wellington was resting his relatively insignificant army on the shores of Portugal in anticipation of another campaign, he was all the time wearing out the vitality of a host numerically far superior to his own, and was producing in it that process of wastage which saps the power of a military force in war when casualties from exhaustion and disease cannot be made good. He, in fact, was treading his opponents down by doing nothing. And there is perhaps no portion of the military career of the Duke which more clearly proves his claim to be accounted one of the foremost of the masters of the art of war, than the period of the Peninsular struggle when his operations

were wearing their least active appearance. The traditions of British strategy were totally opposed to the course which he adopted. His plan of campaign was in defiance of all precedent. It sounded an absolutely new note in the military history of his country.[94]

Although the Crimean War suffered even greater neglect than the Peninsular War, and although it did not fight its way back onto Staff College or Sandhurst syllabuses in the years before 1914 as had the Peninsula, in at least some circles it enjoyed a limited renaissance for the same reason the Peninsula had. It was a perfect illustration of the role of the army in support of Britain's maritime power. E. B. Hamley had stressed how in 1854 the sea had provided the secure base required by the allies.[95] Again it was Callwell who took the implications the furthest. By threatening the possibility of a number of landings, the allies prevented the concentration of the Russian armies in the main theater of war. The plan of the allies was to deliver a sudden, crushing blow, but, in the event, war became "the wearing out of the resources of a formidable adversary by prolonged operations during which he was laboring under a crushing strategical disadvantage."[96] The main assets of the allies were seapower and "the ravages which climate, hunger, and exhaustion caused in corps and regiments which strove to reach the theatre of war and never reached it."[97] Thus, "it was by a process of slow exhaustion that their [the allies] fighting forces wore down the hostile capacity for resistance."[98]

However, Callwell's work was to sound a muted note in British military historiography. Like *Small Wars, Military Operations and Maritime Preponderance* is striking not least by virtue of its individuality. The broad point, and the more traditional one, that land power could enable the projection of seapower, was accepted in the mid-years of the first decade of the twentieth century. But talk of "exhaustion" and "wastage" was neglected in preference for more familiar concepts. For some, the Peninsular and Crimean Wars suggested that Britain's role and style in European war might be different from that of other European armies. But this did not mean embracing a "strategy of attrition" per se. It meant, instead, integrating seapower and land power. Britain's maritime supremacy, most of the blue-water school had recognized by 1914, needed to be accompanied by land operations on the Continent to have decisive effect. In 1911 Julian Corbett, probably the outstanding pre-1914 naval thinker, praised the Peninsular War as an ideal example of "applying the limited form to an unlimited war. Our object was unlimited. It was nothing less than the overthrow of Napoleon. Complete [naval] success had failed to do it, but that success had given us the power of applying the limited form, which was the most decisive form of offence within our means."[99] He described the Crimean War in identical terms.[100]

The dominance of Continental thought in the army in the crucial years between 1910 and 1914, and the triumph of its leading advocate — Sir Henry Wilson, then Director of Military Operations — at the Committee of Imperial Defence in August 1911, can be misleading. Over the longer term, many in the British army were much more marked by maritime attitudes than the rapid dispatch of the British Expeditionary Force to Europe would suggest. Until 1905, views like those of Maurice on Corunna, already cited, were probably more frequent. Sir John French was among those who subscribed to them. On 7 February 1905 he drew the attention of the Aldershot Military Society to three features of the Peninsular War — guerrilla operations, the offensive-defensive in strategy, and the need for a strong army to complete the work of seapower.[101] The Peninsular War, he said, is "among the best illustrations of brain power — use of command of the sea, and an efficient organisation of landpower."[102] In the field in 1914 French's thinking was prompted by the tradition of Napoleon, received through Jomini and Hamley. The maneuvers of August-September 1914, and particularly the battle of the Marne, helped encourage faith in a "strategy of annihilation" rather than the "strategy of attrition." But amphibious operations were in French's mind in the winter of 1914–15, as they were in Churchill's. In particular, French nurtured a scheme for a combined land-sea drive along the Belgian coast.

In a wider strategic sense, British strategy in 1914–15 displayed a fondness for "applying the limited form to an unlimited war." Certainly army officers' initiation into naval views of warfare, and their acceptance of naval dominance in British strategy, encouraged them to think of ways of integrating land power with control of the oceans. Kitchener, as secretary of war, was too much of an imperialist to be impervious to this sort of thinking; Hankey, the secretary to the cabinet and a Royal Marine by upbringing, in his diaries and memoirs shows himself to have been a strong advocate of a maritime strategy; and the director of military operations in 1914–15 was none other than Sir Charles Callwell. All three were crucial figures in the formulation of British strategy in 1914–15. Gallipoli may be the classic example of conducting a limited operation which might have unlimited effects, but it does not stand alone; Salonika was conceived in the same vein, and so were the putative landings elsewhere in the Mediterranean. It was this, the maritime legacy of the Peninsula and of the Crimea, that was most in evidence in the First World War.

Moreover, the argument can be pushed one stage further. If seapower was envisaged as Britain's principal contribution to an Entente war effort before 1914, its effect was bound to be attritional. The Royal Navy might dream of decisive fleet action, just as the army manifested similar longings; but, in the event, it was the blockade of German trade and the defense of Britain's own sea communications that became the core of the allied war effort. A maritime perspective may therefore have helped British army officers to grasp the wider dimensions of a grand strategy of attrition — perhaps more readily than was the case with their colleagues in France. But in a narrower, operational sense, attritional warfare was not part of the British army's mental equipment. At this level the influence of the Peninsula and of the Crimea was not to be found where it might have been most valuable — in France and Flanders. There, on the Western Front, the lessons of attrition had to be learned all over again.

NOTES

1. Quoted in Jay Luvaas, *The Military Legacy of the Civil War: The European Inheritance* (Chicago, 1959), 185.

2. Brian Bond, ed., *Victorian Military Campaigns* (London, 1967), 25–26.

3. Hew Strachan, *Wellington's Legacy: The Reform of the British Army 1830–54* (Manchester, 1984); Strachan, "Lord Grey and Imperial Defence," in *Politicians and Defence*, ed. Ian F. W. Beckett and John Gooch (Manchester, 1981), 1–23.

4. Hew Strachan, "The Early Victorian Army and the Nineteenth-Century Revolution in Government," *English Historical Review* 95 (October 1980): 782–809.

5. Hew Strachan, *From Waterloo to Balaclava: Tactics, Technology, and the British Army 1815–1854* (Cambridge, 1985).

6. Delbrück imagined that a "strategy of attrition" was a more limited form of warfare than a "strategy of annihilation" since its object would be a negotiated peace. The Crimean War fits his understanding of a "strategy of attrition" better than the Peninsular War does. But it is the Great War that really exposes the problem of definition: the belligerents espoused a "strategy of attrition" without acknowledging the need (despite Delbrück's own views at the time) to accompany it with more limited objectives. On Delbrück, see Arden Bucholz, *Hans Delbrück and the German Military Establishment: War Images in Conflict* (Iowa City, 1985), and Gordon A. Craig, "Delbrück: The Military Historian," in *Makers of*

Modern Strategy from Machiavelli to the Nuclear Age, ed. Peter Paret (Oxford, 1986), 326–53.

7. Stress should be made that the assumptions inherent in using the words "lessons" and "modern" are the assumptions of pre-1914 military writers—not an assumption on the writer's part that military history can reveal "lessons" for "modern" war.

8. A. W. Kinglake, *The Invasion of the Crimea,* 8 vols. (Edinburgh, 1863–87), 3:224.

9. Evelyn Wood, *The Crimea in 1854, and 1894* (London, 1895), 84.

10. E. Bruce Hamley, *The Story of the Campaign of Sebastopol* (Edinburgh, 1855), 295–337.

11. George Wrottesley, *Life and Correspondence of Field Marshal Sir John Fox Burgoyne, Bart,* 2 vols. (London, 1873), 2:186; also Wrottesley, ed., *The Military Opinions of General Sir John Fox Burgoyne, Bart, G.C.B.* (London, 1859), 197.

12. Wrottesley, *Life and Correspondence of Burgoyne,* 2:330–42.

13. Kinglake, *The Invasion of the Crimea,* 3:220.

14. Hamley, *The Story of the Campaign of Sebastopol,* 220.

15. Thomas Miller Maguire, *A Summary of Modern Military History, with Comments on the Leading Operations* (London, 1887), 180.

16. Harry D. Jones, *Journal of the Operations Conducted by the Corps of the Royal Engineers* (London, 1859), part 2, 10–11, 611.

17. Maguire, *Summary of Modern Military History,* 182.

18. Hamley, *The Story of the Campaign of Sebastopol,* 201.

19. Jones, *Journal of the Operations,* 2.

20. Wrottesley, *Life and Correspondence of Burgoyne,* 2:155, 163; *Military Opinions of Burgoyne,* 293–94, 298–99.

21. Kinglake, *Invasion of the Crimea,* 7:14–17; Jones, *Journal of the Operations,* 1–2, 6; E. B. Hamley, *The War in the Crimea* (London, 1891), 195.

22. Quoted in Kinglake, *The Invasion of the Crimea,* 3:205.

23. H. C. Elphinstone, *Journal of the Operations Conducted by the Corps of Royal Engineers* (London, 1859), part 1, 35.

24. Wrottesley, *Life and Correspondence of Burgoyne,* 2:182.

25. Jones, *Journal of the Operations,* 587.

26. Julian R. J. Jocelyn, *The History of the Royal Artillery (Crimean Period)* (London, 1911), 411, 457–58.

27. Maguire, *Summary of Modern Military History,* 180.

28. Jones, *Journal of the Operations,* 638.

29. Kinglake, *Invasion of the Crimea,* 8:94.

30. H. P. Pétain, *Verdun* (London, 1930), 144–45.

31. Strachan, *From Waterloo to Balaclava,* 133–35.

32. Jones, *Journal of the Operations,* part 2, 577.

33. Wrottesley, *Military Opinions of Burgoyne,* 190–91; Wrottesley, *Life and Correspondence of Burgoyne,* 2:152.

34. P. L. MacDougall, *The Theory of War: Illustrated by Numerous Examples from Military History* (London, 1856), 114–15.

35. P. L. MacDougall, *Modern Warfare as Influenced by Modern Artillery* (London, 1864).

36. Jay Luvaas, *The Education of an Army: British Military Thought 1815–1940* (London, 1965), 90–92.

37. Ibid., 438.

38. F. Maurice, *War* (London, 1891), vii.

39. Ibid., 107.

40. Ibid., 2–5.

41. Ibid., x.

42. Ibid., 32.

43. B. H. Liddell Hart, *Strategy: The Indirect Approach* (London, 1967), 129. Liddell Hart, writing after the First World War, did not understand a "strategy of attrition" as a strategy of limited war: indeed, he would have seen it as the reverse of his "indirect approach." But Delbrück saw a "strategy of attrition" as avoiding a single, decisive battle, and his idea therefore had some common features with Liddell Hart's "indirect approach."

44. Ibid., 128.

45. Ibid., 132, 129.

46. David Gates, *The Spanish Ulcer: A History of the Peninsular War* (London, 1986).

47. J. H. Boraston , ed., *Sir Douglas Haig's Despatches* (London, 1919), 319–21.

48. William Napier, *English Battles and Sieges in the Peninsula* (London, 1866).

49. W. F. P. Napier, *History of the War in the Peninsula,* vol. 6 (London, 1840), 682.

50. Ibid., vol. 4 (London, 1834), 364; also vol. 5 (London, 1836), 355–56.

51. Ibid., 4:365.

52. Ibid., vol. 3 (London, 1831), 13; also vol. 1 (1832, 2d ed.), ix-xi; vol. 2 (1829), 337–52.

53. Luvaas, *The Education of an Army,* 19–20.

54. Liddell Hart, *Strategy,* 131–32.

55. Napier, *War in the Peninsula,* 2:460.

56. Ibid., 3:254–55.

57. Ibid., 3:270, 339–40, 398–401.

58. Ibid., 3:339–40.

59. Ibid., 3:492.

60. [Murray], *Quarterly Review* 56 (April 1836): 132.

61. Ibid., 61 (January 1838): 56–57.

62. Ibid., 61:157.

63. Ibid., 61:54.

64. Ibid., 61:95.

65. Ibid., 56 (April 1836): 138.

66. A committee of the Corps of Royal Engineers, ed., *Aide-Memoire to the Military Sciences,* 2d ed., 3 vols. (London, 1853–62), 1:15–16.

67. E. B. Hamley, *The Operations of War,* 7th ed. (Edinburgh, 1922; 1st ed. 1866), 214–16, 239, 423; see also Hamley, "Wellington's Career," *Blackwood's Edinburgh Magazine* 87 (April 1860): 397–417, and (May 1860): 591–610.

68. Lt. Col. Chesney and Henry Reeve, *The Military Resources of Prussia and France and Recent Changes in the Art of War* (London, 1870), 18, 56.

69. C. W. Robinson, *Lectures upon the British Campaigns in the Peninsula, 1808-14; Introductory to the Study of Military History* (London, 1871), 121.

70. Thomas Miller Maguire, *Summary of Modern Military History, with Comments on the Leading Operations* (London, 1887), 112.

71. Ibid., 113.

72. See, for example, Colonel F. Maurice, *War* (London, 1891), x, 32.

73. Chesney and Reeve, *The Military Resources of Prussia and France*, 32.

74. G. F. R. Henderson, *The Science of War* (London, 1919), 101, 104, 127; Maurice, *War*, 54–55; General Lord Roberts, *The Rise of Wellington* (London, 1895).

75. Henderson, *Science of War*, 97–98, 101–4, 127. The leading contemporary biographer of Wellington developed the same argument, Sir Herbert Maxwell, *The Life of Wellington: The Restoration of the Martial Power of Great Britain* (London, 1907; 1st ed. 1899), 177–207.

76. Lord Roberts' introduction to Spenser Wilkinson, ed., *From Cromwell to Wellington: Twelve Soldiers* (London, 1899), ix.

77. F. Maurice, "Wellington 1769-1851," in *War*, 469–70.

78. T. Miller Maguire, *The British Army under Wellington 1811-1813: A Summary* (London, 1906), v.

79. For the scheme of examination, see the preface of J. H. Anderson, *The Peninsular War March 1, 1811, to October 31, 1813* (London, 1906), 5.

80. Maguire, *British Army under Wellington*, 38.

81. J. W. E. Donaldson, *Military History Applied to Modern Warfare*, 2d. ed., revised and enlarged by A. F. Becke (London, 1907), 228, 261, 267.

82. Captain Lewis Butler, *Wellington's Operations in the Peninsula (1808-1814)*, 2 vols. (London, 1904).

83. Major-General C. W. Robinson, *Wellington's Campaigns 1808-15;* also Moore's *Campaign of Corunna*, 3 parts (London, 1905-6), part 1, 14.

84. Ibid., part 1, 148; part 3, 653.

85. Ibid., part 2, 345.

86. Ibid., part 1, 76; part 2, 172; part 3, 653.

87. Ibid., part 3, 428–30.

88. Roberts in Wilkinson, *From Cromwell to Wellington*, xi–xii.

89. J. F. Maurice, *The Diary of Sir John Moore*, 2 vols. (London, 1904), 1:x.

90. F. Maurice, ed., *Sir Frederick Maurice: A Record of His Work and Opinions* (London, 1913), 111.

91. C. E. Callwell, *The Effect of Maritime Command on Land Campaigns since Waterloo* (Edinburgh, 1897), 6–7.

92. C. E. Callwell, *Military Operations and Maritime Preponderance: Their Relations and Interdependence* (Edinburgh, 1905), 300.

93. Callwell, *Effect of Maritime Command*, 12.

94. Callwell, *Military Operations and Maritime Preponderance*, 298–99.

95. Hamley, *The Story of the Campaign of Sebastopol*, 17–18; Hamley, *The War in the Crimea*, 163.

96. Callwell, *Military Operations and Maritime Preponderance*, 303.

97. Callwell, *The Effect of Maritime Command,* 186; also 174, 180, 197.

98. Ibid., 185.

99. Julian S. Corbett, *Some Principles of Maritime Strategy* (London, 1972; lst ed., 1911), 62.

100. Ibid., 54, 59, 292.

101. Cited in Maguire, *The British Army under Wellington,* Appendix I.

102. Ibid., vi.

Afterword

Tools of War:
Concepts and Technology

━━━━━━━

SIR MICHAEL HOWARD

THE ORIGINAL *concept* of war was the control of territory, for in the preindustrial age territory was the source both of manpower and of wealth. The principal *tool* of such control was the castle or fortress, and it is in some ways a pity that this volume does not contain a chapter dealing specifically with the science of fortification. But the general point has been addressed, particularly in the contribution by Simon Adams. Adams reminds us that, in the early seventeenth century, the main task of European armies was to garrison territory, providing both internal order and external defense. Indeed, in a broader perspective, siege warfare should be seen as the normal form of military activity from the eleventh to the eighteenth centuries, with an atypical half-century from 1480 to 1530. During those years the defense of castles built according to traditional patterns had been neutralized by siege artillery. The *trace italienne* had not yet restored the effectiveness of fortifications; so field armies could be used as instruments of outright territorial conquest. For a brief period warfare became mobile and decisive.

This was when writers on strategy began to focus upon battles, and all the calculations as to the best deployment and combination of weapons with which to conduct them. But no sooner did this study begin than it became largely academic. In spite of all the beautifully illustrated textbooks produced by Maurice of Nassau and his contemporaries, in spite of the bold innovations of Gustavus Adolphus, defensive fortifications had regained, by the seventeenth century, an ascendancy that made set-piece battles unusual and indecisive. The tempo of the Thirty Years' War was dragged out by long inconclusive sieges. Nevertheless, this period witnessed a development far more important than that of military weapons or techniques: it saw the rise of the professional army.

This phenomenon has been widely discussed in the contributions to this volume, but little has been said about the factors that made it possible, and one factor in particular: the introduction of efficient administration into European armies, and with it regular pay. It was the inability of the great princes of the Renaissance, Charles V, Francis I, and Philip II, to maintain paid and disciplined armies continuously in the field that explains the spasmodic and inconclusive nature of their wars. For this a regular supply of wealth, usually based on taxes levied on a thriving trade, was necessary to pay not only the armies but the officials who administered them. Venice had set the pattern in the fifteenth century, to be followed by the United Provinces in the sixteenth, and, in the seventeenth, by the Swedes, the French, and ultimately the Electors of Brandenburg-Prussia. As significant as any field commanders, if not more so, were the French bureaucrats Le Tellier and Louvois, whose patient administrative skills made it possible for Louis XIV, by the end of the seventeenth century, to maintain continuously armies on foot numbered in six figures.

For armies on such a scale, increasingly equipped with firearms demanding a large and continuous supply of ammunition, administration and discipline became preeminently important. Self-control and obedience gradually displaced the heroic virtues as the primary military requirement; and such obedience, especially in the firing line, made possible by the beginning of the eighteenth century that coordination of arms on the battlefield, which, a hundred years earlier, had been little more than a pious aspiration.

Campaigns in Western Europe continued to revolve around sieges until well into the eighteenth century: the increased dependence of "modern" armies on their lines of supply, if only for ammunition, indeed made siege warfare more important rather than less. But during that century the siege was gradually to lose its central significance. The proliferation of roads made it easier for armies to move fast across country. The improvement of agriculture made it easier for them to support themselves as they did so. At the end of the century the sheer size of the armies raised by revolutionary France enabled them to sweep past enemy fortresses and leave them to wither on the vine, but already eighteenth-century military writers such as Lloyd and Tempelhoff had taken it for granted that the objective of a campaign was defeat of the enemy army. Napoleon spelled out what was already implicit in the campaigns of Frederick the Great, and both Jomini and Clausewitz were to base their dogmas on the Napoleonic experience. Throughout the nineteenth century, the central concept of war was to be the Decisive Battle, and the tools of war were designed to fight it.

What were the techniques that made battle decisive? The answer had been the same ever since firearms had first appeared on the battlefield in the fifteenth century—the appropriate combination of fire and shock. Artillery could provide the first, cavalry the second, and, with the development of the flintlock musket and bayonet, the infantry could deliver both. Fire without shock was indecisive—at least, until the invention of breech-loading firearms. Shock without fire was suicidal, or at best it turned the battlefield into an uncontrollable melee. The imposition of order on the conduct of war, both by land and by sea, was anyhow characteristic of an era that sought to derive from the fundamental principles governing the universe appropriate norms of social behavior, and to apply the touchstone of rationality to all human activity. As Dr. Maltby shows in his chapter, the simultaneous evolution of the firing line on the battlefield and of line-ahead formations at sea, the attempt to constrain the violence of war within the limits of orderly, calculated, rational control, was of a piece with other contemporary forms of social behavior.

It was not any superiority in weapons systems, neither the fieldpiece nor the musket, that set eighteenth-century Europe on the road to world conquest. Rather it was these disciplined professional armies with their volley firing, their capacity for maneuver on the battlefield, and their steadiness under fire. Their adversaries had to imitate them or go under, whether it was the Indian princes against the British or the Russians against the Swedes; and they had to imitate not just the weapons, which was easy, and the discipline and the drill, which was harder, but the administrative efficiency that produced the regular pay making both drill and discipline possible. In Russia, as Professor Hellie has shown, Peter the Great set about creating a state whose control of its internal resources would rival that of its western neighbors. The Indians (like the princes of Renaissance Europe two centuries earlier) went into debt, and Dr. Lenman has explained how they thereby lost the wealth that was the source of their power. Money rather than technology was the principal requirement for eighteenth-century warfare: *point d'argent, point de Suisses*—or sepoys for that matter.

American readers will not need to be reminded that these paid professional soldiers were tools, not only of war, but also of social control. King George III's "Redcoats" enforced the taxation system that supported the British ascendancy. So everywhere, and in every sense, these professional armies both symbolized and sustained the ancien régime. In Europe for forty years after the Napoleonic wars, social control was seen by governments as being the principal function of their armies. Not till the 1850s were they again to use their arms against one another.

But the work of the revolutionary wars could not be undone. If the disciplined ranks of the professional armies symbolized the ancien régime, the undisciplined, self-motivated heroism of the French citizen-armies symbolized the revolution. In the era of romanticism what mattered in war, as in the creative arts, was the free spirit of man, liberated from all artificial and external constraints. As Professors Lynn and Higginbotham make clear in their chapters, the "myth" of revolutionary war was of central *political* significance. It was the unquenchable, irresistible courage of free men (what Dr. Showalter has termed "the vitalistic heritage") that was to overcome the serried ranks and disciplined fire of the Prussian (or Hessian) automata. In France the bayonet was the weapon of the free man, and the cry *à la baïonnette!* was a summons to a political, as well as to a military, offensive. In the United States the symbol of freedom was to be the weapon of the sharpshooter, the rifle. Unfortunately, it still is.

But even free men needed leaders, and those leaders had themselves to be heroic. Napoleon fitted the role a great deal better than George Washington, a figure who has remained as obstinately and admirably resistant to romanticization, as has the Duke of Wellington. For the generation of Stendhal, Napoleon epitomized the spirit of freedom much as Fidel Castro or Che Guevara did for the romantic young twenty-five years ago. He was a hero of classic proportions: single-handedly he had overthrown an entire order based upon feudal privilege and carried the banners of liberty, equality, and fraternity to the farthest corners of Europe. Was this due to military professionalism or to innate genius? Jomini tried to reduce the Napoleonic performance to replicable formulae and bequeathed to later generations of strategists the concept of "principles of war." Clausewitz was more skeptical. Throughout the nineteenth century there was waged all over Europe a battle of the books, as liberals attributed the successes of the Napoleonic armies to the heroism of free men and conservatives, to the professional skills inherited from the ancien régime.

What part did technology play in all this? It has been often and properly pointed out that the transformation of warfare occurred before the transformation of technology and that Napoleon used only weapons that would have been familiar to Saxe and Frederick, if not Marlborough and Turenne. It was skill in the use of familiar tools, not the invention of new ones, that brought Napoleon his success; especially the use of the artillery arm, in which his social obscurity had compelled him to seek his own professional fortunes. If liberal historians saw the bayonet as the instrument par excellence of the revolutionary armies, conservatives were able to point to the old royal artillery cadres, which stopped the Prussians dead in their tracks at Valmy and whose guns were increasingly to dominate not only the battlefields of Napoleon but those of Helmuth von Moltke and, ultimately, of Douglas Haig.

Artillery was no business for amateurs. For many years it was not one for soldiers at all, but a "mystery" for specialist craftsmen. Only in the eighteenth century did artillerists become totally integrated into European armies; as also did engineers, their techniques broadening out from siegecraft to the road and bridge and, ultimately, railway building, which would make and keep armies mobile. Trained in special academies—the Ecole Polytechnique, the Royal Military Academy at Woolwich, and, not least, the U.S. Military Academy at West Point— in skills that had as much civil as military application, these men developed a new kind of professionalism; themselves taking part in and contributing to the technological evolution that was to transform the world in the nineteenth century, and warfare with it.

It is to these *armes savantes,* rather than to a cavalry and an infantry that retained their ancien régime character well into the twentieth century, that we must look if we are to understand the achievement and significance of the British army in the nineteenth century. By European standards it was, in Kaiser Wilhelm II's words, "a contemptible little army"; contemptible not only in size but in its capacity to adapt to the revolution in the scale and nature of war taking place on the Continent. But European warfare was not what the British army was for. After 1815, the Crimean expedition excluded, it virtually abjured serious European intervention and, as Dr. Strachan has shown us, failed to study its Continental experiences to learn how to do better next time. Its true political function—once the police force took over the maintenance of internal order within the British Isles—was the long-range projection of military power, to Africa, to India, to China.

This it did very well. It did not develop a capacity for amphibious warfare: its record in this respect, from Walcheren to the Dardanelles, remained disastrous. But it developed ports, it built railways, it exploited riverine transport, it pioneered cartography in remote areas—in short, it became expert in logistics on a very large scale. Its tightly bonded regiments, self-contained worlds of their own, did not care where they fought, and were as effective in West Africa or China as they were in India. They had of course, as Hilaire Belloc reminds us, the Maxim gun, and their opponents had not; but, more to the point, they had the logistics and organization to support the Maxim gun. Eventually they encountered, in South Africa, an adversary who was also armed with the Maxim gun, as well as with Mauser rifles and Krupp artillery, and the honeymoon was over. The British army had to adjust to the harsher world of the twentieth century—and had very little time in which to do it.

One of Britain's tools of conquest, like that of other colonial powers, was the railway—the most effective instrument for projecting military power overland that the world had yet seen. The late Victorian British defense specialists watched apprehensively as the Russian railway system crept over Central Asia toward the Indian frontier. It was the Russian Empire's capacity to deploy military power against Japan in the Far East, which the Trans-Siberian Railway provided, that led Halford Mackinder to propound in 1904 his theory of "the Heartland" and found the specious "science" of geopolitics. The two most decisive wars of the mid-nineteenth century, the American Civil War and the Franco-Prussian War, were decided largely by the advantage that the skillful use of railways gave to the victorious side; and in the developments leading to the First World War, strategic railways were seen as a force multiplier potentially decisive in its impact. Like fortifications, railways deserve a place in this study which it has not been found possible to give them. Strategic thinking in Europe between 1870 and 1914 was obsessed with railways. But tactical thinking was still, inevitably, concerned with a more traditional problem—the relationship between fire and shock on the battlefields for which these rail-borne armies were destined.

As the development of the breech-loading rifle enlarged the range of firearms, so the effectiveness of the bayonet as the weapon of the citizen-soldier became more difficult to sustain. Indeed, in Europe, as already in America, the rifle—accurate, easy to load and maintain, the weapon of the individual rather than of the disciplined mass—proved ideal both for the volunteer and for the short-service conscript; and as the French found in 1870, the Turks in 1877, and the Boers in 1899, it was the weapon of defense par excellence. But technology was producing the antidote in the form of mobile and powerful field artillery. The Prussian infantry had been shredded to pieces by the French chassepot rifles at Gravelotte, but at Sedan, a few weeks later, they stood by and watched Krupp's steel breech-loading cannon batter the French into surrender. The future pattern of tactics seemed to be emerging: *l'artillerie gagne, l'infanterie occupe.*

But the future was not there yet. Rifles extended their range, making it impossible for the guns to accompany infantry in the attack, forcing them to remain behind cover and give indirect support. Smokeless powder and entrenchments gave the defense the further lethal advantage of surprise. Even though artillery kept pace, growing ever more powerful and accurate with mobile heavy artillery adding its weight to the battlefield, there would always come a moment when the covering fire lifted and the infantry had to charge across "a zone of death." How could this be done? Common sense and experience both dictated open formations, with the maximum use of individual or small-unit initiative and cover. But could conscripts and volunteers be trusted on their own? If they went to ground and made use of cover, would they ever get up again? Regular officers and NCOs, gloomily eyeing their annual intake of conscripts, very much doubted it. So whatever staff officers might write into infantry regulations for the attack to encourage individual flexibility, initiative, and the use of cover, battalion commanders in all armies played it safe and practiced close formations for the assault, with officers in the lead and NCOs bringing up the rear. It looked better on maneuvers, apart from anything else. The French defeats in August 1914 are the best documented of the subsequent catastrophes, but the German performance at Langemarck the following November, when young volunteers were played into action by their regimental bands, was no better. The British took two years to get their citizens' army into action. When they did, the same mistrust of the volunteers' reliability on the battlefield made the army commanders send their men to attack the German defenses above the Somme in broad daylight in extended line. Britain was never to be quite the same country again.

At the end of the nineteenth century Ivan de Bloch, in *La Guerre Future,* had prophesied just such an outcome. Statistically he proved that no attack could succeed in face of the fire deployed by the defenders. There would therefore be stalemate on the battlefield; the war would become one of attrition; the fabric of industrial society would be unable to stand the strains imposed upon it; and the belligerents would collapse into revolution and chaos. The First World War seemed to fulfill this prophesy so precisely that subsequent generations wondered how Bloch's clear warnings came to be ignored.

But they were not ignored. They were taken very seriously, and Bloch's views were extensively debated in military periodicals. There were two reasons why they were discounted. The first was that within five years of the publication of *La Guerre Future* two wars were fought with modern weapons, in South Africa and Manchuria, from which the attacking forces emerged clearly victorious. European military specialists regarded the Boer War as atypical, but the Russo-Japanese war as a fair model, both in naval and military terms, for European powers — and the Japanese had won. Given enough artillery support and infantry "who know how to die," it was believed the tactical problem of the assault could be solved. Strategically the lesson of the Russo-Japanese War was more depressing. Victories on the battlefield produced no strategic decision. There was no breakthrough. The Russians were simply pushed a few miles back along their line of supply, where they dug in again. Effectively the war became one of attrition, as Bloch had predicted, and Russia collapsed in the manner he had foreseen. But European experts explained this by the logistical problems confronting both sides. Dependent on long supply lines, neither could deploy its full capabilities to decisive effect. In Europe, where shorter distances and efficient mobilization ensured more effective "front-loading," the position would be very different.

And it would need to be. This was the second reason why Bloch's warnings were discounted: *they were believed.* No one thought that the nations of Europe, beset as they all were by social and nationalist unrest, would be able to sustain a war lasting for years without internal collapse. The war *had* to be short. The initial battles *had* to be decisive. The greatest possible weight, therefore, had to be put into the offensive.

European states had to win a short war because they could not afford to fight a long one. "The short war" in 1914 was not an illusion: it was a necessity.

So the nations of Europe went to war in 1914 in expectation of a gigantic and decisive Napoleonic Battle, or series of battles, that would settle the fate of their continent as swiftly as it had been settled in the summer of 1870. Unfortunately their technology did not match up to the concept, and it was more difficult to adjust the former than the latter. In 1915 the major belligerents accepted that they were fighting a war of attrition and slowly adjusted their techniques accordingly. Cavalry disappeared, infantry was transformed, and gunners and engineers came into their own. But the story of that transition demands another volume.

Notes on Contributors

SIMON ADAMS is Lecturer in History at the University of Strathclyde, Glasgow, Scotland. He has published over twenty articles or contributions to books on British and European politics and international relations during the Renaissance-Reformation period, and is completing *England's Foreign Policy, 1529–1640* for the Longman Press.

RICHARD HELLIE is Professor of History at the University of Chicago. Author of a numerous articles and papers, he has written *Enserfment and Military Change in Muscovy, Slavery in Russia, 1450–1725,* and edited several collections and documents including *The Plow, the Hammer, and the Knout,* and *The Ulozhenie of 1649* in two volumes.

DON HIGGINBOTHAM is Dowd Professor of History and War and Peace at the University of North Carolina, Chapel Hill. His books include *Daniel Morgan: Revolutionary Rifleman, The War of American Independence, George Washington and the American Military Tradition,* and *War and Society in Revolutionary America.* He is a former member of the Board of Editors of the *American Historical Review.*

SIR MICHAEL HOWARD is Robert E. Lovett Professor of Military and Naval History at Yale University. He was previously Professor of War Studies at the University of London (1963–68), Chichele Professor of History of War at Oxford (1977–80), and Regius Professor of Modern History (1980–1989). His extensive list of publications includes *The Franco-Prussian War, War in European History,* and *The Causes of Wars.*

BRUCE LENMAN, a native of Aberdeen, is Reader in Modern History at the University of St. Andrews. He has authored over forty scholarly articles, several concerning the history of Indian military institutions. His bibliography includes *An Economic History of Modern Scotland, The Jacobite Risings in Britain, 1689–1746,* and *The Jacobite Clans of the Great Glen, 1650–1789.*

JOHN A. LYNN is Associate Professor of History at the University of Illinois, at Urbana-Champaign. His first book was *Bayonets of the Republic:*

Motivation and Tactics in the Army of Revolutionary France, 1791-94 (1984). He is currently writing *The Wars of Louis XIV, 1667-1714* for Longman Press. He chairs the Midwest Consortium on Military History.

WILLIAM MALTBY is Professor and Chair at the Department of History, University of Missouri, St. Louis. Since 1977 he has served as executive director of the Center for Reformation Research. In addition to several articles, his books include *The Black Legend in England: The Development of Anti-Spanish Sentiment, 1558-1660* (1971) and *Alba* (1983). He is now writing *Before the Military Revolution: Warfare in the West, 1494-1648*.

DENNIS SHOWALTER is Professor of History at Colorado College. He has written fifty articles and several books, including *Railroads and Rifles: Soldiers, Technology, and the Unification of Germany, Little Man, What Now?: Der Stürmer in the Weimar Republic,* and *German Military History Since 1648: A Critical Bibliography.* He has held several offices in the American Military Institute, including Trustee.

HUGH STRACHAN is Senior Tutor at Corpus Christi College, Cambridge University. He is the author of five books, including *European Armies and the Conduct of War, Wellington's Legacy: The Reform of the British Army 1830-54,* and *From Waterloo to Balaclava: Tactics, Technology and the British Army 1815-1854.* He is currently writing a history of World War I for Oxford University Press.

Index